The FILMS of Tom Hanks

The FILMS of Tom Hanks

Lee Pfeiffer and Michael Lewis

A Citadel Press Book
Published by Carol Publishing Group

A Citadel Press Book
Published by Carol Publishing Group
Citadel Press is a registered trademark of Carol Communications, Inc.

Editorial, sales and distribution, rights and permissions inquiries should be addressed to:
Carol Publishing Group, 120 Enterprise Avenue, Secaucus, N.J. 07094

In Canada: Canadian Manda Group, One Atlantic Avenue, Suite 105, Toronto, Ontario M6K 3E7

Carol Publishing Group books may be purchased in bulk at special discounts for sales promotion, fund-raising, or educational purposes. Special editions can be created to specifications. For details, contact:
Special Sales Department, 120 Enterprise Avenue, Secaucus, N.J. 07094

Designed by Andrew B. Gardner

Manufactured in the United States of America

10   9   8   7   6   5   4   3   2   1

Library of Congress Cataloging-in-Publication Data
Pfeiffer, Lee.
        The films of Tom Hanks / Lee Pfeiffer and Michael Lewis.
            p.   cm.
        "A Citadel Press book."
        ISBN 0-8065-1717-4 (pbk.)
        1. Hanks, Tom. I. Lewis, Michael (Michael D.), 1962—   II. Title.
    PN2287.H18P44   1996
    791.43'028'092—dc20
                                                                    95-19786
                                                                    CIP

To my mom, Catherine,
who always knew I'd
be "big" someday
M.L.

For Allan J. Wilson,
for believing in my writing
all these years
L.P.

Contents

Acknowledgments

The authors extend their gratitude to the following corporations and individuals:

M-G-M/UA, Paramount Pictures, 20th Century-Fox, Columbia Pictures, ABC TV, Touchstone Pictures, Universal Pictures, Orion Pictures; from Citadel Press and Carol Publishing: Steve Schragis, Bruce Bender, Allan J. Wilson, Gary Fitzgerald, Kevin McDonough, Margaret Wolf, Steve Brower, Alvin Marrill, Andy Gardner, Don Davidson; Jerry Ohlinger's Movie Memorabilia Store in New York City; Bob Klepeis; Ron Plesniarski; and of course our long-suffering families, who temporarily agreed to convert our homes into "Tom Hanks Museums" as we researched this book: Janet and Nicole Pfeiffer and Amy and Samantha Lewis.

The FILMS of Tom Hanks

Tom Hanks:
All-American Everyman

In 1980 Tom Hanks made his big-screen debut with a minor role in *He Knows You're Alone*, an undistinguished film, even by the standards of the low-budget genre affectionately termed by critics Roger Ebert and Gene Siskel as "dead teenager movies." Within four years, he was a genuine star, thanks to his performance in 1984's sleeper hit *Splash*.

Since that time, Hanks has had his share of career missteps, but he has consistently ranked among the most popular screen presences of his generation. By the mid-nineties, he had emerged as a major force in the motion-picture industry—surely the *youngest* actor in recent memory to earn that distinction.

Yet Hanks's upbringing certainly did not betray what fate had in store for him. Born on July 9, 1956, in Concord, California, he lived an early life that was distinctly middle class but not ordinary. His father, Amos, worked as a chef, and his mother, Janet, stayed home to raise Tom and older siblings Larry and Sandra as well as younger brother Jim. His childhood was distinguished by his parents' frequent moves as well as a number of marital separations and reconciliations. He would later recall the effect this had on him: "I was only five when we first started

An early publicity shot

moving around. I just felt lonely; I felt abandoned, in the dark. 'How come no one's telling me?' No one is telling you the 'why,' just the 'what': 'Pack your bags, get the stuff you want, and put it in the back of the station wagon.' "

He was five when his parents divorced for the first time. They would later remarry "any number of times," such situations becoming so commonplace that Hanks never saw anything unique about his lifestyle. "We were just a completely more or less normal broken family. Everybody was married a bunch, and everybody lived different places, and nobody thought much of it. It was a pretty laissez faire relationship. I pretty much called my own shots. I was the third kid, and by the time you come along, the folks—well, they pretty much don't care. I mean it's 'Are you coming home anytime soon? Are you in jail?' We're all pretty close now, but it was rough for a while. My dad's third wife, Frances, is a wonderful lady, but we made it very hard on her at first. We were awful. There was lots of tension and craziness, for all the classic reasons. I was only ten at the time when she came along, and I'd been living alone with my dad for a long time, and it was like no one's going to tell me what to do. It took a while to adjust."

Despite his parents' unorthodox relationship, the family did not lack for love or affection. Hanks recalled, "I never felt unloved. I was always in some sort of a family structure. And when we were alone, my [older] brother and sister and I hung together. The coolest place to be was at home, because we were always cracking each other up. I was surrounded by goodness. No one was hitting me or telling me I was stupid or drinking themselves into oblivion. My dad was not a guy who had his fingers on the pulse of his own feelings, but he was a good guy. And my mom, even though she was far away, was always concerned about my well-being and always happy to see me. So I felt blessed. The skeletons in our closets were only a couple of femur bones." Hanks found particular solace in the company of his older brother, Larry, who was ironically considered the funniest member of the family.

Hanks's parents finally decided that their "on-again, off-again" relationship was too frustrating; they divorced for the final time in 1961. Tom, his sister Sandra, and his brother, Larry, lived with their father, while Jim resided with their mom. When Hanks was ten years old, his father married Frances Wong, a woman with a large extended family. At one point, up to twenty-two people were living in the same modest household. Yet Hanks remained philosophical about his situation and fondly remembers the dubious distinction of "blowing people away by saying, 'I have three mothers, and I've lived in ten different homes.' " He said, "By the time I was ten, I had lived pretty much in every kind of configuration, from big houses in the country to tiny apartments in big metropolitan areas. I think I moved every six months when I was a kid. But I had a solid core of my older brother, my sister, and my dad. We lived with my aunt for a while, sleeping on the sofa bed; my dad slept in a trailer in the backyard, and we had tiny apartments in those complexes that stretch to the horizon on a landfill. I never had one single point of view that said, " 'This is the best way to live.' "

Hanks's chaotic home life left him with a need for attention—easy to understand, given the "cast of thousands" which inhabited his household. He attended Skyline High School in Oakland, California, where he channeled his extroverted nature by becoming a self-proclaimed "class clown." This was a trait Hanks had already mastered in many different grammar schools. "I loved being the new guy in class. It was a new classroom; they had different books— 'Oooh, they're using these pencils!' The class-clown-ish type of thing was a defense mechanism, but I was pretty good at making people laugh. If the adrenaline

rush that comes with performing is addictive, I got it at an early age. I could make kids laugh standing in line for handball. And it would perk me up. *That's where I learned timing.*"

Hanks's life was greatly influenced by two people who helped steer him toward acting: drama teacher Rawley Farnsworth and classmate John Gilkerson. With their encouragement, Hanks made his stage debut in a school production of *South Pacific*. He gained enough confidence to later perform in *The Night of the Iguana*.

Hanks also dabbled in religion and became quite dedicated to spreading the Word. He recalled that he did his "own little theological search for a while. Very conservative, very Bible-oriented, the Sunday morning service, and the Sunday evening service. It beat smoking pot." Hanks says his church group was actually "fun and social. The core of it was a conservative— not theological—base that was centered on the more traditional Protestant interpretations of the New Testament. We didn't speak in tongues or anything like that. We had to accept Christ as our savior, but we didn't have to go down to the well." It is ironic that a man with these conservative values should become the darling of one of the most liberal professions.

Academically, Hanks was a mediocre student in high school but could not blame his grades on a hectic social life with girls. Years later, he confessed that he was hardly a teenage Hugh Hefner: "I was never particularly good-looking. I was death with women in high school—absolutely strikeout king. I was a little too geeky, a little too gangly, and much too manic."

Upon his graduation in 1974, he enrolled in a two-year program at Chabot Junior College in Hayward, California. To make ends meet, Hanks moonlighted as a bellhop at the local Hilton Hotel. Here he had his first brushes with genuine show-business people by way of carrying Cher's bags and driving Sidney Poitier to the airport. Hanks had enrolled in acting classes in college simply because he felt it would be a fun way to kill time. "When I was in junior college, the drama classes were easy," he later told Barbara Walters. "You just kind of go in and you do scenes from plays and you do Chekhov and stuff like that and it's all very funny. You get to pretend and the hour just goes by real fast and you can

The cast of *Bosom Buddies* (*left to right*): Wendie Jo Sperber, Donna Dixon, Tom Hanks, Telma Hopkins, Peter Scolari, and Holland Taylor (ABC-TV)

Both Scolari (a.k.a. Hildegarde) and Hanks (Buffy) agree that the show's cross-dressing theme got old *real* fast. (ABC-TV)

O'Neill's *The Iceman Cometh* at the Berkeley Repertory Theater, he was so impressed by the caliber of the acting and the production that he called the event a turning point in his life, and from then on he devoted his time to finding a niche in the theater. "I have to stress that because of that performance I didn't decide to become an actor. It was so much more than that. I didn't care what I did—build sets, string lights, paint props, or act. The main thing was to somehow be a part of this life."

Determined to use college as a springboard to a theatrical career, Hanks earned a scholarship to California State University in Sacramento. His initial goal was to become a stage carpenter, but the school allowed him to cross-train in virtually every other aspect of the theater. Hanks's stint at Cal State provided another benefit—a romantic relationship with an aspiring producer-actress named Susan Dillingham. For marquee value Dillingham changed her professional name to Samantha Lewes, and she and Hanks soon became inseparable. Eventually, Hanks—perhaps further inspired by Samantha—took to the stage as a performer, appearing in a production of *The Cherry Orchard* at the Sacramento Civic Theater. The play's director, Vincent Dowling, was the artistic director of the Great Lakes Shakespeare Festival in Cleveland. When the run of *The Cherry Orchard* was over, Dowling extended an invitation to the cast members to return with him to Ohio and study acting as interns in future stage productions. Hanks could not resist and impulsively left college, never to return.

Vincent Dowling was impressed with Hanks from the beginning. He told *Premiere* magazine in 1989, "When I came home that afternoon [after seeing Hanks act for the first time], I told my wife there was one kid there who had star quality. I said, 'He's like a young Tony Curtis, but I think he has even more potential.'" Dowling later elaborated on his enthusiasm for Hanks's talents, saying, "Tom's magic as an actor comes from an abundance of life . . . he was always happiest onstage, even at eighteen. You'd always see him moving about. Even sweeping up with those big awkward brushes, every-

get an A and that's the way drama class is. But being an actor? I didn't think I could cut it."

Nevertheless, the reluctant thespian enrolled in a course called Drama in Performance, thinking it was an acting class. To his surprise, the curriculum consisted of studying plays and then attending performances. Hanks found his creativity stimulated by the plays, and he became hooked on the works of the great writers. "I spent a lot of time going to plays. I wouldn't take dates with me. I'd just drive to a theater, buy myself a ticket, sit in the seat and read the program, and then get into the play completely. I spent a lot of time like that."

When Hanks attended a performance of Eugene

thing would be something to conquer—humorously but efficiently—to work, master, twirl around.... He's always kept his instrument at concert pitch: voice, body, imagination. He's lived with discipline all these years, not dissipation."

Hanks loved his days in Cleveland, particularly when he began to land roles in local Shakespearean productions which actually earned him a modest paycheck. Samantha had moved to Cleveland with him, and together they seemed on top of the world. Hanks began to get opportunities to flex his acting muscles in a number of demanding roles: as Grumio in *The Taming of the Shrew*, as Rosencrantz in *Hamlet*, as Montano in *Othello*, as Fabian in *Twelfth Night*, and as Faulconbridge in *King John*. He costarred with other actors who had trained in some of the most exclusive drama schools in the world, and with every performance he seemed to learn something new about technique. He likened the demanding experience to "learning to play the violin on a Stradivarius."

Slowly, Hanks began to be noticed by the local critics. In 1978 he received the Best Actor Award from the Cleveland Critics Circle for his performance as the evil Proteus in *The Two Gentlemen of Verona*. Encouraged, Hanks worked tirelessly, accepting one demanding role after another. Eventually, he and Samantha agreed to head to the Big Apple. Hanks had earned a year's salary at the Great Lakes Shakespeare Festival and qualified for unemployment compensation. The money was desperately needed: Samantha had become pregnant, and she and Hanks married. The two set up house near Times Square, in the heart of New York's theater district, and Hanks labored, unpaid, in plays produced by the Riverside Shakespeare Company. The experience he gained was invaluable, but money was tight. Hanks was now barely supporting himself, Samantha, and newborn son Colin. Things became so bleak that Hanks's sister Sandra recalls cashing in empty soda bottles to send him twenty dollars. Hanks tried to land jobs in television commercials, but a Shakespearean background didn't prove advantageous to people who market Big Macs. In the summer of 1979, he returned to Cleveland to work at the Great Lakes company.

A typical manic moment on *Bosom Buddies* (ABC-TV)

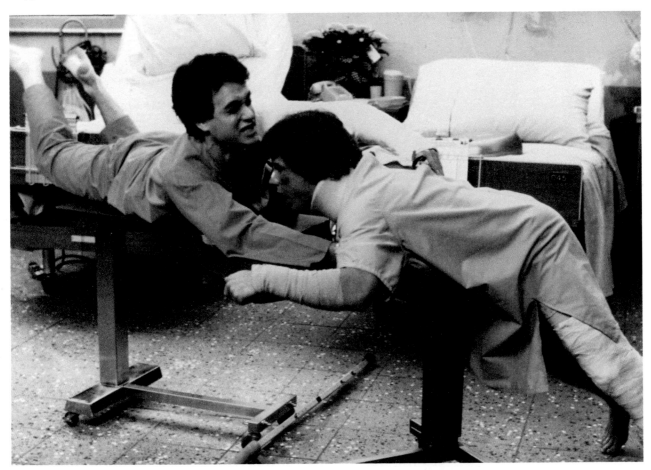

Relaxing on the set. Hanks and Scolari became fast friends and have stayed that way ever since. (ABC-TV)

When he came back to New York he was to find his fortunes changed dramatically.

Hanks was offered a seven-minute role in an exploitation film: *He Knows You're Alone*. The story, Hanks recalled, was about "that very particular group of psychotic killers that only stab women who are about to be married." The low-budget affair was shot on Staten Island, New York, and Hanks still remembers not even having the distinction of getting a memorable death scene. Instead, he makes a brief but pleasant impression as a friend of one of the killer's targets. The role paid him $800, but the real value of the movie was that it allowed him to join the Screen Actors Guild.

Hanks's luck improved dramatically when he won a leading role in *Rona Jaffe's "Mazes and Monsters,"* an above-average television movie with Hanks (top-billed) giving a fine performance as a vulnerable young man whose obsession with a role-playing game contributes to his mental breakdown. The

film allowed Hanks to be seen by his widest audience to date and to make a significant impression on people in the industry, leading to a screen-test for an ABC comedy series called *Bosom Buddies*. The show was produced by the same team which had launched the very popular *Laverne and Shirley*, and ABC planned to premiere it in fall 1980.

Bosom Buddies, loosely based on *Some Like It Hot*, featured Hanks and Peter Scolari in the Jack Lemmon and Tony Curtis roles. The actors portray two young advertising executives who, upon finding that their New York apartment has been condemned, move into a hotel which is restricted to women. In order to maintain their living arrangements, the men have to dress in drag. The real ladies, of course, never suspect the obvious, and the situation allows for endless double entendres. While the premise of the show was hardly original, sharp writing and the genuine chemistry between Scolari and Hanks made it work. The two developed a strong friendship both on camera and behind the scenes.

Bosom Buddies was a ratings smash when it was originally telecast on Thanksgiving, 1980. Sandwiched between two hot series—*Mork and Mindy* and *Barney Miller*—the series could not fail to attract a large audience. However, after its second season began, ABC inexplicably placed the show on temporary hiatus. When it returned, it was bounced around, and viewers were never sure when, or if, the series would air. After two seasons and thirty-seven episodes (plus the pilot), *Bosom Buddies* was canceled. Like so many other promising shows, poor scheduling had deprived the series from ever regaining popularity.

Despite its demise, *Bosom Buddies* was a gigantic boost to Hanks's career. He earned $9,000 per episode and, more important, learned how to improvise dialogue and material quickly. (He and Scolari always had contests of one-upmanship to see who could improvise the wittiest lines.) Hanks fondly recalled: "We had a lot of fun doing the show, and the good time we were having came across on-screen. It was a major learning experience to me." Due to

Hanks's success in recent years, many episodes of the series were released on video in 1995.

After *Bosom Buddies*, Hanks appeared on such shows as *The Love Boat*, *Family Ties*, (playing a recurring high-profile role as Meredith Baxter-Birney's alcoholic brother in two episodes), *Taxi*, and *Happy Days*. It was on the last that Hanks befriended Ron Howard, the series' star. When Howard graduated to full-time feature-film director a couple of years later, he struck box-office pay dirt with the comedy hit *Night Shift* and became a "name" director. He was developing his follow-up film, *Splash*, for Disney's newly established Touchstone Pictures division. The year was 1983, and Howard and producing partner Brian Grazer were having trouble finding a star for their project. The plot, as everyone now knows, centers on a likable young man who falls in love with a mermaid in present-day Manhattan.

Tom Hanks later said, "The only reason I got that part was because absolutely no one else would do it. . . . Ron Howard was so desperate, he had to try his luck with me—a complete novice who had no idea what he was doing. Thank God." Hanks was as surprised as anyone when *Splash* became a smash. It instantly catapulted everyone involved with it into the upper echelon of Hollywood, including Hanks, Ron Howard, mermaid Daryl Hannah, and chubby John Candy, in his first major supporting role.

Sure beats cross-dressing . . . we *think*! (ABC-TV)

Hanks sustained momentum at the box office with another surprise hit: the sophomoric 1984 comedy *Bachelor Party*. He was cast as an irresponsible wise guy who finds that his bachelor party is the catalyst for some of the wildest and most catastrophic events to hit California since the Great Earthquake of 1906. The relatively low budget film was still in a higher class than most of the similarly themed comedies which flooded theaters in the early to mid-eighties. Hanks would later dismiss the film: "The movie is just a sloppy rock-and-roll comedy that has tits in it. It was made when the studios were making lots of *Porky's* and *Animal House* kinds of things." Still, Hanks has a fondness for it and readily admits that it helped cement his newfound status as a bankable leading man. It also led to the ultimate in 1980s status: being asked to host *Saturday Night Live* (an honor he has accepted six times to date).

Hanks's hot streak took a detour with the release of *The Man With One Red Shoe*, his ill-fated 1985 espionage comedy, a misfire which wasted a talented cast that included Dabney Coleman, Carrie Fisher, Jim Belushi, and Charles Durning. At the same time, his home life was undergoing rough times. Samantha, whose career was languishing, was frustrated by her husband's success as an actor. Hanks tried to help by producing a play in which Samantha starred, but it did little to ease the tension which afflicted their marriage. Not helping matters was Hanks's nonstop work schedule, which frequently found him away from his family. (In the ensuing years, he and Samantha had also adopted a daughter, Elizabeth.) Still, the couple made every attempt to resolve their differences, with only mixed results. They divorced in 1987.

Hanks flew to Mexico for his next film, *Volunteers*, and fell in love with his costar, Rita Wilson, of whom he would say, "I'm mad about the woman. She's fabulous. We got to know each other over the course of four months. It was a slow dawning. There's something incredibly special about her." These not-so-subtle remarks were not the typical backslapping quotes devised for a film's press kit. Hanks had found his true love with the sexy and funny Wilson, and the chemistry between the two is apparent in the final cut of *Volunteers*. Wilson said in an 1994 interview: "Tom is the kind of person you find yourself being very comfortable around, so you're much more in a relaxed state. It's not the same thing as when you set your sights on somebody and you say, 'He's a cute one! I want to go out with him!' . . . It was very easy to talk to him, and we laughed readily. It was very nonsexual at the beginning. . . . I had thought that I was the person who would never really fall in love in her life. I just didn't think that would happen."

Hanks described his own spin on their relationship in a mid-nineties interview with *Vanity Fair*: "We're not opposites at all. But we certainly are complements somehow. My notches fit her nooks. When we met, it was just bona fide friendship and delight, which rapidly became a kind of passion. I mean, there was a substantial amount of stuff I had to go through. I was married. I had two kids. I could not just . . . ah . . . well, the thing that drove me to the couch was . . . that all I was doing was repeating this kind of life that my parents had gone through, with an incredible amount of pain. Because my parents broke up when I was five, there began this kind of disconnectedness that hung in there until I was thirty. But, I mean, everybody's got something that comes along and chews 'em up for a bit. My loneliness came out of that. . . . There just didn't seem to be a table that I truly felt accepted at unconditionally. Coming across Rita, I found someone who could not understand that, and I got a glimpse of how life could be. . . . Los Angeles, before I met Rita, was this hideous place where you ended up not out of some choice but because they paid you to go there. It was a place where the holidays were always going on somewhere else. The only real discussions you ever made were whether to get off at Woodman or Coldwater."

Despite being married while madly in love with another woman, Hanks rallied to star opposite Shelley Long in *The Money Pit*, an underrated 1986 slapstick comedy for Steven Spielberg's production company. His next project was far more ambitious. In *Nothing in Common* he costarred with one of his idols: the Great One himself, Jackie Gleason. Never stooping to the obvious to play for sentiment, the smartly written contemporary comedy/drama, centered on the rocky relationship between a cantankerous old man and his son. In it a life-threatening illness befalls the Gleason character, much as Hanks's own father had once been afflicted. Hanks enjoyed every minute of the filming even though the domestic drama probably brought back some painful memories of his relationship with his real father. *Nothing in Common* was not a substantial hit, but Hanks reveled in the type of glowing notices he had not enjoyed since *Splash*. The film unfortunately also made him the last actor to costar with Jackie Gleason. The Great One died soon after the movie was released.

During the filming of *Nothing in Common* Hanks separated from Samantha and moved in with David Chambers, an old friend from the *Bosom Buddies* days. When the press broke the story, Hanks responded by saying, "I had some personal problems. Big deal. Everybody has them. We're not talking about nuclear holocaust. I was a little bit crazy. . . . In some ways, I guess I've been like a classic absentee father. My work has taken me away a lot—and certainly being separated, even more so. I think my marriage broke up for many of the reasons that any other marriage breaks up. Lack of communication plays a huge part, and the basic nature of the relationship."

In a 1993 interview Hanks reflected on those days: "The first thing that went through my mind was Oh, my god; my kids are going to feel as lonely as I did. That was very bad. I did everything I could to avoid the same circumstances. When you know it's absolutely over and finished—not only is there no way to reclaim, but you don't want to—the options are pretty dismal. You know any of those choices was going to have repercussions for a long time. You know it's going to take three years to get over. . . . I sought professional help. So you go and sit in somebody's office and say, 'Man, I'm depressed.' And you

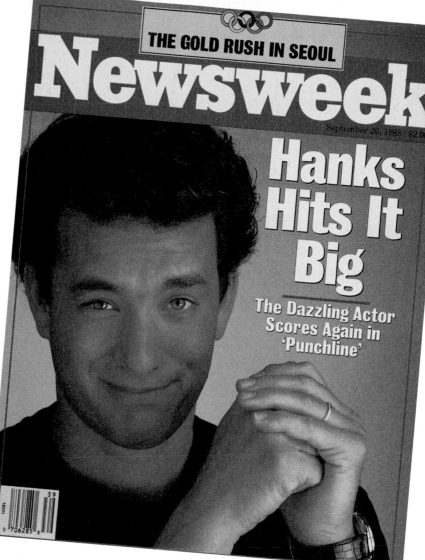

"Big" time: On the cover of *Newsweek* in that magical year 1988 (*Newsweek*)

give them a litany of what's going on in your life and they say, 'No wonder; look at all the stuff you're going through.' "

Hanks plunged deeply into his work to distract himself from the troubles in his personal life. He concentrated on dramatic roles, but his Israeli-made starring vehicle *Every Time We Say Goodbye*, a World War II romance about a Jewish woman and an American air force pilot—a non-Jew—trying to find love against the background of societal prejudices, did little to keep the momentum going. The well-intentioned film deserved more attention than it received, but its modest budget and downbeat story line made it the least seen Tom Hanks movie to date.

Hanks was nevertheless grateful for the fame he had achieved and tried to give something back to his alma mater when he returned to Skyline High School in 1986 to address the student body. Afterward, he stood patiently and shook hands with the school's more than six hundred students. Hanks tried to keep his fame in perspective, saying, "[I started acting] out of a desire to have fun. . . . It's not so much that [acting] was hugely challenging or broadened my horizons—which were both true—but simply because it was fun. That's why I got into this in the first place. And fun comes out of the challenge and the struggle. If you don't have that, how can you enjoy the other side of it?"

Hanks returned to the world of over-the-top comedy with *Dragnet*, a 1986 spoof of the classic TV series. Although this movie was not a blockbuster, it did well enough to (at least temporarily) revive Hanks's sagging numbers at the box office.

By all accounts, Hanks's fame and fortune had not affected his ego. How many other stars would have the nerve to describe themselves in such loving terms to *Esquire*: "I've got kind of a bizarre body, a big ass, and fat thighs. I've got a goofy-looking nose, ears that hang down, eyes that look like I'm part Chinese and are a funny color. I've got really small hands and feet, long limbs, narrow shoulders, and a gut I've got to keep watching. My hair makes me look like a Talmudic scholar." Such self-deprecating candor only served to endear Hanks to the public. His views were refreshing, and more than one critic

began to compare him to Jimmy Stewart—an accurate analogy but one that would become increasingly tedious as the years went by. In fact, Jimmy Stewart's was not the image Hanks always dreamed of having. He said, "I would hope to come off as a guy that's hip. Richard III was hip. Iago was hip. Brando. *Star Trek*. And, of course, Cary Grant. He was the embodiment of hip." On another occasion, Hanks confessed that his true idol was a fictional character: "I wanted to be James Bond. All of my friends did. We all wanted to be that guy." Ironically, Hanks's public image would remain closer to Jimmy Stewart than Agent 007.

By the end of 1987, Hanks and Rita Wilson were among Hollywood's most compatible couples. On a trip to St. Barts on New Year's Eve, Hanks suddenly proposed to Wilson while at dinner with actor Peter Weller, newscaster Diane Sawyer, and director-husband Mike Nichols. "We were all at this table together," he recalled. "I had just asked Rita to marry me, and she said, 'You bet!' " With that, the couple began to plan for their wedding day, which occurred on April 30, 1988. Among the eclectic group of friends attending the wedding: Dan Akyroyd and his wife, Donna Dixon, Jon Lovitz, Kathleen Turner, Roger Moore, and Peter Scolari, along with many of the cast of *Bosom Buddies*. Hanks jokingly reflected on marriage the second time around: "I think thirty-one is about the right age to be married twice, don't you?" However, by all accounts, he and Rita Wilson were true soul mates.

As for Hanks's relationship with his ex-wife, Samantha, he candidly told *Vanity Fair* in a 1994 interview, "[She] and I don't talk a lot anymore, but we're very respectful of each other. I wouldn't say we were friends or even friendly. But we're very respectful of each other's place and position. All that other stuff that can go along with it? It has not existed. I see my kids at my leisure and at their request and my request. There was certainly a period of discomfort and trouble. But once the legal stuff got worked out, it's been quite, well, I wouldn't say pleasant, but it's been easy. And their mother has been a wonderful parent."

In 1988, Hanks's career would get a *Big* boost with the release of a film which would gain him an Oscar nomination. *Big* was not only the most challenging role of Hanks's career to date; it would also be Penny Marshall's breakthrough film as a director. In the role of the grown man in the body of a twelve-year-old, Hanks got unanimously enthusiastic reviews from the international press. He had been skeptical about the fantasy/love story and confessed: "When I told a friend what *Big* was about, he goes, 'Oh, it's like Peggy Sue goes back to the future and meets *Tootsie*.'" Hanks's wonderfully natural performance caught all of the nuances of a young boy's behavior from innocence to naïveté to being incredulous at his first exposure to the pleasures and frustrations of adult life, including sexuality.

Prior to the film's release, there was very little show-biz "buzz" about it. Hanks himself told an interviewer, "Am I big box office? I guess so; I hope so. It's good if I am, but I wouldn't out-and-out lay claim to that. Supposedly, I am. But nothing I've done has really gone over the roof or entered into the

Hanks remains a diehard Cleveland Indians fan, although his fame makes it increasingly harder to visit the ballpark.

national consciousness." Hanks's modest self-appraisal was about to be contradicted by the box-office gross of *Big*, his first blockbuster. Significantly, the film played equally well around the globe, thus forming the genesis of Hanks's international appeal. He didn't win the Oscar that year, but the nomination alone earned him renewed respect in the industry.

His next project was *Punchline*, a thoughtful comedy/drama about an obsessively competitive amateur comedian who will do anything to make it in the "big leagues." The movie was shot before *Big* but released after it. Hanks shared the screen with Sally Field, who received top billing for her role as the housewife who turns to Hanks for career advice. The two form a fragile friendship that almost leads to romance, but, refreshingly, it does not. Hanks saw more than a little of himself in his character, for he has always cited competitiveness among his shortcomings. His role was the most unsympathetic part he had played to date, and one of the most challenging. The movie did not benefit much from Hanks's recent success in *Big*.

Comedy with a bittersweet edge: An underlying sadness permeates many of Hanks's roles.

Perhaps it appealed primarily to urban audiences and not enough to middle America. Artistically, though, Hanks was on a roll, and many critics cited the irony of an actor's giving *two* Oscar-worthy performances in one year.

Hanks was philosophical about the phenomenal success he was enjoying. He told the *Los Angeles Times*, "I know a year like I'd had comes once every fifteen years, if you're lucky. Once every ten years if you're amazingly lucky and once every five years if you're a phenomenon, and I'm not laying claim to being that. I just knew that it had been wild and that it would probably fall apart somewhere down the line. I said that I'd feel bad about it for a while when it happened, but in the end I'd be okay."

Hanks's choice of his next few roles wouldn't cause the "bottom to drop out" of his recent success story, but they did little or nothing to provide him with anything other than marginally interesting characters who served as the catalyst for incredible events. *The 'burbs* (1989) was a goofy, off-the-wall comedy which mingled social satire, juvenile sight gags, and psychic phenomenon with predictably uneven results. A good cast and a few moments of inspired lunacy

made it watchable and a modest success at the box office. *Turner & Hooch* (also 1989) was even more anemic. Hanks was upstaged by the ugliest dog in movie history in a glorified TV movie that was cuddly-cute right up to its controversial and completely uncalled for climax in which the lovable canine is senselessly killed. The film was a fairly big hit—largely because of Hanks's box-office clout—but critics (and later Hanks himself) dismissed the movie as an uninspired time killer.

Hanks's nonstop work schedule became the talk of the industry. He no sooner would finish shooting one film when he was en route to a new location for another. He told *Premiere* in 1989, "Things are so much different now; the motivations for having to make all those movies don't exist anymore. I'm not living with parents who are remarrying or splitting up or taking a job somewhere. And I'm not having to do the same. For most of my twenties I think I moved every six months. Enough's enough! I'm *tired!*"

Despite his protests, Hanks was unable to avoid the lure of two other seemingly promising scripts. *Joe Versus the Volcano* (1990) was the brainchild of director-writer John Patrick Shanley, who was briefly

Hanks directed and made a cameo appearance in an episode of Showtime's *Fallen Angels* series. (Showtime)

the darling of the Hollywood set. The movie was too strange to allow for a successful marketing campaign, and although Hanks's fans initially turned out, the film was classified a box-office disappointment. Its savage reviews were somewhat undeserved. The movie was at least an original, and Hanks had given a very funny performance. Significantly, it represented his first teaming with Meg Ryan, with whom he would later costar in *Sleepless in Seattle*.

While *Joe Versus the Volcano* met with critical scorn and did only mild business, it looked like *Citizen Kane* compared to Hanks's next and greatest career misstep: director Brian De Palma's ill-fated and watered-down adaptation of Tom Wolfe's bestselling novel *Bonfire of the Vanities*. One of the biggest publishing phenomenons of recent years, *Bonfire* would seem to have been a sure thing as a blockbuster motion picture. However, from the very beginning, every wrong decision was made. The film was miscast, with Hanks all wrong for the part of the cynical Wall Street egghead Sherman McCoy whose fateful accident involving a black youth on a South Bronx street leads to a scandalous trial that rocks New York's fragile relationship between the races. Faring no better were Hanks's costars Bruce Willis and Melanie Griffith. Released during the Christmas season of 1990, *Bonfire of the Vanities* was available on

home video only a few months later. The resounding rejection by the public made *Bonfire* one of those legendary flops which critics love to write about.

Having experienced his first cinematic disaster, Hanks said: "We were either making something on the order of *Gone With the Wind*, or we were the biggest clowns in the business and we'd be laughed off the screen. We were laughed off the screen." Such candor helped ease critical resentment toward Hanks in the wake of the *Bonfire* debacle. He would later tell Larry King, "You learn more from getting your butt kicked than you do by getting it kissed. I think that's my quasi-philosophy. I learned what to do and what not to do. . . . I think it's better when you really get shellacked; it's not nearly as heartbreaking as losing by two points."

One bright spot following the *Bonfire* fallout was the birth of Hanks's first child with Rita—Chester Marlon Hanks. In a 1994 interview Hanks spoke about his feelings of raising a second family: "Kids are great, and I love them. They're more entertaining than television. But the only difference between my first crop and my second is that I have a better understanding of what my responsibilities are: how you need to love them and how you need to let them go. I'm much calmer now and much more prone to just hanging out with all of my kids at the age I am now than I was at twenty-five or twenty-seven. I was in the thick of trying to establish a beachhead in this world. I went off and pounded out nine movies in a row. I'm not doing that anymore."

Hanks's career returned to the big leagues—literally—with Penny Marshall's 1992 hit comedy-drama *A League of Their Own*, which depicted the women's baseball leagues that helped keep the sport alive during the war years of the forties, when most of the male players were in the service. The film seemed like an uncommercial project. Sports-related movies rarely do big box-office business; *female*-oriented, sports-related films generally do even worse. *League* depicted a baseball league which the average person didn't even realize existed, and Tom Hanks was still suffering from the burnout of *Bonfire*. However, under Penny Marshall's heartfelt direction, Hanks gave a wonderful performance as the washed-up, alcoholic team manager who sees the women's leagues as his last hope to remain on the periphery of baseball. Most of the screen time belonged to Geena Davis as the country girl who finds fame, fortune, and an almost-illicit affair with Hanks's character, Jimmy Dugan. The movie drips with sentimentality, but it is so superbly acted

Relaxing with a friend between takes on the set of the *Tales From the Crypt* episode which Hanks directed (HBO)

that the public overlooked the lukewarm notices, and the film grossed over $100 million. An unconventional role in one of the year's most unconventional films had returned Hanks to the ranks of top box-office attractions. (The film would inspire a short-lived television series, and Hanks directed an episode.)

Just as reteaming with *Big* director Penny Marshall on *League* proved to be a wise choice for Hanks, so, too, was his decision to reunite with Meg Ryan, the costar of the ill-fated *Joe Versus the Volcano*. Hanks teamed with Ryan for *Sleepless in Seattle*, a low-key but highly sentimental film, with Hanks as a young widower trying to raise a ten-year-old boy alone.

Sleepless stretched credibility and logic in its

attempt to milk every tear from female audience members, but the strategy worked. Hanks had a chance to play a totally normal guy without eccentricities or "cute" personality quirks. Audiences responded with overwhelming enthusiasm, and suddenly Hanks was a romantic leading man. Marc Platt, president of TriStar Pictures, which released the film, summed up Hanks's appeal thusly: "No question that Tom is a very unique individual. I think that when you're standing out in acting, you go where the opportunity is. But comedians often make wonderful actors. There's a kind of vulnerability that makes for real expression. Robin Williams, Steve Martin, and now Tom Hanks are just a few who came straight from comedy but later demonstrated broad range as

The many faces of America's favorite actor

actors. . . . Tom is very much an actor for the nineties. He exudes intelligence, and at the same time he's very passionate. In *Sleepless* he made it safe for audiences—male and female—to experience emotions, to laugh and cry. That's very much a notion of the period we're living in, and Tom fits that bill."

Beyond being one of the biggest hits of 1993, *Sleepless* paid other dividends: It gave Hanks and Rita Wilson a rare opportunity to share some screen time together. (Wilson had a supporting role.) Hanks said of the experience, "I'd love to work with Rita again. We had a great time on *Sleepless in Seattle*. . . . It brings options to lunchtime that you don't have with a lot of other costars. . . . [But] it would be hard, I think, to do a movie where somehow our own relationship was kind of put on public display. I don't ever want to mine whatever it is we have at home for . . . some sort of story we would eventually cash in on. I'd love to be in a movie where we have no knowledge of who we are against each other. Now this is interesting—I think something bleeds through on the screen that says the audience knows these people are married, therefore we cannot get involved in a story as to whether or not they're going to get together." In essence, don't look for Mr. and Mrs. Hanks going the Burton-Taylor route and doing a remake of *Who's Afraid of Virginia Woolf?*

Hanks reflected on the more personal side of his marriage, telling *Interview* magazine in 1994, "I felt lonely for a real long time. That's why I say my wife saved me, because I don't feel lonely anymore. I did right up to the point where she crossed my path. The union of two of you is better than the actual sum of the two of you. You don't just add two people; you multiply. That's what I think I've got. And it's not a purely romantic thought; it's much better. Rita and I have been through a lot just as a couple and certainly as a husband and wife. It takes a while to pound out a relationship, but I think that process ends up being the great hope. Somehow it's the great hope that is reflected in a lot of the movies that I do."

Despite the happiness his marriage and career have brought him, Hanks still admits to having some frustrations in his life, including a common one for actors—regretting those great roles which got away. "I would have loved to have been given the opportunity to play the concentration-camp commandant in *Schindler's List*, he said. "Sadly—and I guess not surprisingly—I wasn't even considered. But I know I would have been a great choice for the part, because everyone thinks I'm Mr. Happy Haircut Guy. I know it would have worked."

Politically, Hanks keeps his opinions to himself. He told the *New York Times*, "When I saw Sonny Bono at the Republican National Convention with Gerald Ford in '76, all I could think of was 'What the hell is Sonny Bono doing there?' I was eighteen years old and thought that was the stupidest, dumbest thing I've ever seen. I don't feel that anybody is influenced in any way by the fact that a public figure on the show-business level embraces any sort of political cause. The images just balance out after a while. For every Warren Beatty, there's Charlton Heston."

Hanks's success in films did not result in his turning his back on television. He directed and made a cameo appearance in "I'll Be Waiting," based on the Raymond Chandler story, the second episode of the film noir anthology series *Fallen Angels*, which aired on Showtime in 1993. (The show featured *Bosom Buddies* pal Peter Scolari.) While Hanks received praise for his directorial efforts, he dismissed the experience as "a big pain in the ass." He admitted to *Vogue*, "Most actors I've come across have the idea that they can do it all—that they can direct. I'm not so sure I can, but I would like to find out. And I'm in the position where I can barter my way into these unearned situations." Hanks would also direct an episode of the popular HBO series *Tales From the Crypt*.

On the acting front, Hanks was about to embark on the riskiest, most challenging role of his career:

playing in *Philadelphia*, Andrew Beckett, the AIDS-stricken young attorney who sues his law firm for discrimination when he is "coincidentally" fired once news of his affliction is made known. The movie, directed by Jonathan Demme, was considered a high commercial and artistic risk. Despite platitudes about sympathizing with AIDS victims, the motion-picture industry is as guilty as any other when it comes to discriminatory practices. There was not only speculation that such a downbeat story line would fail to appeal to holiday audiences (the movie was released in the Christmas, 1993, season); but there was also concern that Hanks might well be ostracized from romantic leading parts due to his determination to portray a gay man. He explained his motivation for doing the film, saying, "Well, I got older. And at some point, not too long ago, my sense of responsibility to my work began to shift. And I think we've been through a lot of stuff and we're ready for the nineties, you know? You can't be thirty-seven years old and still be tripping over suitcases in a house that never gets finished or being confounded by that dumb dog who just won't listen to you."

The skeptics were proved wrong once *Philadelphia* was released. Not only did it become a sizable commercial hit for Tri-Star Pictures; Hanks would win his first Oscar for Best Actor.

Hanks's acceptance speech at the Academy Awards proved to be more controversial than the film itself. In a long, heartfelt (some say rambling) "thank you," he added: "I could not be standing here if it weren't for two very important men in my life: Mr. Rawley Farnsworth, who was my high school drama teacher, who taught me to act well the part. There all the glory lies. And one of my classmates, Mr. John Gilkerson. I mention their names because they are two of the finest gay Americans, two wonderful men that I had the good fortune to be associated with, to fall under their inspiration at such a young age. . . . I know that my work in this case is magnified by the fact that the streets of heaven are too crowded with angels. We know their names. They number a thousand for each one of the red ribbons that we wear here tonight. They finally rest in the warm embrace of the gracious creator of us all. A healing embrace that cools their fevers, that clears their skin, and allows their eyes to see the simple, self-evident, common-sense truth that is made manifest by the benevolent creator of us all and was written down on paper by wise men, tolerant men, in the city of Philadelphia two hundred years ago. God bless us all. God have there—the level of the [AIDS] tragedy that has been going on so long is just too big. And I thought that was connected to the Constitution."

The controversy of *Philadelphia* and his acceptance speech notwithstanding, Hanks had arrived at the top of the "A" list of bankable actors. Everyone agreed that he was one of the most likable screen presences, but few suspected the depth of his dramatic talents.

In the wake of his Oscar triumph, Hanks declared, "I'm secure and comfortable. I feel loved and embraced. I don't waste an awful lot of time on trying to figure things out. That's very relaxing. Because of the love that Rita and I have, I feel I've been freed up to do a whole different kind of work than I had prior to experiencing that." Certainly, "different" would be an understatement for Hank's next film venture—one of the most original American movies of recent years: *Forrest Gump*. This was a sentimental tale of a slow-witted but likable country boy who, through various twists of fate, becomes an American legend. The film is part soap opera, part comedy, part love story, and part history lesson. Small wonder that *Gump* was considered too offbeat to find its niche among audiences. However, a brilliant marketing campaign stressed Hanks's star power, along with the sweeping events and gentle humor depicted in the film. Indeed, the movie's understated ad campaign—consisting of Hanks sitting on a bench with the now-famous box of chocolates at his side—was to become one of the great success stories in recent movie advertising history. By the time *Gump* opened, in the summer of 1994, *Gump* mania instantly—and unexpectedly—swept the world.

mercy on us all, and God bless America."

Despite the sincerity and poetic quality of Hanks's words, the press focused almost exclusively on his "outing" his former teacher and classmate. Did he have their permission and blessing, or had Hanks just made the most intrusive violation imaginable of these men's private lives? It turned out that Hanks had asked Farnsworth's permission before giving the speech. He praised Hanks for his words and was very moved by the speech. Tragically, Gilkerson had died of AIDS a few years before, thereby making Hanks's words all the more poignant. While Hanks confessed, "I could have gotten off a little sooner, I guess," he said he had no regrets about the speech: "I knew the only thing I truly wanted to say was something germane to the more important aspect of why I was

The nuances Hanks brought to the role and his incomparable skill in making Forrest a model of dignity and respect positioned Hanks as one of the foremost actors of recent years. He was rewarded with a second consecutive Oscar for Best Actor, a feat unrivaled since Spencer Tracy won back-to-back statuettes in 1937 and 1938. (*Gump* would also win several other key Oscars, including Best Picture and Best Director.) So great was the public's appetite for anything *Gump*-related that a merchandising boom was

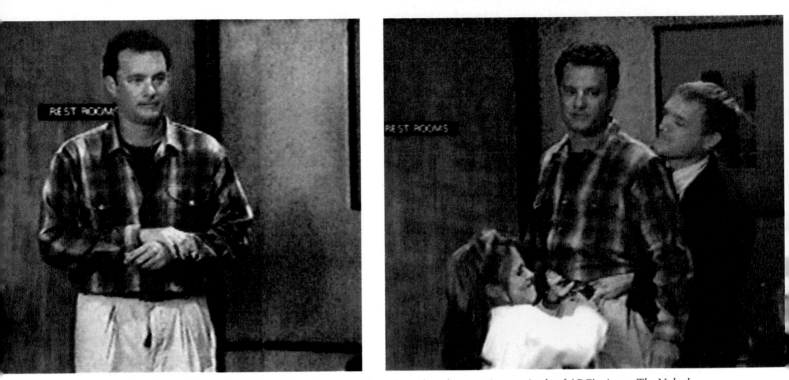

Hanks returned to the small screen in 1995 and faced an especially awkward predicament in an episode of ABC's sitcom *The Naked Truth*. (ABC-TV)

launched by Paramount. With a flood of *Forrest Gump* items vying for shelf space in stores and the public constantly quoting dialogue from the film, even Hanks admitted he was tired of hearing the film's famous line "Life is like a box of chocolates . . ." However, it should not be overlooked that *Forrest Gump* is a masterpiece.

Hanks's phenomenal success had one downside: He was finding it increasingly impossible to perform the day-to-day things that the average person often takes for granted. He told *USA Weekend*, "I've been getting cuts in line at the airport for quite some time, so it has its advantages. It's not so much the loss of privacy; it's how you protect what privacy you have. I made my peace with that a long time ago. I go to a restaurant, and people will take pictures. I go on vacation, and people come up and introduce themselves. Some things I just don't do anymore, like go to the bank, because It's too much trouble. I try to go to the same restaurants and stores, so they're used to me. Every once in a while, I'll go to a new one, and all hell breaks loose. Sometimes it's funny, and sometimes it's a hassle. But if the tragic loss of being a celebrity is that I don't get to go to baseball games as much as I'd like to, that's a price I can pay without much difficulty."

With *Forrest Gump* still making cash registers ring internationally, Hanks decided on his next film project, one that was very much an ensemble piece, teaming him with a talented cast who each get their moments to shine. The film was director Ron Howard's *Apollo 13*, based on the book *Lost Moon* by former astronaut Jim Lovell. Lovell was the commander of the ill-fated 1970 space mission in which a planned landing on the moon had to be aborted when an explosion all but stranded the astronaut's capsule in space with little hope of rescue. The highly dramatic tale of courage and heroism in the face of almost impossible odds seemed like a promising proj-ect for Hanks in more ways than one. In addition to reuniting him with Ron Howard for the first time since *Splash* a decade before, playing Jim Lovell prompted Hanks to say, "I think this is kind of every boy's dream come true. Every little boy . . . wants to play an astronaut."

Since the last big-budget astronaut film, *The Right Stuff*, had been a box-office disappointment, though highly-praised, a decade earlier, there was some wonder whether *Apollo 13* would do any better, especially since everyone knew that the astronauts do make it back to earth (albeit by the seat of their pants in a capsule that was disintegrating with every second). No one was surprised, however, when the movie opened huge in the summer of 1995 and continued to break records in its international engagements. Hanks received solid reviews but dismissed any talk of a third Oscar nomination by saying that the film belonged to everyone and that no particular actor dominated. Modesty aside, however, there was little doubt that Hanks's name above the title was greatly instrumental in the film's stunning reception. The film would later be nominated for Best Picture at the 1996 Academy Awards.

As *Apollo 13* opened, the workaholic Hanks made the surprising announcement "I'm going to relax. I have nothing to do all summer. I've fulfilled my space fantasy. I'm not sure what my other film fantasies are. I'm going to have to dig something up." And relax he did. Hanks and Rita Wilson spent a good deal of time cruising on a yacht through the Mediterranean with Steven Spielberg and wife Kate Capshaw. He also found some time to indulge in hobbies as diverse as surfing, juggling, jogging, scuba diving, golfing, and—his one known eccentricity—collecting antique typewriters. He is also an ardent baseball fan who attends games whenever and wherever he can. He confessed to *Teen* magazine, "I'm your average family Joe. When I'm not working, I like the routine of getting up in the morning, taking care of the house and the kids, then sitting down and having some coffee. Then I just like to piddle around. I talk on the phone, watch television, read, and that's about it. I like boredom—I save the exciting stuff for work." Hanks also admits to having a passion for organizing his CD collection. "I don't know how to fix a screen door, but man, oh, man, can I organize my CDs! I do it five or six times a year, arranged by musical type or theme. I'm constantly looking for the perfect five CDs to put on shuffle so no matter what comes up it's never too jarring from one song to the next. You know, mix in a little Charlie Parker jazz and a movie soundtrack, maybe put the Pretenders in there and come up with the perfect background music." His sister Sandra agreed that he is quite low-key off camera: "His idea of a big day on the town is a double-header at Dodger Stadium, a diet Coke, and a hot dog. I mean, that's Tom!"

Following *Apollo 13*, Hanks provided the voice of a pull-string cowboy opposite Tim Allen's astronaut action figure in Disney's highly innovative *Toy Story*, an ambitious fantasy film which had the distinction of being the first feature-length movie to be created entirely with computer animation. During his well-deserved post-*Apollo* vacation, Hanks was inundated with scripts. For once, he did not feel compelled to choose a new project quickly. He declined the title role of director Oliver Stone's *Nixon* and considered such diverse properties as a biography of Walter Winchell and the sci-fi classic *Stranger in a Strange Land*. By this time, his salary per film—before "perks" and bonuses—had risen to $15 million, making him among the highest-paid actors in the world. Still, he eventually chose a rather low key film for his follow-up to *Apollo*. In *That Thing You Do*, Hanks stars in a tale centering on the adventures of the members of a rock band in 1964. Although he had earlier said, "I don't think I have the wherewithal to direct [a feature-length film] all the way from start to finish," *That Thing You Do*, will indeed mark Hank's debut as a big-screen director. With the success of actors who have tested their talents behind the cameras (Robert Redford, Warren Beatty, Mel Gibson, to name a few), Hanks might very well prove to be an impressive talent in this area. He also is developing films via his own production company, Cla Vius Base (a name he first heard in *2001: A Space Odyssey* referring to the biggest crater on the moon). It does not appear, however, that he and his wife, Rita, will be collaborating on any projects in the near future. In January 1996, Mrs. Hanks gave birth to their son Truman, and the couple decided that either she or Tom will stay home with the children to provide a stable environment. Beyond that? Hanks jokingly says, "Well, yes . . . I am battling Kevin Costner for the rights to *Snagglepuss: the Movie!*"

Few actors have accomplished so much before reaching their fortieth birthday. There is enthusiasm by Hanks's admirers about the work which can be accomplished by this actor in the years to come. Yet, by all accounts he remains remarkably free of ego and pretentiousness. Perhaps friend Steven Spielberg described Hanks's qualities most succinctly when he said, "Tom doesn't fit into the molds of the other American icons. It's too easy to find a couple of people that share that same all-Americanness that you can compare him to. But Tom Hanks will always be remembered for being Tom Hanks. He is without peer." As for Hanks's own succinct self-analysis, he simply says, "I really like this high-paying movie-star gig, and I'd like to hold on to it as long as they'll let me."

Hanks accepting the Oscar for *Forrest Gump*, 1995

The FILMS

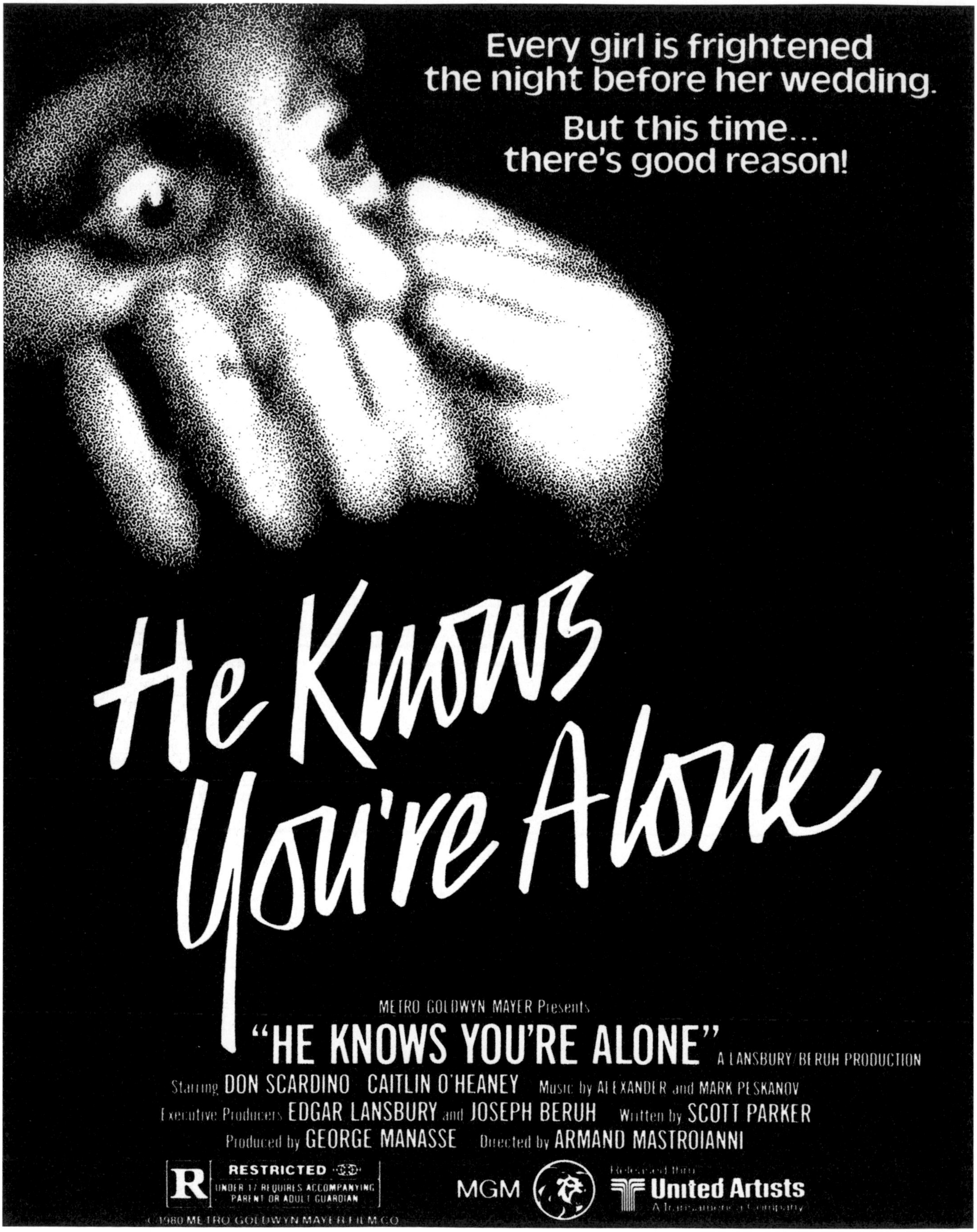
Every girl is frightened
the night before her wedding.
But this time...
there's good reason!
He Knows You're Alone
METRO GOLDWYN MAYER Presents
"HE KNOWS YOU'RE ALONE"
A LANSBURY/BERUH PRODUCTION
Starring DON SCARDINO CAITLIN O'HEANEY Music by ALEXANDER and MARK PESKANOV
Executive Producers EDGAR LANSBURY and JOSEPH BERUH Written by SCOTT PARKER
Produced by GEORGE MANASSE Directed by ARMAND MASTROIANNI
R RESTRICTED
UNDER 17 REQUIRES ACCOMPANYING PARENT OR ADULT GUARDIAN
MGM
United Artists
©1980 METRO GOLDWYN MAYER FILM CO

He Knows You're Alone

Metro Goldwyn Mayer, 1980

"It was one of those hack-and-slash movies they made out on Staten Island for about forty bucks."

Cast
Don Scardino (*Marvin*); Caitlin O'Heaney (*Amy*); Elizabeth Kemp (*Nancy*); Tom Rolfing (*Killer*); Lewis Arlt (*Gamble*); Patsy Pease (*Joyce*); James Rebhorn (*Professor*); Tom Hanks (*Elliot*).

Credits
Director: Armand Mastroianni; producer: George Manasse; executive producers: Edgar Lansbury and Joseph Beruh; screenplay: Scott Parker; director of photography: Gerald Fell; editor: George T. Norris; art director: Susan Kaufman; music: Alexander and Mark Peskanov. Running time: 94 minutes.

Original pressbook ad (M-G-M/United Artists)

Tom Hanks's inauspicious big-screen debut occurred in this run-of-the-mill slasher film. The genre has its roots in the 1972 shock-shlock exploitation "masterpiece" *Last House on the Left*, a gore fest which proudly boasted a budget slightly higher than the average home movie. The film set the tone for virtually every copycat movie which would follow: A lot of pretty young women and their typically hapless boyfriends are slashed, hacked, and mutilated by a mysterious fiend who has the good timing to generally make his strike while couples are engaged in sexual activity. This gives some justification for enough frequent nudity to allow audience members to temporarily lift their noses from their "barf bags."

The genre peaked in the late 1970s and early 1980s upon the release of the first *Friday the 13th* film and John Carpenter's original *Halloween* (which retains its status as the only worthwhile slasher movie made to date). While most of these movies proved to be somewhat less artistically satisfying than the works of Alfred Hitchcock, they would occasionally serve as a showcase for promising actors and actresses who would later move on to legitimate stardom in A movies. (Jamie Lee Curtis, once seemingly hopelessly typecast as a "scream queen," is one of the more notable alumni of the "Dead Teenager Movies.")

3

As Elliot, a brief bright spot in an otherwise-run-of-the-mill slasher film (M-G-M/United Artists)

By 1980, Tom Hanks was already feeling the pangs of frustration which every actor experiences. He recalled: "I never assumed I'd get out of TV. I always thought, This is all there is. I thought that after this series gets canceled, maybe I'll land another TV series. I don't know how people operate like that, consciously thinking, Now I will move to features. I just thought that I have to do well and that if my luck held out I would always work in the same medium, but maybe with better material."

At this same point in time, an aspiring director named Armand Mastroianni, an American cousin of Italian screen legend Marcello Mastroianni, had been suffering frustrations of his own trying to interest studios in a light comedy he had written about two Brooklyn families. With no professional credits on his resumé, Mastroianni was rejected at every turn despite the fact that studio brass were basically complimentary about his writing skills. He would later say, "There was interest [in the comedy script] but who wants to take a chance on an unknown director?" Finding that necessity was the mother of invention, Mastroianni quickly switched gears and told the studio that he would drop his comedy project in favor of exploiting the recent popularity of slasher movies. Ultimately, he interested executive producers Edgar Lansbury (Angela's brother) and Joseph Beruh into backing his directorial debut with a low-budget thriller. (Mastroianni may have been encouraged by Lansbury's experience with bringing cinematic horror to the screen. After all, he was the executive producer

of the disastrous film version of *Godspell*, a movie which did more to aid the cause of atheism than all the writings of Madalyn Murray O'Hair.) Ultimately, M-G-M agreed to distribute the film—if and when it could be completed on its meager budget.

Mastroianni boasted to the press that *He Knows You're Alone* would take moviegoers "on a trip where they have not been taken before." Unfortunately, his destination did not prove to be some far-flung planet or the dark recesses of the human mind but rather Staten Island, a respectable but unremarkable middle-class borough of New York City. Mastroianni had grown up on Staten Island and had attended school there. He decided to use the place as the sole location of his film because of its "cheery sites"(!). This must have come as news to native Staten Islanders, who have long been critical of being treated as the second-class stepchild of the other boroughs. So resentful are the residents of being deprived of any meaningful cultural attractions that they have long threatened to secede from the rest of New York City. Indeed, the borough's main claim to fame is that it is about the only major population center in the United States that won't allow its residents to make a round trip outside the borough without incurring a seven-dollar toll!

Nevertheless, Mastroianni pretentiously claimed that he was basing his film on his home turf for atmospheric reasons: "When people see a spooky old castle, with lightning flashing around it, they know they are supposed to be scared. It's been done—pardon the expression—to death. But when the scene of the crime is friendly and familiar, they're lulled into a false sense of security.... The most friendly and familiar places are the most terrifying if you look at them the right way. You can't take people on an old, familiar trip to a graveyard or a haunted house and expect them to be terrified. They've been there. You've got to give them a different ride—and their money's worth. By making the scene of the crime an ordinary, everyday locale, the terror is magnified. Any house can become a house of horrors if the audience is aware of some danger which the character of the film has not yet discovered. That's when you start screaming at the screen, 'Don't open that door,' or 'Don't go back inside!' "

The ill-fated Amy (Caitlin O'Heaney), who's about to face a killer who has something against brides (M-G-M/United Artists)

Mastroianni's prediction of people's reaction proved to be true. The audience did scream, "Don't open that door!" and, "Don't go back inside." Unfortunately, it was when they were leaving the theater and warning those who were waiting on line to see *He Knows You're Alone*. All of Mastroianni's talk about finding terror in everyday settings is valid enough when one is dealing with Hitchcock directing Cary Grant in the crop-dusting sequence of *North By Northwest*. However, one feels that Mastroianni criticizes the use of using a "spooky old castle with lightning flashing around it" simply because there is not an abundance of such castles on Staten Island and his budget wouldn't allow him to travel to more exotic locales—or at least across the bridge to "spooky" New Jersey or "frightening" Brooklyn.

He Knows You're Alone centers on a young woman named Amy (Caitlin O'Heaney) who gets second thoughts about her pending wedding when her fiancé goes on a bachelor weekend with his buddies. She receives conflicting advice from her girlfriends and is constantly pursued by ex-beau Marvin (Don Scardino), who is relentless in trying to charm her into marrying him. Simultaneously, a mad killer (Tom Rolfing, looking like a greasy version of Desi Arnaz Jr.) with a penchant for stalking women who

have recently become engaged, is shadowing Amy's every move. (The reason is never explained. Neither is Amy's skittishness. Before she ever sees the killer, she is jumping out of her panty hose at every turn.) At first, she thinks she is imagining things, but it becomes apparent that she is indeed being targeted by the mysterious, threatening presence of the stranger. In the true tradition of female movie victims, Amy never makes more than a cursory attempt to alert her friends or seek help and always ensures that she has ample time to jog alone through secluded woods, walk through dark basements, and otherwise provide ample opportunities to be assaulted.

The killer begins to murder all of those close to Amy, although in this small town news seems to travel slowly. Despite a spree of brutal killings, no one seems unduly alarmed except Detective Gamble (Lewis Arlt), whose fiancée was murdered on what would have been their wedding day years ago. Obsessed with finding his lover's killer, Gamble for some strange reason is allowed free reign to use Amy as bait for his personal vendetta. Meanwhile, Amy goes blithely on her way, like Mr. Magoo, oblivious to the destruction she is causing those around her, as the killer systematically eliminates her closest friends. The film limps toward a ludicrous conclusion in

The killer (Tom Rolfing) "drops in" on Amy, who's taken refuge in a morgue. How convenient! (M-G-M/United Artists)

Tom Hanks appears briefly as Elliot, a charming, if somewhat pretentious, psychology student who escorts Amy and her girlfriend to a local carnival—in the dead of winter! Hanks's raison d'être seems to be to give a rather obvious and heavy-handed lecture on people's need to place themselves in terrifying situations. The purpose of his dialogue is to awkwardly blend in a mention of the impact the shower scene from *Psycho* had. Incredibly, his lecture is followed almost immediately by—you guessed it—a young woman taking a shower while the killer roams the house. (At least this rip-off is intentional, as Mastroianni even duplicates some exact camera angles. In one of the film's rare moments of original-ity, the inevitable murder does *not* occur in the shower, although we are treated to a rare and unexpected nude scene that is refreshingly devoid of any redeeming social value, nor is it even slightly integral to the plot.)

which Amy and Marvin are stalked by the killer in the local morgue. (Keep in mind, this setting was used by a director who wanted to illustrate how terror could be found in locales that are "cheery" and not cliché. If Mastroianni considered the local morgue a disarming and pleasant atmosphere, one can only wonder about his social life. Does he picnic in cemeteries?)

He Knows You're Alone uses practically every cliché known to moviegoers and throws in a few we've probably forgotten. The film also keeps intact the requisite pattern of behavior for all potential victims of a cinematic mass murderer: Despite knowing the danger they are in, everyone makes sure they go off in different directions to investigate the weird and terrifying events by themselves. Why don't all of these folks ever just decide to stay in one room until they are rescued? We are also given a number of the required "false scares" which are mandatory in films of this type (i.e., a curtain menacingly pulled back to reveal a friendly face).

Except for Lewis Arlt as Detective Gamble, the cast of *He Knows You're Alone* isn't good enough to help compensate for the weak script, nor is it bad enough to provide the unintentional laughter which so often makes movies like this somewhat enjoyable. Although Arlt's screen time is very limited, he is one of those larger-than-life bad actors who makes you yearn for his next fleeting appearance. He single-handedly helps keep this otherwise forgettable chop-and-slasher potboiler from being a bore.

While it would be an exaggeration to say that Tom Hanks gave a memorable performance, he does manage to impress during his few minutes on film. His likable nature is apparent even at this early stage, and unlike some of his costars, he seems perfectly comfortable in front of the camera. Hanks has occasionally been asked to recall this film during interviews. At one point, he said of the movie: "It was hack 'n slash made for about ninety bucks on Staten Island. I got the role because I walked into an audition and did a reading and they said, 'Oh, okay.' I had three days on this movie. I didn't know what I was doing. I just showed up and learned how to hit a mark and then moved on. I mean, *c'mon*, it was a long time ago. . . . It certainly went to the *top* of my resumé!"

Hanks was paid $800 for his seven-minute appearance portraying a character he would later describe as "some geek who appeared out of nowhere and then disappeared. . . ." He would add almost mournfully, "I don't even get killed as I remember!" On another occasion, he referred to the film by saying, "You remember it, of course. It swept all the major awards!"

Having pointed out that *He Knows You're Alone* is by no means a classic thriller, it should be stated that it is not the worst film of its kind. Mastroianni restrains himself from the rampant bloodbaths found in other movies of this genre. (The murders generally occur off camera, and nary a drop of blood splatters on the lens.) At times—against all logic—the film manages to convey a bit of suspense. However, the baffling conclusion is more bewildering than scary, and the sloppiness of Scott Parker's script is not much help throughout the rest of the story.

Elliot, philosophizing about the human need to be scared. Perhaps Hanks himself was scared that someone might see this film! (M-G-M/United Artists)

Trivia Note

Martial-arts fans might recognize the late actor Steve James (of the *American Ninja* movies) in an early sequence in which he and his on-screen girlfriend are questioned by Detective Gamble about a murder.

Although the producers bragged that on the basis of advance previews of the film "[Mastroianni] is being deluged by offers," the truth is that the only Mastroianni best known to moviegoers today is still the Italian lover, dear old Marcello. Obviously, a cinematic dynasty was not to be.

M-G-M released *He Knows You're Alone* in

1980 with the realization that it was slightly less prestigious than other films associated with the studio (i.e., *Ben-Hur*, *Mutiny on the Bounty*, *Singin' in the Rain*). The skimpy press book advised theater owners of clever marketing plans to entice the public. Among the more notable brainstorms: "You might want to put the title at the bottom of your buttered popcorn cups so when patrons look for the last few kernels they'll get the unexpected warning!" (Just how many moviegoers have a habit of trying to read the bottom of the butter-soaked popcorn cup in a darkened theater while the film is playing is left unclear.) Another imaginative game plan suggested: "The idea is to urge singles to get together to see *He Knows You're Alone*, since a good scare is a shared experience—and there's no better way to meet a new friend than to clutch at the nearest arm!" Shockingly, droves of "singles" didn't make their initial date a movie about a maniacal killer stalking desperate women.

Perhaps more theaters should have implemented the most elaborate publicity ploy suggested by the studio to replicate one of the movie's more gruesome scenes: "Install a large tropical fish tank in your lobby—complete with gravel bed, plant life, an aerator and, of course, fish. Then place a mannequin's head—its eyes opened wide and its hair billowing out—on the bottom. For further shock value, place your aerator so that bubbles seem to escape from the mannequin's lips. And if a local mechanical whiz kid can make the head's eyes seem to blink from time to time, you've got the display of the year!" The only thing lacking might have been a recording of Dionne Warwick singing "Going Out of My Head."

Despite such marketing gimmicks, *He Knows You're Alone* played a few short weeks in theaters and vanished from the minds of moviegoers. It's only claim to fame is that it presented Tom Hanks with his first feature-film role. The movie is available on tape, and to M-G-M Home Video's credit, they have not adopted the misleading tactics of some of the other studios and repackaged the movie to suggest that Hanks is the star of the film. In fact, the star is neither Hanks nor any of the actors. The *real* star of *He Knows You're Alone* is the arsenal of knives employed by the maniacal on-screen killer. The abundance of cutlery leads to the movie's biggest (and perhaps intentional) laugh—a special "Thank You" in the closing credits to the Hoffritz Corporation!

Reviews

"The latest in a ghoul's parade of cheaply made horror movies by young and unknown filmmakers. It is the first theatrical film for the 30 year old director . . . and it shows in uncertain pacing, halting performances and innumerable technical flaws. Some of the footage is obviously overexposed, the sound has a persistent echo and the music is tinny and intrusive. Scott Parker's screenplay is as full of holes as the victims. In fact, the film's only asset is Don Scardino, who was last seen as Al Pacino's neighbor in Cruising *and who is the only member of the cast with significant professional experience."*

—Tom Buckley, *New York Times*

"Yet another entry into the slice-and-dice genre, this one with the minor novelty of brides-to-be as victims. A bit less bloody than others of its like, otherwise, business as usual."

—*Leonard Maltin's Movie and Video Guide*

"Standard, grisly rampaging killer fare. . . . It marks a no-more-than-competent feature debut for director Armand Mastroianni. Scott Parker's script is but a pretext to pile up as many stabbed and slashed corpses of pretty young women as the traffic will bear. Mastroianni works up a fair amount of fright, but the effect is, needless to say, morbid in the utmost. . . . There are the usual bows to Hitchcock and even the time-honored trick of opening the film with a scene that proves to be a movie-within-a-movie. Scenes depicting the police are particularly inept and derivative. . . . That people should pay money to see such films is ridiculous when you think about it."

—Kevin Thomas, *Los Angeles Times*

Rona Jaffe's "Mazes and Monsters"

CBS–Lorimar, 1982

"The most difficult part of this role is fighting my own personality—toning myself down."

Cast
Tom Hanks (*Robbie Wheeling*); Chris Makepeace (*J. J. Brockaway*); Wendy Crewson (*Kate*); David Wallace (*Daniel*); Susan Strasberg (*Meg*); Vera Miles (*Cat*); Anne Francis (*Elle*); Lloyd Bochner (*Mr. Wheeling*).

Credits
Director: Steven H. Stern; producers: Tom McDermott and Richard A. Briggs; teleplay: Tom Lazarus, from the novel by Rona Jaffe; director of photography: Laszlo George; art director: Trevor Williams; editor: Bill Parker; music: Hagood Hardy. Running time: 103 minutes.

Tom Hanks's first lead role in a motion picture (albeit a TV movie) came in *Rona Jaffe's "Mazes and Monsters,"* an offbeat Canadian-made production which aired on CBS while Hanks was making waves with *Bosom Buddies* on ABC. The film revolved around a real-life incident in which a college student became so enthralled with the fantasy game Dungeons and Dragons that he took his role-playing to an extreme and seemingly vanished off the face of the earth. The well-publicized case launched an exhaustive search for the eccentric student, which led to underground caverns and endless man-made tunnels that stretched for miles beneath the campus.

Novelist Rona Jaffe became intrigued by the power this game held over some of its players, those who seemed to become obsessed with the fantasy elements to such an extreme that they could no longer function in the real world. In essence, the game is a long, complicated "adventure" in which the participants take on the identities of sword-and-sorcery heroes and villains. Each tries to outwit the other in order to survive various obstacles. Although intended to be played as a board game, by the time the craze peaked in the early eighties, some of the more impressionable players had gone to the extremes of actually enacting the story at remote locations, while dressed in medieval garb. (Remember this was in the days before "safe" computer games like Nintendo would transform such impressionable youth into a generation of couch potatoes.)

The TV movie opens with Robbie Wheeling (Tom Hanks) arriving at a new college after having gotten poor grades at a previous school. His disappointed parents warn him that he'd better shape up and improve his performance this year and "not to play that dreadful game" again. Robbie intends to do just that, but shortly after settling into his dorm, he becomes friends with brilliant J.J. Brockaway (Chris Makepeace), who is well into his college studies despite being only sixteen. J.J. introduces Robbie to his two best friends, Kate (Wendy Crewson) and

to move into his dorm room. When she tells him he is moving the relationship along too fast, Robbie becomes sullen and withdrawn. He increasingly turns to Mazes and Monsters to fulfill his fantasies, which include an obsession to find his long-lost brother who ran away from home years before. Taking the advice of a mythical game character he sees in a dream, Robbie officially breaks off his relationship with Kate, although they remain friends. However, he seems to be increasingly taking on the characteristics of his Mazes and Monsters alter ego—Pardieu—a fictional holy man from centuries ago.

Robbie launches a search for his lost brother, using directions from the character he dreams of. The

J.J. (Chris Makepeace), Kate (Wendy Crewson), and Robbie (Hanks) play with their toys. (CBS-Lorimar)

Daniel (David Wallace). The three attempt to entice Robbie into participating in their frequent games of "Mazes and Monsters."

Robbie initially declines the invitation; obsession with the game caused his problems in the previous school. However, he agrees to try just one game, only to be hooked again. He also forms an attachment to Kate, and before long the two are lovers. Several times a week, they meet with J.J. and Daniel to develop even more complicated "Mazes and Monsters" scenarios. Ultimately, the games become the center of their lives, and when J.J. suggests they dress in costume and play the games in a series of nearby secret caves, his friends readily agree.

Now deeply in love with Kate, Robbie asks her

mysterious being in Robbie's imagination also begins to give him instructions about how to live his life. If Robbie "purifies" his body and soul, he will be given clues as to how to be reunited with his brother. Ultimately, Robbie disappears from campus, leaving his worried friends to search frantically for him. They enlist the help of the police, but to no avail. Fearing Robbie is dead, Kate is initially relieved to get a phone call from him informing her he is in New York City and desperately in need of help. Before Kate, J.J., and Daniel arrive, however, Robbie again lets Pardieu take over his personality. His friends track him to the top of the World Trade Center and rescue him just as he is about to leap—the final act in his quest to find his brother. Robbie regains his senses and is emotionally reunited with his friends.

The film has a twist ending which finds Kate, Daniel, and J.J. visiting Robbie at his home three months later. Although his mother assures them he is coming along well, they are shocked to find he has totally reverted back to the personality of Pardieu—presumably forever.

Tom Hanks described the challenges involved in playing a complicated character like Robbie: "It's completely different than anything I've ever done. You know that something terrible will happen, that this guy, Robbie, is going to go through pure hell. It's a real workout for me. I have to let Tom Hanks disappear into the background when the cameras roll. But that is what is the most fun about it. I feel I'm working at a much more intense level than I've had at various times in the past."

He described the character of Robbie Wheeling thusly: "Robbie is as dark as India ink—he could be dangerous, but he doesn't have the chutzpah. I tried to find a piece of music I could latch on to and think about it, or styles of paintings or movies—things that would impress Robbie. . . . He would like to see himself as a hero in a Wagner opera—one of those holier-than-thou, greater-than-great types you find only in Wagner."

Hanks said that he based part of his characterization on his own experience playing Dungeons and Dragons: "I had a perception of it that people who haven't played the game wouldn't have. It's pretty indescribable because it's a game completely within your own imagination. So, if you have a particularly vivid imagination, it can be quite scary. The deeper, darker demons we all have inside us can really come to the forefront. That's what happened to Robbie. . . . At one point or another we all have lost a real slant on reality. Some people jump to conclusions very easily, some exaggerate. But Robbie's a paranoid schizophrenic. . . . I'm an actor, but I'm not that crazy."

Hanks's description of his character is somewhat misleading in that it makes it appears as though it will be obvious from the start of the story that Robbie is

Robbie begins to take on his *Mazes* character's persona. (CBS-Lorimar)

an emotionally unstable person headed toward personal disaster. In fact, that is not the case. The screenplay has a number of intriguing twists, the most interesting of which is the presumption that the jealousy J.J. holds over Kate's dating Robbie will lead him to be the center of the oncoming crisis. Until this point, we feel that J.J. is the most disturbed member of the group. He may be the intellectual equal of his classmates, but at age sixteen he is too young to truly fit in on campus (as telegraphed by his tendency to don silly hats). When the story veers in another direction and establishes Robbie as the most unstable individual, it comes as a genuine surprise.

Meeting his fears head-on in the cave (CBS-Lorimar)

Fearing he may have killed someone, Robbie calls his friends for help. (CBS-Lorimar)

As TV movies go, *"Mazes and Monsters"* suffers from some of the lesser production values inherent in the medium. However, compared to many other films made for television, it is an ambitious, consistently interesting effort that at least dares to be different and thought provoking. The film can't resist stooping to a number of clichés: Kate explores the inside of a dangerous maze of caves by herself at night; Robbie's sweat-drenched nightmares (are there any other kind?) come complete with a shadowy figure standing at the end of a tunnel, calling out to him, mist swirling at his feet—like a Woolworth version of Auntie Em calling for Dorothy from inside the old hourglass; and the students' parents are all self-centered, troubled stereotypes.

Nevertheless, director Steven H. Stern keeps the action moving rapidly and avoids almost as many clichés as he indulges in. The sequences inside the caves are scary despite the phony sets, and the script dares to give us an ending that is anything but uplifting. The performances are a mixed bag. Chris Makepeace and David Wallace are acceptable most of the time, but occasionally they slip into the kind of "Hey, kids, we can put a show on in the barn!" enthusiasm that reminds one of an early sixties sitcom. Hanks dominates with a daring, truly fascinating performance. Wendy Crewson is excellent as Kate. This very talented actress has worked consistently in Canadian films in recent years. Even this early in his career, he displayed the subtle nuances and low-key, natural mannerisms that helped create so many interesting characters in his work over the years to follow.

Reviews

"Miss Jaffe takes her story and characters through some fairly predictable turns as the game proceeds to its 'logical extension.' But gradually, her carefully diagrammed contraption begins to work with reasonable effectiveness. Several guest stars . . . are on hand as the assorted parents, but their parts add up to little more than extended walk-ons. The younger actors are required to carry the film and they do so with remarkable skills. The plot takes some startling turns . . . But the game-players take it all in stride. And in the end, the film achieves a broader 'rites of passage' experience than most viewers might be expecting."

—John J. O'Connor, *New York Times*

"In this silly made-for-TV drama about fantasy role-playing adventures, Hanks plays a neurotic college kid who 'flips into the game' and becomes convinced he really is 'Pardieu, the Holy Man.' He almost keeps a straight face, too."

—Ty Burr, *Entertainment Weekly*

The made-for-TV movie's subsequent video release capitalized on Hanks's star power. (CBS-Lorimar)

TOM HANKS in
Rona Jaffe's
MAZES
AND
MONSTERS

KARL·LORIMAR
HOME VIDEO

VHS

MERMAID FOUND
HELD BY FEDS
...man to be released today

Splash
Touchstone, 1984

"I was very fortunate to get the role. It served as an important opportunity for me to get away from doing straight-out comedy. The challenge was invigorating."

Cast
Tom Hanks (*Allen Bauer*); Daryl Hannah (*Madison*); John Candy (*Freddie Bauer*); Eugene Levy (*Walter Kornbluth*); Dody Goodman (*Mrs. Stimler*); Shecky Greene (*Mr. Buyrite*); Richard B. Shull (*Dr. Ross*); Bobby DiCicco (*Jerry*); Howard Morris (*Dr. Zidell*); Tony Di Benedetto (*Tim the Doorman*).

Credits
Director: Ron Howard; producer: Brian Grazer; executive producer: John Thomas Lenox; screenplay: Lowell Ganz and Babaloo Mandel and Bruce Jay Friedman; screen story: Bruce Jay Friedman, based on an idea by Brian Grazer; director of photography: Don Peterman; underwater director of photography: Jordan Klein; production designer: Jack T. Collis; editors: Daniel P. Hanley and Michael Hill; costume designer: Mary Routh; special visual effects supervisor: Mitch Suskin; mermaid design and construction: Robert Short; music: Lee Holdridge. Running time: 111 minutes.

A fortuitous guest spot on *Happy Days* helped Hanks land the role of Allen Bauer. (Buena Vista Distribution Co.)

A scant four years after Tom Hanks made his feature-film debut in the dismal *He Knows You're Alone*, the aspiring star would hit pay dirt with *Splash*, a modestly budgeted comedy that would become a watershed (no pun intended) movie for virtually everyone concerned. It would establish Ron Howard as a major director; elevate Howard's partner-producer Brian Grazer to the level of a true Tinseltown power player; ensure that Disney's new "mature" distribution arm Touchstone Pictures would debut with a smash hit; make the previously unknown Daryl Hannah a media sensation; and raise Tom Hanks from the ranks of lightweight television actor to a leading box-office draw literally overnight.

Yet the success of *Splash* was anything but a foregone conclusion. The modern-day fantasy/comedy about an everyday man who finds himself in love with a mermaid had a troubled origin. Producer Brian Grazer had been driving along California's Pacific Coast Highway and, as he observed the pounding surf, began to daydream about mermaids. He developed the idea into a potential film project along with writer Bruce Jay Friedman, and the project was approved by United Artists. However, the film was soon put into "turnaround" by the studio due to concern over well-publicized plans relating to producer Ray Stark's proposed rival comedy, *Mermaid*, which

futility to compete with a film of a similar nature, not to mention its high-priced talent. Therefore, *Splash* was dropped as an active project.

Undeterred, Grazer pitched the project to his friend and partner Ron Howard, with whom he had recently completed the comedy *Night Shift*. Howard, in the process of establishing himself as a director of some consequence, was initially reluctant to participate. He had already passed on the sleeper hits *Mr. Mom* and *Footloose* and now wondered if his judgment would be questionable again by directing films for Disney. He only had two other films to his credit—the low-budget Roger Corman exploitation film *Grand Theft Auto* and the yet-to-be released *Night Shift*. "I wasn't sure I wanted to do another comedy after *Night Shift*," he explained. "But I started thinking about the romantic possibilities of the project, and we came up with a new structure. Lowell (Ganz) and Babaloo (Mandel) did a one-page rewrite, and it became a character comedy, more of a love story." Still, Howard found the story needed work. "There was too much time underwater in the first draft," he recalled. "There was this kind of underwater kingdom with scenes, dialogue, and jokes, and it was not going to be believable. Now it's mostly above water, and it's really the guy's point of view. We had nothing to lose. We were the underdogs. The people at Disney were the only ones to believe in us."

Howard's reference to the Disney people's enthusiasm was based on the studio's plan to create a distribution company that specialized in more mature fare. The new outfit, Touchstone Pictures, was the subject of widespread industry speculation. In recent years, Disney had reestablished itself as a leader in the genre of children's films. However, there was skepticism that the studio "suits" were hip enough to create and market movies for the dating crowd.

Splash was given a modest budget of $8 million by Touchstone, and industry analysts felt that the film was destined to fight a David versus Goliath battle with *Mermaid*. Complicating matters was a pending

was to be written by Robert Towne and directed by Herbert Ross. Warren Beatty had committed to the project, and his likely costar would be Jessica Lange. With *Mermaid* budgeted at a then astronomical $30 million, United Artists felt it would be an exercise in strike by actors which could cripple production. Both *Splash* and *Mermaid* had to complete filming before the strike went into effect or delay production until it was settled. Ultimately, the *Mermaid* project fell apart, allowing *Splash* to proceed without worrying about the competition.

In *Splash*, the protagonist, Allen Bauer, is a non-descript young New Yorker who fears commitment in relationships. While vacationing on Martha's Vine-

she is a mermaid. When a suspicious scientist reveals Madison's secret, she is captured by the government and treated like a circus freak until Allen rescues her.

Ron Howard's foremost challenge was to find a male lead. John Travolta, Michael Keaton, Bill Murray, Chevy Chase, and Dudley Moore all turned down the project. Howard remembered having worked with Tom Hanks in an episode of *Happy Days* in which Hanks played a childhood victim of

Brotherly love: The scenes Hanks and John Candy (big brother Freddie) share number among the film's funniest. (Buena Vista Distribution Co.)

yard as a youngster, he encountered a beautiful mermaid his age. He has convinced himself that it was a figment of his imagination, although the "vision" is the only girl he has truly ever loved. As an adult, Allen now finds his life thrown into chaos when he encounters a strange but beautiful woman who seems completely unfamiliar with modern society. The girl—who is named Madison by Allen (after seeing the street sign for Madison Avenue)—is actually the same mermaid he briefly glimpsed while a boy. Now Madison, who has been equally haunted by Allen, has come to New York to seek out her would-be lover. Allen is instantly smitten, although he never suspects

Fonzie's bullying. Years later, he became a karate expert and returned to town for vengeance on the Fonz. Hanks's performance impressed Howard, who was starring in the show as Richie Cunningham at the time: "Tom was just hysterically funny and made a lasting impression."

Initially, Howard and Brian Grazer considered Hanks for the part of Allen's boorish, womanizing brother Freddie. It soon became obvious, however, that Hanks could handle the wide emotional range that the role of Allen required. Recalled Grazer: "The character was funny but not quirky. Most comedians have a cute, idiosyncratic quality. We didn't want

17

Daryl Hannah plays Madison, the beautiful mermaid who comes to shore at the Statue of Liberty in search of Allen. (Buena Vista Distribution Co.)

that. Tom is warm. Men like him. Women like him. But it was odd. There he was with everything at stake. And his career was stalled. They wouldn't even let him read for *Policy Academy*. But he walked into the audition in jeans, construction boots, and a work shirt. I've seen thousands of actors read for parts, and I've never seen anyone who looked as if he felt comfortable with himself."

Howard asked Hanks if he was a stand-up comic. "No, I won't do stand-up." replied Hanks. "I'm a chickenshit. Give me something written down and I think I can be funny. But don't tell me to get up there and be funny." Howard liked this candor. Gradually, he began to envision Hanks in the role of Allen: "Tom had to be serious and poignant as well as romantic and vulnerable. I think of him as a terrific leading man, like Jack Lemmon or James Stewart." Hanks would recall ten years later: "The only reason why I got the part was because absolutely no one else would do it. Ron Howard was so desperate, he had to try his luck with me—a complete novice who had no idea what he was doing."

Despite his nervousness, Hanks quickly formed his own interpretation of his character: "The guy was a potato, he was a lox, and that's what I was trying to portray, a swept-away character. If he hadn't met this girl, he would have ended up in forty years as a bitter guy sitting on a park bench who doesn't even come alive for the baseball season."

With Hanks firmly on board, Howard and

Grazer next faced the equally daunting task of finding their Madison, the innocent but sensual mermaid. It was essential that they find an actress with those qualities, who would be willing to endure the rigors of spending much of her time underwater wearing the gigantic tail which had been constructed for the film. (Early prototypes of the tail did not hold up in salt water, and for a while it was considered that these wrinkly rejects might be used for the character of an older "bag lady"–type mermaid. And it was originally planned that the sequence in which the audience views Madison's transformation from normal woman into a mermaid would be rather shocking, à la *An American Werewolf in London*. This was rejected in favor of a more blissful sequence.)

Howard finally found the perfect Madison while auditioning Daryl Hannah, a stunning blonde. "I asked her to jump in [the water] just for size and shape," recalled Howard. "She started dolphin kicking, smiling, and gliding. It was lyrical and beautiful. I told her, 'Do yourself a favor. Get in shape with the tail and do as many of the shots as you physically can.' She studied the moves and twists of dolphins, and after filming ended she said she 'didn't understand how people swam around with these sticks at the ends of their bodies.'"

Having landed the role of Madison, Hannah was determined to perform most of the swimming herself, and did four or five daily dives of forty-five minutes each. (Ultimately, her double was used only once—in silhouette). However, the worst part of the ordeal was having to lie still for three hours each day as technicians continuously applied grease to the mermaid fin. (The trial application took over seven hours!)

At the end of every day, Hannah would literally have to have the thirty-five-pound tail cut away from her body. There was also the problem of minimizing the nudity while Hannah swam through the water. (Walt Disney's ghost would only stand for so much.) Originally, synthetic body appliances were tested, but they did not look real enough. Ultimately, toupee tape was used to adhere Hannah's hair to her breasts. (Hannah, uncomfortable with the nudity, also taped Band-Aids on her nipples.)

Splash was on a very abbreviated production schedule, which included seventeen days in New York City, twenty-nine in Los Angeles, and sixteen in the Bahamas. Hanks and the crew had to undergo extensive underwater training, including lessons in swimming and CPR. Hanks said, "I went through a whole semirigorous scuba-diving instruction course in the cold Pacific before leaving to shoot in the Bahamas. By then, I was a certified diver. Not that there was any danger. We weren't really diving in more than forty feet of water. In fact, it was kind of fun—for me. I'm sure it wasn't fun for Daryl. She had that fin on her!"

Ron Howard had to learn to direct with hand signals, a slate board, and underwater paper. A special Plexiglas and aluminum triangular enclosure was constructed which had an air bubble built into it, allowing Howard to actually talk if hand signals failed to be effective. Still, the logistics of shooting underwater were daunting. "There wasn't enough time for me to look through the camera. We did five or ten setups per dive, with only fifty minutes at our disposal," Howard said.

Madison brings home a special treat for Allen. (Buena Vista Distribution Co.)

The film's underwater director of photography was Jordan Klein, long regarded as a master in his field. (Among Klein's achievements was the phenomenal photography for the undersea battle in *Thunderball*.) He reflected on the unrelenting cold when filming under the sea: "Once anyone gets cold in the water, even if it's eighty degrees, they're working on sheer guts," he said. "This is truly what slowed down the picture. With conventional equipment and divers, the underwater photography might have taken three days instead of close to three weeks."

Despite the difficulties in bringing the film in on

The Imagine team at work: producer Brian Grazer (*left*) and director Ron Howard (Buena Vista Distribution Co.)

schedule, Hanks developed an immediate respect for Howard as a director. He said shortly after filming completed, "My forte was manic comedy, but from the beginning Ron pointed out to me that this was not what I was expected to do, that it was not my job and that if I did that, the movie was going to be terrible. So I was never saying, 'Let's do this 'cause it would be funny.' I was saying, 'Let's do this because it would be interesting. It would fill the guy out a bit. 'Cause he's not stupid, he's not a moron, he has a certain amount of wit.' . . . Ron always told me, 'Don't worry! You're gonna get laughs. But you're gonna get laughs on the look, not the action.' And that's essentially the case. The laugh after the laugh. There is the bona fide thing that makes you laugh, and then there is a character looking at this or reacting in some way that makes you laugh again. So that's what I got, but at the same time I think I got some old-fashioned laughs, too. Things that make people go, 'Hey, pretty

funny guy!' And that's important to me, you know."

With Hanks and Howard both so even-tempered, the atmosphere on the set was anything but tense. The closest thing to a confrontation was recalled by Hanks in 1995: "Ron . . . has first-rate common sense. He gave me one of the best lessons I ever got as an actor. First of all, I couldn't believe I was an actor in a movie, and I hadn't paid attention to the call sheet. And there was a scene with a huge plot point and a huge character point, and it caught me by surprise. He was calm. We did it. We did it again and again. Eventually, we got it. It wasn't like we lost a day or anything. Ron was calm. But he summed up the whole experience by telling me, 'It would have been nice if you were a little more prepared today.' " For his part, Howard was sympathetic to his star. He said at the time, "Tom really has the toughest role. He had to be serious and poignant as well as romantic and vulnerable. There were also moments when he had to be funny, not to mention the difficult scenes where he had to act underwater."

Hanks also enjoyed working with the late John Candy, then primarily known for his work in SCTV. Candy was cast as Hanks's obnoxious (but oddly lovable) brother, and despite their physical differences, the two found they had an immediate rapport. Hanks said at the time, "John and I have developed a surprising dual relationship. And it's not at all competitive or 'Can you top this?' It has been, from the beginning, 'What shall we do here?' John is a pacer—he'll start pacing around and he'll say, 'What if we try this?' By the time we get to actually doing it, it's a meshing of gears that makes some pretty good music. John is an ambassador of goodwill. I never met a guy as sweet and giving. I don't pal around with him off camera. But the things he thinks are funny also crack me up. He also knows how to improvise from his days with Second City. We're striving for the same end result, to be funny and interesting and to get the audience involved."

The joy the cast and crew found in working together is very apparent on-screen and helps make *Splash* a truly delightful and innovative comedy. Despite his low-key mannerisms, Hanks commands the screen and proves that when it comes to getting laughs, Howard's theory of "less is more" is completely accurate. With this film, Hanks established himself as the archetypical Everyman. His reactions to encountering extraordinary circumstances are so believable that they somehow make a love story about a New Yorker and a mermaid seem plausible.

Hanks also proves to be a convincing romantic lead. Both he and Hannah convey innocence and passion with such skill that the audience experiences a full range of emotions—from joy to pity. In addition to Hanks, Hannah, and Candy, the film also boasts a wonderful supporting performance from scene-stealing Eugene Levy, also a veteran of SCTV, as the nerdy scientist who first exposes Madison's identity

On the verge of greatness: early wardrobe test shots for *Splash* (Buena Vista Distribution Co.)

21

as a mermaid, only to later aid in her rescue.

From the film's wonderful, sepia-tone flashback sequence in which the young Allen first encounters Madison to the suspenseful and romantic finale, there is nary a dull moment or an extraneous frame of film. In between are such inspired scenes as Madison devouring a lobster whole (shell and all!) while in a posh Manhattan restaurant; her frantic attempt to prevent Allen from discovering her "secret" as she bathes in his apartment; and Levy's hilarious effort at exposing Madison by showering her with water as she sits near a dais at which the president of the United States is speaking.

Splash opened in March 1984 and grossed $6.1 million in its premiere weekend—then a phenomenal figure. It would ultimately earn over $110 million and become a huge hit on video. Hanks would later say of the film's surprise success, "I didn't think it would be a stinker, maybe a little cartoonish, but the first weekend I get a call. 'Six million bucks at the box office.' You're in your first big film. It's beyond my comprehension. That's a lot of money. You can't get much better right out of the box. It's perfect.'" While Hanks was obviously thrilled at being in "the big leagues," he jokingly complained that he didn't have "points" or a percentage of the film's gross: "The last time [Disney] gave an actor points, I think it was Fess Parker for *Davy Crockett*."

For Ron Howard, who called the movie "the most challenging film" he'd ever done, *Splash* forever ended his reputation as being an overgrown child star. While his previous film *Night Shift* was a surprise hit, many thought its success was just a fluke. *Splash* proved that he was an innovative talent behind the camera, much as he was in front of it. From this point on, Howard would concentrate solely on directing (with the exception of a well-received reprise as Opie Taylor in the 1986 TV reunion movie *Return to Mayberry*). Although he and Hanks worked extremely well together, it would be another ten years before they would team up again on *Apollo 13*.

Hanks joked that the success of *Splash* had truly made him a changed man: "Now I'm sullen and arrogant!" He also said that he was being "deluged" with scripts for which there was no financing. In fact, from this point on, Hanks would find there would never be a shortage of projects. He has always been careful to remember the impact his first starring role had on his career. In 1989 he said, "It was a miracle I was in it, but nobody else wanted to do a Disney movie about a mermaid. If *Splash* had disappeared, I wouldn't be here today."

Reviews

"*Splash* *may feature a heroine with fins, but it's mostly a standard love story, albeit one with some delightful new twists. . . . accomplishes the improbable with some enchanting underwater sequences, scenes that make credible the thought that Daryl Hannah might really be a mermaid. As likable a leading man as Mr. Hanks is, though, and as beguiling as Miss Hannah is in her Boticelliesque incarnation here, the film would not be nearly so successful without the bulldozing presence of John Candy. . . . The mere sight of the tubby Mr. Candy is funny enough.* Splash *could have been shorter, but it probably couldn't have been much sweeter. Only purists will quibble with the blissfully happy ending, which has the lovers swimming through a shimmering underwater paradise that is supposed to be the East River.*"

—Janet Maslin, *New York Times*

Just a simple story of a man who falls in love with a fish! (Buena Vista Distribution Co.)

"A charming mermaid yarn notable for winning suspension of belief and fetching byplay between Daryl Hannah and Tom Hanks . . . whose desperate vulnerability is on the mark. Although film is a bit uneven, production benefits from a tasty look, [and] an airy tone. . . . Hanks makes a fine leap from sitcom land. . . ."

—"Loyn.," *Variety*

"[Hanks and Candy] aren't remotely conceivable as brothers. Hanks is slender and dark with curly hair and crinkly eyes, while Candy is a roaring tub of guts, looks like a lascivious Charles Laughton throwing Christians to the lions in The Sign of the Cross. But the implausibility is itself funny, and the two men complement each other. Hanks, a TV and theater actor, is an expert comic, with steel springs in his legs, but he's also good-looking and relaxed enough to be a leading man. He commands the emotional center of the scenes, holding your sympathy in place, while Candy, a libidinous blond bull, frightening to behold, frolics madly at the edges. . . . It's been a long time since we've had a good boy-meets-fish story, and Splash is a fairly irresistible one."

—David Denby, *New York* magazine

Bachelor Party

20th Century-Fox, 1984

"The entire cast has incredible comedy talents, and I was impressed with the script the moment I read it. It was the only of the the many youth-oriented comedies with genuine wit."

Cast

Tom Hanks (*Rick Gassko*); Tawny Kitaen (*Debbie Thompson*); Adrian Zmed (*Jay O'Neill*); George Grizzard (*Mr. Thompson*); Barbara Stuart (*Mrs. Thompson*); Robert Prescott (*Cole Whittier*); William Tepper (*Dr. Stan Gassko*); Wendie Jo Sperber (*Dr. Tina Gassko*); Barry Diamond (*Rudy*); Gary Grossman (*Gary*); Michael Dudikoff (*Ryko*); Brad Bancroft (*Brad*); Martina Finch (*Phoebe*); Deborah Harmon (*Ilene*); Tracy Smith (*Bobbi*).

Credits

Director: Neal Israel; producers: Ron Moler and Bob Israel; executive producer: Joe Roth; screenplay: Neal Israel and Pat Proft; story: Bob Israel; director of photography: Hal Trussel; art directors: Kevin Conlin and Martin Price; editor: Tom Walls; music: Robert Folk. Running time: 106 minutes.

The calm before the storm. The boys toast Rick on his engagement. (20th Century-Fox)

*B*achelor Party is significant in the career of Tom Hanks in that it proved that the young actor's charisma made him a bankable star and that the success of *Splash* was not merely a fluke. The script is basically an undistinguished vignette about a bachelor party from hell, blown up to big-screen proportions, in which virtually every imaginable disaster occurs. A late-breaking successor to *Animal House*, it was among the last of the "gross-out" comedies which capitalized on that film's phenomenal success. While the Hanks vehicle lacks the wit or manic energy of *Animal House*, it looks like *The Gold Rush* when compared to such sleazy entries in the genre as *Porky's*.

If the plotline of *Bachelor Party* celebrated non-conformity, then at least the film's producers Ron Moler and Bob Israel practiced what they preached in real life. The premise for the script originated when Moler and Israel attended a bachelor party for the latter's brother Neal, who—with Pat Proft—had written the screenplay for *Police Academy*. The ill-fated fete, which was held at a Holiday Inn in Hollywood, proved to be a wild affair which caused Neal to say later, "The lid came off that night." Immediately, the Israels and Moler realized that they had not only survived a truly memorable homage to decadence but had also stumbled upon a highly commercial idea.

The manic mayhem of *Bachelor Party*, with Hanks at the center of the action (Aaron Rapoport, 20th Century-Fox)

ner Pat Proft. All of this on the basis of a striking poster which appealed to everyone's baser instincts.

Initially, Paul Reiser and Kelly McGillis were to star in the comedy of errors about a non-comformist bridegroom-to-be's battle to remain faithful to his fiancée amid the zaniness of an out-of-control bachelor party. However, after only two days of filming, the results were less than encouraging. Claiming that Reiser and McGillis were miscast, the producers fired their two leads and scrapped the modest amount of footage which had already been shot. Moler and Israel went to Fox and successfully lobbied for an increase in their distribution fees to allow them to recast. A month later, Hanks and Kitaen were chosen for the lead roles.

Ultimately, the script was passed along to Tom Hanks, who was in postproduction on *Splash* at the time. Hanks recalled, "When I read the script, I thought it was a formula film, a rock 'n' roll sex comedy essentially, and I wondered what the challenge was going to be. How was this going to be interesting as opposed to cashing in on the craze? Being *Surf II* or *Porky's IX*. Well, the creative people actually wanted to get as far away from that as possible. Okay, fine, so this time, it was my turn to say, 'Let's turn on the creative juices and see what happens. Let's see what makes this cook.' At the same time, I wasn't interested in throwing myself at a wall or dropping my pants. We needed to get something better."

Despite being a low-profile production, *Bachelor Party* hit several potholes on its road to theater screens. The production ran into union difficulties when it was learned that half the crew belonged to the International Alliance of Theatrical Stage Employees despite the fact that the producers never signed a formal pact with the union. When the producers refused to do so, picket lines were set up around the film locations. According to producer Ron

The bizarre odyssey in bringing *Bachelor Party* to the screen had its origin in a ludicrous strategy which paid off brilliantly. Moler and Israel were searching for backers to finance their film, but the threadbare plotline was hardly conducive to eliciting enthusiasm among potential investors. Ultimately, Moler and Israel decided to market their property as though it were a completed film despite the fact that they only had a general premise for the story. The pair created a poster which prominently featured horny guys ogling a girl's legs. Moler and Israel gave the poster maximum exposure, and the ad campaign appealed to Raju Patel and Gutman Das, who headed a small production company called Twin Continental Films. They formed a partnership with Moler and Israel, and the group successfully closed a distribution deal with 20th Century-Fox. Appropriately, Neal Israel was hired as a screenwriter, along with his part-

Moler, "the I.A. was in a militant mood. They told us, 'It's all or nothing at all,' expecting us to buckle under. The I.A. singled us out. But we didn't have the extra million it would have cost to go union." Instead, the union members on the film had to be replaced with nonunion workers. Following this debacle, the producers had to sort out a title dispute, since *Bachelor Party* was the name of a 1957 film starring Don Murray and E. G. Marshall which was written by Paddy Chayefsky and owned by M-G-M/UA.

When these problems were eventually resolved, director Neal Israel surprised the cast and crew by insisting on a two-week rehearsal period prior to actual shooting. This was a highly unusual procedure for such a low-budget film, but Israel (who once apprenticed under famed Broadway producer-director-playwright George Abbott) was adamant about bringing craftsmanlike zeal to this less-than-highbrow project. He explained his rationale: "That had to do with my theater background. Directing for me comes out of character, and I like to have actors interrelate as the characters without the script, using improvisation. But most of the movie was written down by the time we came to shoot—even Tom Hanks's monologue in the kitchen as he throws around the meatballs."

The movie was shot in various Los Angeles locations and in an art-deco hotel-suite set built on a soundstage at Hollywood's Laird Studios. The room was modeled after a similar $1,000-per-day suite at L.A.'s famed Biltmore Hotel. In fact, the Biltmore itself was used for scenes in the lobby, restaurant, hallway, and parking lot.

Bachelor Party rises above the run-of-the-mill "gross-out" comedies largely because of its talented cast. Tom Hanks would be reunited with a number of actors

with whom he had worked on *Bosom Buddies*, including Barry Diamond, Wendie Jo Sperber, Adrian Zmed, and Martina Finch. Veteran actor George Grizzard was cast as Hanks' snobby father-in-law-to-be. Director Neal Israel recalled that Hanks appeared to be having the time of his life interacting with the wildly diversified cast: "[Hanks] provided the perfect foil for all his crazy buddies. Like his character, he's basically a nice guy. No Hollywood nonsense. The best time he had was playing tennis like baseball, hitting the ball clean out of the court, with George Grizzard."

The plot—such as it is—concerns a flippant,

Disguised as hookers in an attempt to infiltrate the bachelor party, Debbie and her friends accidentally drop in on some amorous Japanese businessmen. (20th Century-Fox)

antiestablishment school-bus driver named Rick (Hanks) and his efforts to remain faithful to his fiancée despite the promises of his buddies to explore the limits of sexuality at his upcoming bachelor party. Rick assures his bride-to-be, Debbie Thompson (Tawny Kitaen), that he will not succumb to peer pressure. As the date of the party approaches, Rick tries to make peace with his future father-in-law, a

out to be disasterously dull but quickly escalates to a party of Roman-orgy proportions. Convinced that Rick is engaging in sordid sex, Debbie and her friends masquerade as hookers to gain access to the party. The scheme backfires when they are kidnapped by a pimp who mistakes them for real prostitutes and delivers them to a group of horny Japanese businessmen. Ultimately, Rick proves his fidelity and convinces Debbie to marry him, although the memory of the world's wildest bachelor party will never be forgotten by either of them.

Jay (Adrian Zmed) tries to fire Rick up for his big night with the guys, but Rick's mind is on his loyalty to Debbie. (20th Century-Fox)

Tom Hanks best described the film by saying, "It's as raunchy as you can get within the realm of decency." He would later tell *Rolling Stone*, "Doing *Bachelor Party* is not like doing *Richard III* or *Henry IV, Part II*, but that doesn't diminish the joy of scoring off something that somebody else has written. In fact, at times, it can be more difficult just walking down a hall and talking to somebody and making that interesting. That's what I find to be the biggest challenge in making movies. Doing Shakespeare and *Bachelor Party* is not that different, actually. The cerebral processes are the same. The demands are certainly different. The overall appreciation is going to be different. Doing Shakespeare, doing classical theater, is a luxury." When the interviewer continued to press about Hanks's presence in a low-brow film, he replied curtly, "This is what I do. I'm an actor. An actor has to act. What else am I supposed to do—sit around the house?"

snooty aristocrat who is appalled at the thought of Debbie marrying a man he considers to be a modern-day Neanderthal. Mr. Thompson encourages her jealous, blue-blooded, would-be lover Cole (Robert Prescott) to use every means necessary to break up Debbie and Rick's relationship. Everything comes to a head at the bachelor party, an event which starts

Hanks need not have been so defensive. While it is true that had he anticipated the overwhelmingly positive reaction to his performance in *Splash* he may not have signed for this film, it is not a movie to be ashamed of. In fact, Hanks has many moments which are truly inspired. And, like all good actors, he is not afraid to allow his costars to exhibit the full range of

Everyone survives the wild night, and the wedding goes (almost) without a hitch. (20th Century-Fox)

their talents. Hanks's interaction with the cast provides many memorable moments of amusement, and his chemistry with Tawny Kitaen is delightful to watch.

Much of *Bachelor Party* is too sophomoric to provide the sustained wit of *Airplane* or *The Naked Gun* films. Its unabashed reliance on nudity, gross jokes, and a (now) distastefully casual attitude toward drug use often cause potentially funny situations to fall flat. However, the film does have its share of memorable moments, gross as they are. The best involve an ill-fated donkey, a scene in which nerdy Gary Grossman discovers that his new love is a transvestite, a sequence in which Debbie and her girlfriends visit a male strip club, and one in which Rick's future mother-in-law has a hilarious encounter with a beefy waiter and what appears to be a hot dog. (There is no dignified way of describing the scene further!) Throughout, Hanks is the glue which holds the threadbare plot together. Just when the script becomes overly predictable and routine, Hanks's

manic energy produces some genuine laughs. (And at the risk of being politically incorrect, we must confess to taking lascivious delight at the nude scenes, which are gloriously gratuitous.)

Bachelor Party cost $5 million to make, became the surprise hit of 1984, and helped reaffirm Hanks as one of the screen's top young stars. Undeniably, the following he had built with *Splash* was largely responsible for the success of *Bachelor Party*. Other gross-out comedies with lesser leading men had bombed at the box office, but with this film Hanks proved to the industry that he could already be counted on to "open" a major studio release on the basis of his name.

While reviews for *Bachelor Party* were less than glowing, critics were somewhat kinder to this movie than they had been to other, less ambitious films of the genre. Hanks received the lion's share of the praise for his highly energetic performance. "*Bachelor Party* was a movie that knew no rules whatsoever," Hanks later reflected. "The point of it was to make people laugh—sometimes it did, and other times it didn't at all. But that's all right. Because even within those confines, there still has to be something that you're going to look at, so you come up with things even if they're not built into the script."

Bachelor Party is crude, obnoxious, offensive, gross, and demeaning to both men and women. We look forward to seeing it again.

Reviews

"*Merely the latest youth comedy to confuse grossness with hilarity in a vain attempt to emulate the success of the* Animal House/Porky's/Police Academy *triumvirate. Those three worked because their exuberant excesses were matched by an unstinting inspiration that's absent here. Actually,* Bachelor Party *is a cut above routine summer raunch because it has a sprinkling of genuinely hilarious moments and because it*

has the good fortune to have Tom Hanks, fresh from Splash, *as its star. Hanks really is a likable, spontaneous zany . . ."*

—Kevin Thomas, *Los Angeles Times*

"*It takes much longer than might be expected for* Bachelor Party *to degenerate into a mindless mob scene. Until it takes that turn for the worse, the movie is actually funny. That is, it's as funny as* Police Academy. . . . *And it's certainly funnier than it has been made to look by its advertising campaign, which seems to feature the usual gang of suspects enjoying the usual sophomoric sex romp. . . . Mr. Hanks's suave smart-alecky manner owes a lot to Bill Murray, but he's funny and engaging even if he isn't doing anything new."*

—Janet Maslin, *New York Times*

Rick really didn't do much chandelier swinging, with Hanks playing one of the most faithful grooms-to-be in history. (20th Century-Fox)

Director Neal Israel sets up a shot with his future bride and groom. (20th Century-Fox)

"This low-brow comedy is elevated slightly out of the food-fight rut by the amiable presence of Tom Hanks."
—Kim Newman, *Monthly Film Bulletin*

"Another case of adults giving the kids what they think they want. Picture is too contrived to capture the craziness it strains for and ultimately becomes offensive rather than funny.... Main reason to see the pic is for Hanks's performance. Recalling a younger Bill Murray, Hanks is all over the place, practically spilling off the screen with an overabundance of energy."
—"Jagr.," *Variety*

"1984's version of the Annual Summer Food Fight Movie....The first half of the movie sets up the party and the second half of the movie is the party. Both halves of the movie are raunchy, chaotic and quite shameless in aiming at the lowest possible level of taste, of course.... I didn't think [Hanks] was all that terrific in Splash—*I thought he was miscast, and they should have gone for somebody who was less of a conventional leading man—but in* Bachelor Party *he's a lot more funny and I enjoyed the performance.... It tries hard, and when it's funny, it is very funny.... * Bachelor Party *has some great moments and qualifies as a raunchy, scummy, Blotto Bluto memorial."*
—*Roger Ebert's Movie Home Companion*

The Man With One Red Shoe

20th Century-Fox, 1985

"I wasn't shocked it failed. I saw the original and felt about the same as I do about our movie. It's not Star Wars."

Cast
Tom Hanks (*Richard Drew*); Dabney Coleman (*Cooper*); Lori Singer (*Maddy*); Charles Durning (*Ross*); Carrie Fisher (*Paula*); Edward Herrmann (*Brown*); Jim Belushi (*Morris*); Tom Noonan (*Reese*); Gerrit Graham (*Carson*); David L. Lander (*Stemple*).

Credits
Director: Stan Dragoti; producer: Victor Drai; screenplay: Robert Klane, based upon the motion picture *The Tall Blond Man With One Black Shoe* written by Francis Veber and Yves Robert; director of photography: Richard H. Kline; production designer: Dean E. Mitzner; editors: Bud Molin and O. Nicholas Brown; music: Thomas Newman. Running time: 92 minutes.

As symphony violinist Richard Drew (20th Century-Fox)

Released soon after the surprise success of *Bachelor Party*, *The Man With One Red Shoe* was an Americanized remake of a 1972 French farce about an innocent man mistaken for a secret agent. The film proved to be a major disappointment on every level. At the risk of writing an unpardonable pun, Hanks should have given the *Shoe* script the boot.

The razor-thin plot finds Charles Durning as Ross, the embattled director of the CIA, who is trying to stave off attempts by his second in command, Cooper (Dabney Coleman), to frame him for allowing agents to deal in drugs. Cooper is obsessed with gaining control of the CIA, and Ross is equally determined to remain in power. Ross concocts a scheme to throw Cooper off balance. He pretends that a key witness in the drug investigation will be arriving in Washington, D.C., to exonerate him of all charges. Although no such person exists, Ross informs Brown (Ed Herrmann), his long-suffering underling, to choose an innocent man to use as bait for the ruse.

As fate would have it, Brown's choice for the bogus spy is Richard Drew (Tom Hanks), a professional violinist whose main distinction is that he is wearing one red shoe—or sneaker, to be precise. Before long, the unsuspecting Richard is being followed and bugged by Cooper's men in an attempt to

With Jim Belushi (Morris) and Lori Singer (Maddy): The three give inspired performances, but the movie ultimately blows a flat. (20th Century-Fox)

that they have won the Publishers' Clearing House Sweepstakes ("the one with my picture on it!").

The project came about when producer Victor Drai obtained the rights to remake several French films for the American market. His first, *The Woman in Red*, was a fairly well received 1983 Gene Wilder comedy patterned after the French film *Pardon Mon Affaire*. Drai's first objective with the *Shoe* film was to find a director. He secured the services of Stan Dragoti, who had previously made TV commercials and scored with the comedy hits *Love at First Bite* and *Mr. Mom*. Dragoti was immediately captivated by what he felt were the ironies of the script: "The picture makes a statement. Caught in a crazy, totally immoral conflict, two men act morally and are rewarded—one with love, one with success. . . . This is a classical cause-and-effect story in which everything builds logically from the initial premise. You don't see much of that anymore: first act, second act, third act. What you get today is mostly 'and then' writing: This happened and then that happened and then something else, with no causal link connecting them."

Initially, Victor Drai had hoped to cast a more mature actor as Richard Drew. However, he settled on Tom Hanks, perceiving him as a "refreshing and new" face. He also felt that Hanks's background as a classically trained stage actor would allow him to play romantic sequences, light comedy, even slapstick—all elements essential to his character. Stan Dragoti was enthusiastic about having Hanks as his star: "Tom's greatest strength is that all audiences can relate to him. He's not staggeringly handsome, but he's so appealing and hip and interesting that you always care about what he's doing on the screen. He's

learn the secret information they believe he possesses. Cooper orders one of his agents, Maddy (Lori Singer), to seduce Richard in order to "crack him." Instead, Maddy not only becomes convinced that the bumbling Richard is not an agent but also finds herself falling for him. The climax of the woebegone tale is an elaborate chase sequence in which Richard must rescue Maddy from the clutches of Cooper's assassins. The screenplay wraps up everything in a predictable, "feel good" ending in which Richard and Maddy become lovers; Richard's best friend's wife, who has made blatant sexual passes at him, is reconciled with her husband; Cooper is arrested for his crimes; and Brown has the satisfaction of taking over Ross's job as the head of the CIA. All that's missing is having Ed McMahon appear to tell the entire cast also the consummate actor. In *Red Shoe* he approached each scene fearlessly. For instance, at one point, his character is shot with tranquilizer darts. I asked him if he wanted me to hire some mimes who could show him how to react to being tranquilized, but Tom told me not to waste my money. And the scene worked perfectly." (Any man who refuses to employ mimes can't be *all* bad!) Dragoti later counted Hanks's "pixieish quality" among his on-screen attributes.

Hanks admitted: "When I sat down with [Stan

klutziness was too limiting—a one-joke thing. The character, as we developed him, tends to be myopic because of his passion for music, but he has many other interests as well, and he's not an incompetent when the girl he loves is threatened." Hanks also reminded the director that the film should undergo a title change because he is neither tall nor blond. A member of the crew suggested changing the color of the shoe. (Presumably, "red" evokes much more laughter among audiences.)

Hanks was impressed with the quality of the

Richard unwittingly involves himself in Brown's (Ed Herrmann) spy caper. (20th Century-Fox)

Dragoti] three months before I went into the movie, I was still kicking around whether I wanted to even go about doing a remake, especially something that was so affectionately remembered as *The Tall Blond Man With One Black Shoe*, a movie that can really only be done by the French because that's the way they view the world."

Hanks became committed to the project because he found the character to be multifaceted and challenging. "It was never a question of what was funnier or would get the most laughs, but of making it as interesting as possible," he recalled. "The guy is totally reactive, and Stan and I agreed that playing it for

production itself: "Our movie was incredibly constructed, the kind of thing where one person is observing me in a room and there are people observing him observing me. . . . It's like boxes within boxes. It was almost like a battle to clear the head away from doing anything that is going to take away from the main thrust of that big beat. It was very tough and almost confining—it was an opportunity for me to get the juice out of the refrigerator. That is literally what I had to do. . . . I had to discover ways of doing that which wouldn't be pedestrian. That is the most nitpicking, nickel-and-dime stuff about making a movie, the hardest to really comprehend."

Filming on *The Man With One Red Shoe* began in Washington, D.C., in August 1984 and continued through early November. To research his role as a violinist, Hanks visited with classical musicians who lived in Washington. His opinion of these individuals influenced his on-screen portrayal: "They were bright, stimulating people, eclectic in their interests and varied in their personalities. But they were all bad dressers, which they blamed on lack of money. You can see that reflected in my wardrobe on-screen."

If the role of Richard Drew did not garner Hanks a tidal wave of critical praise, it did at the very least allow him the benefit of learning the basics of playing the violin. For several months, Hanks took lessons, until he finally "mastered" the violin to the point at which he could play a few pieces of music that were actually recognizable. He said at the time, "I wanted something that would be a severe stretch. Although I'd played the violin for a couple of years in

elementary school, all I really knew was how to hold the bow. In the movie, I have to play the solo from *Scheherezade* with the symphony and also the love song I write to Lori Singer, and we were determined that it would be authentic on the screen." Ultimately, however, Hanks was not pleased with the result in the final cut of the film: "It was a mistake. I should have learned to act playing the violin. I thought I botched it." In fairness to Hanks, whatever his shortcomings were as an amateur musician, they do not negatively affect relevant sequences in the film.

In addition to his musical woes, Hanks also had to cope with some special-effects work that proved to be a considerable challenge; specifically, a sequence in which the harried Richard Drew accidentally brushes his teeth with shampoo, which results in his blowing giant soapy bubbles every time he opens his mouth. The seemingly simple scene was actually a nightmare to perform for Hanks and special-effects director Al Lorimer. Lorimer explained: "It *sounds* like a real easy thing, but when you want to get a six-to-eight-inch bubble coming out of a guy's mouth and the director wants a dead shot, straight at his face, you can't use an appliance from the side and shoot a profile. With Tom, we took approximately three weeks to develop a formula that would not irritate his mouth or be detrimental to his health. We had to make the bubble come out and last while having that special appliance—which Tom would blow through—to keep the solution inside his mouth, and then some special ointment for his lips so the bubble wouldn't break when it hit them. The audience won't know about the bubble's development or how many guys in my crew got that nasty stuff in their mouths until we found the right formula. They'll just think that Tom had something in his mouth and blew a bubble!"

Hanks's take on the bubble-blowing scene: "I'm foaming at the mouth like a rabid dog. I've already got the runs. But I'll swallow as much of the stuff as possible. I'm a team player. I think there's a Vegas act like this. . . ."

Lorimer was also impressed with Hanks's ability to improvise during an amusing sequence in which Richard Drew must cope with the erratic plumbing in his bathroom. The scene required Hanks to deal with the frustration of having to turn on one faucet in order to get another working. (i.e., to get water in the

Dabney Coleman as Cooper provides some all-too-infrequent laughs. (20th Century-Fox)

sink, he must put the shower on; to get the shower to work, he must flush the toilet, etc.) In Lorimer's opinion, "one of the cutest things was the bathroom scene where everything is working wrong. Tom Hanks kidded me afterward and said, 'The star of this scene is the toilet and the sink, not the actor.' But it worked very well because Tommy makes things work very well. Many actors can't really deal with props, effects, gags, and mechanical things—it's like the old saying, 'You can't chew gum and walk at the same time.' But Tommy really enhanced everything."

For all the effort required to bring the film to the screen, *The Man With One Red Shoe* proved to be a disappointment on almost every level. The main problem is the screenplay by Robert Klane, which is manic but uninspired. In order to bring off a farce like this, the characters must behave either in a believable fashion or be so "over the top" (à la *The Naked Gun*) that absolutely nothing can be taken seriously. The script's fatal flaw is that it is too farcical to reflect real life but never absurd enough to rely on pure slapstick. The result is an unsatisfactory compromise that never quite works. The characters are all cartoons, and the situations become increasingly unbelievable.

Most depressing of all is the waste of an outstanding cast, none of whom can be blamed for the film's failure. Hanks is amiable and pleasant, but director Dragoti gives him little to do but look bewildered. Hanks is the catalyst of all the madcap events which occur in the film, but the script and direction never capitalize on his comedic skills. Potentially hilarious sequences, such as the aforementioned bathroom plumbing scene, are instead only moderately amusing. Likewise, another scene with great possibilities—Hanks inadvertently catching Lori Singer's hair in his zipper while she attempts to seduce him—falls almost completely flat because Dragoti does not have the comedic instinct to capitalize on its potential.

Surprisingly, Hanks and Singer do create some genuine chemistry in spite of the mediocre dialogue. Singer is well cast as the sultry spy who falls in love with the bumbling Hanks, and the scenes in which she seduces him are among the film's highlights. The most amusing scenes belong to old pros Charles Durning and Dabney Coleman as the warring CIA bigwigs who catch Hanks in their crossfire. Coleman has played the immoral executive so many times, he could perform the role in his sleep. Still, his wild-eyed insistence that Hanks is indeed a clever spy provides the movie with most of its all too infrequent laughs. Ed Herrmann is completely wasted as Durning's stooge, and the final sequence in which he delivers Durning his "just desserts" seems an afterthought.

Even worse are the lame roles written for Jim Belushi as Hanks's best friend and Carrie Fisher as Belushi's horny wife, who makes continuous, albeit unsuccessful, attempts to seduce Hanks. Belushi is reduced to wandering around in a daze as he discovers bodies in Hanks's apartment which keep disappearing. If someone like Don Knotts or Jerry Lewis appeared in such a scene, the result could have had a great deal of promise. However, Belushi is not an actor known to excel in slapstick, so the sequence is as dead as the on-screen murder victims. Fisher is given an embarrassing supporting role which requires her to dress in leopard-skin panties in order to seduce Hanks into fulfilling her sexual fantasy of playing Tarzan and Jane.

The Man With One Red Shoe opened in the summer of 1985 to poor reviews and meager box-office receipts. Hanks remained immune from most of the blame, which justifiably fell on the writer and director. However, his role did not continue the momentum he had gained from *Splash* and *Bachelor Party*. Following the film's flop, Hanks remained somewhat defensive of *Red Shoe*. In a 1986 interview he said, "Listen, I loved my character. . . . I thought it was great, that he was totally oblivious to all the craziness around him. Yet the movie went down the tubes. I think sometimes you put all this work into a film but the actual theme—the thing that makes people out there really *care* about the movie—gets lost along the way." In a later interview, he reflected on the film again, saying, "People say, 'Oh, you must feel so bad about remaking a brilliant French comedy like *The Tall Blond Man With One Black Shoe*.' Well, I saw that film about five days before we started filming, and I didn't think it was so brilliant. I liked the guy I played. On the other hand, it is getting tough to find variations on that character."

Despite the lukewarm reception for *Red Shoe*,

Hanks continued to build his reputation as a likable, professional actor who gives his all to any project. Unfortunately, it would take a few more films and a few more years before Hollywood recognized his ultimate potential.

Reviews

"A noisy remake of a French spy farce that makes the mistake of casting Hanks as a clueless shmo. The shoe doesn't fit."

—Ty Burr, *Entertainment Weekly*

"Has a good cast, decent sight gags and a couple of terrific one-liners going for it. If it only had a better plot, it could have been one of the funniest movies of the summer. . . . Hanks is as charming here as he was in Splash. *. . . Actually, it would have been nice to see* all *the talent in this movie tested more than it was. As it is, you have to have a special sense of humor to enjoy this movie."*

—Carl Pisano, *Newsday*

"Too bad the look of the movie has nothing to do with its content. The style isn't the message . . . it's imposed on the material to make it feel hip. It does feel hip, and it also feels boring, because Dragoti doesn't give the story any momentum. [The movie] manages to be sleek and sludgy at once. It's miscast, too. Hanks isn't a physical clown; he's a talker. He was hilarious with loutish material in Bachelor Party *because he put a spin on his lines like a Little League Bill Murray. But his work here consists of blinking and looking dazed. . . . There are fitfully funny scenes, but most of [the movie] feels like sleepwalking. What could be the joy in duplicating someone else's movie, especially if the original is hack work?"*

—David Edelstein, *Village Voice*

Morris tries to convince Richard—and himself—that he is not crazy, that he *did* see dead bodies that suddenly disappeared. (20th Century-Fox)

"*A calamitous attempt to turn a successful French farce into a Hollywood comedy. In the lumbering hands of Victor Drai and director Stan Dragoti, the title is not the only thing that changed. Somewhere along the way they also shredded the pace, tempo, humor and coherence. They not so much as adapted it as put it through La Machine. I've seen tortoise races move faster than [this].*"

—Rex Reed, *New York Post*

"*Victor Drai . . . appeared to be making a career out of demonstrating how poorly French farce can travel . . . [the movie] loses a lot in the translation . . . it's just slight, and none of it elicits more than the mildest of chuckles. The real trouble, though, is what was once an airy comedy of errors has been staged in a more literal sitcom style, which makes the story's silly turns of circumstance look absurd.*"

—Janet Maslin, *New York Times*

Hanks good-naturedly endured countless takes of this bubble-blowing scene. (20th Century-Fox)

Volunteers

Tri-Star, 1985

"[Lawrence] is a guy as far removed from me as anybody I've played because it's 1962, he's a rich kid who went to Yale, and he turns out to be the guy you love to hate and hate to love."

Cast
Tom Hanks (*Lawrence Bourne III*); Rita Wilson (*Beth Wexler*); John Candy (*Tom Tuttle from Tacoma*); Tim Thomerson (*John Reynolds*); Gedde Watanabe (*At Toon*); George Plimpton (*Lawrence Bourne Jr*); Ernest Harada (*Chung Mee*); Allan Arbus (*Albert Bordonaro*).

Credits
Director: Nicholas Meyer; producers: Richard Shepherd and Walter F. Parkes; screenplay: Ken Levine and David Isaacs; story: Keith Critchlow; director of photography: Ric Waite; production designer: James Schoppe; editors: Ronald Roose and Steven Polivka; music: James Horner. Running time: 106 minutes.

Hanks as snobbish boor Lawrence Bourne III, with John Candy, as Tom Tuttle from Tacoma (Tri-Star Pictures)

Immediately following production of *The Man With One Red Shoe*, Tom Hanks plunged into *Volunteers*, his next comedic showcase, a cynical and satirical look at one effete snob who thumbs his nose at the idealism of the Kennedy-Camelot era. The film casts Hanks as Lawrence Bourne III, a young, narcissistic aristocrat whose penchant for compulsive gambling leads to his being targeted for death by the mob. When his father (George Plimpton) balks at bailing him out of trouble again, Lawrence is forced to flee to Thailand with a planeful of ambitious, starry-eyed Peace Corps recruits who are eager to "save" the native population.

Bourne is immediately at odds with his fellow travelers, especially Beth (Rita Wilson), a beautiful young Peace Corps worker who is repulsed by Lawrence's blatant sexual innuendos and his self-centered attitude. The two end up serving in the same village, where they must unite to stave off the demands of a local warlord who insists they build a bridge which would enable him to conquer the village they have been sent to aid. When Beth and the villagers are imperiled, Lawrence's latent compassion awakens, and he engages in a dangerous rescue mission which saves the day and leaves the warlord in defeat. Along the way, Lawrence learns about values and wins over Beth.

The idea for *Volunteers* came about when producer Walter F. Parkes and writer Keith Critchlow were on a seventeen-hour flight to Iran in the late 1970s to attend the Tehran Film Festival, considered a prestigious international event during the days of the shah. To pass the time, they began to formulate outlines for potential film scripts. Parkes said: "We thought it would be interesting to take the least likely Peace Corps candidate, somebody totally devoid of any altruism, and plunk him down in the middle of the jungle. After a couple of decades of angst-ridden heroes, Lawrence is kind of wonderfully unneurotic. Compared to almost everybody he meets, his motives are crystal clear: He's out to have a good time and doesn't care who knows it. But at the same time, he's kind of like a Rick Blaine character. He starts out as a guy who, like Bogart in *Casablanca*, sticks his neck out for nobody. By the end of the film, he's risking that neck for the sake of a village he's grown to love."

Eventually, a script was completed by Ken Levine and David Isaacs, who had made a name for themselves by writing many *M*A*S*H* television episodes. Producers Richard Shepherd and Walter F.

Parkes then presented the idea to Nicholas Meyer, not generally known for his handling of comedies, who directed such films as *Time After Time*, *Star Trek II: The Wrath of Khan* and the shattering television movie *The Day After*, about nuclear war. Meyer happened to be looking for a lighthearted vehicle for his next project. He later said: "I read the screenplay when I was on my honeymoon. I couldn't stop laughing. But what appealed to me the most was its extreme literacy. It's somewhat reminiscent of *A Midsummer's Night's Dream* in the same way that *Bringing Up Baby* was its cinematic equivalent. There is plenty of blue-collar moviemaking these days, with everybody saying, 'Fuck you.' I prefer to see—and make—movies of a different kind."

In a *New York Times* interview, Meyer expanded on his views about *Volunteers*: "When I first read the screenplay, it seemed to be addressing the same things that I had been going through over *The Day After*. I was coming to realize what my selfishness was all about. The Peace Corps fascinates me. I've always thought of it as being the one useful thing the federal government has done since the New Deal. But

I have always wondered, 'Is it altruistic?' No. It's not altruistic if you accept my fundamental principle, which is 'Everything is connected.' By helping people to make a better life, you ultimately help to preserve your own skin. That's as selfish as you can get." Poignant thoughts, but how does Meyer manage to find a common denominator between a film which depicts the horrors of a nuclear holocaust and a light-weight comedy about a sex-crazed snob?

Meyer's cynical theory that people who choose to live in mud huts to help famine-plagued people are being selfish made him the perfect person to direct a film with a character such as Lawrence Bourne. If one believes Meyer's rationale, Mother Teresa must rival the Gabor sisters when it comes to being self-indulgent. Nevertheless, with Meyer aboard, the next goal was to find a suitable star for the role of Lawrence. It was essential that they find someone who could pretend to be completely self-centered, devoid of any semblance of compassion, and yet retain the ability to be charming and lovable.

Producer Richard Shepherd had Tom Hanks in mind from minute one: "It was while we were . . . firming up the deal for *Volunteers*. I had an afternoon free, so I went to Westwood to see a movie. It just happened to be the day *Splash* opened, so I caught that. Minutes after getting out of the theater, I called Walter and said, 'The guy that *has* to play Lawrence Bourne III, *if* we can get him, is in a movie called *Splash*. His name is Tom Hanks.'"

Coincidentally, since the script for *Volunteers* had been kicking around for some time, Hanks had read it as far back as 1981. He said, "I wanted to do it right then, but I wouldn't have been ready to. The stuff I've been able to do in this has been culled from all the work I've done up to this point because this is the most constantly demanding role I've ever had. The concentration and disciplinary factors I've been notoriously lacking in my entire career up to this point are now necessary. This is the first job I've had where the gut instinct was not all that necessary. I've had a lot of jobs, especially in TV, where that was all you had to work on because you don't have the time to explore anything else. But on this movie I saw a dialogue coach; there were aspects of fashion and dress I had to get down. When it comes to fashion, I'm basically a lox. I don't care what I wear."

Hanks felt an immediate rapport with Meyer, and the director made some useful suggestions about characterization to his star. "When I first met Nick," Hanks said, "he slapped my face with a challenge

Candy heroically resists Communists' brainwashing . . . for all of fifteen seconds! (Tri-Star Pictures)

right from the very beginning. Things like dialect, which at that point I hadn't even considered. The New England accent adds a whole element to it and doesn't become a joke unto itself. Nick isn't exactly the most hilarious guy you're ever going to meet, but what he does have is a great affection for actors and a massive head. He can hold court better than anybody I've seen."

Truly intrigued by the many facets of his character's personality, Hanks said at the time, "I think I did my best work in developing this role because the guy was unlikable to a degree. I think he was the most dynamic character I ever played in that he was the most perfectly formed on paper. It was literally my job to take all of the necessary steps to fill him out—working on his voice and clothes, stuff like that. . . . My character finally becomes involved, but in his own very particular way and for his own very partic-

The gang is forced to destroy the bridge they just built to thwart the plans of the opium warlord, the CIA, and the People's Army. Did we leave anyone out? (Tri-Star Pictures)

ular reasons. This is a guy you hate to love. He's not a jerk or an idiot. He's very smart but not calculating. When he comes up against an adversary, he'll convince them that they have no reason to hurt him. Or, as he says in the movie, 'You can't do this to me. I have certain rights.' "

Although Hanks is the most prominent comedic talent in *Volunteers*, he is supported by several notable supporting actors. John Candy, his *Splash* teammate, is cast as Tom Tuttle from Tacoma, a big, lumbering goon who arrives in Thailand with a determination to spread American democracy and within minutes becomes a pawn of the Communist troops. Candy's character is so "over the top" it makes his on-screen alter ego in *Splash* look like John Houseman. The screenplay wisely limits his role to sporadic appearances, which leave the audience wanting more. Every time he pops up, it's a highlight, and he complements Hanks even more than he did in their first teaming.

Significantly, Hanks met his future wife, Rita Wilson, on the set of *Volunteers*. Wilson, portraying the exasperated object of Lawrence Bourne's desires in her big-screen debut, is a charming and winning actress with a refreshing presence. She displays the ability to walk the fine line between playing "straight man" to Hanks's quips and being a solid comedic

presence in her own right. Hanks developed an instant interest in her that was more than professional, although his initial comments to the press remained very businesslike: "Rita's great. She was on an episode of *Bosom Buddies*, but I didn't have a scene with her. We just sat across the table from each other. For somebody who's making her first movie, she's amazingly cool, not cocky. She was making a good living doing commercials and TV, but she chucked it all to study in London for a year at the Academy of Music and Dramatic Art." Years after their marriage, Hanks confessed to having less platonic thoughts at the time. "We were both involved with other people at the time, so we took it very, very slowly. But at the same time, it really was undeniable."

While the cast and crew worked together seamlessly, the physical demands of bringing *Volunteers* to the screen proved to be quite a challenge. The Peace Corps was shown an early draft of the script but objected to virtually every aspect of the way the organization was being depicted. They considered the screenplay the equivalent of "spitting on the American flag" and asked Meyer to change the setting from Thailand to Burma because the Peace Corps does not operate there. They demanded that the organization not be mentioned in the same breath as the

There are probably a few million places Lawrence would rather be than in the jungles of Thailand, but he's somehow able to keep his sense of humor. (Tri-Star Pictures)

CIA. There were also requests that the Peace Corps name be replaced by that of a fictitious charity. Meyer stood his ground and ignored these demands. "Anyone can see this is an affectionate spoof and that the people who made this movie went out of their way to endorse the Peace Corps. And if you can twit the army in movies, why not the Peace Corps?"

Logistically, the location shooting for *Volunteers* proved to be a smooth operation for all concerned. Actual filming took place in Mexico, at various locations, which included the jungle near Chiltepec, Oaxaca; at Churubusco Studios; and in the isolated town of Tuxtepec, Oaxaca. For the climactic scene in which Hanks and the villagers attempt to blow up the bridge to thwart the advancing enemy forces, the crew built the longest wooden suspension bridge ever created (over two-and-one-half football fields long) as well as an entire authentic Thai village. The bridge was the biggest challenge. It had to appear flimsy enough to have been built by amateurs but safe enough to support the cast and crew.

Ironically, the shooting was going so well, there was concern that the cast would have to sit idly by awaiting the completion of the bridge. Producer Richard Shepherd said: "Anyway, the clock is ticking. Construction starts on the bridge a little before filming starts, and it's a real rat race. Can they build it fast enough to keep up with the shooting? At one point, we were dressing all the Mexican construction workers in Thai costumes for the long shots. Anyway, we blew it up in January, with eight cameras going to make sure we didn't miss anything."

Despite such problems, Shepherd enthusiastically proclaimed the filming of *Volunteers* "one of the happiest shoots I can remember. Despite just about every conceivable natural problem: coral snakes, for instance, and rain, general bad weather, bugs. And mud. Lots of mud. But even with all those things, it was a very relaxed, happy crew. And I think a lot of that is due to Tom and John, who were just great to

get along with, no star attitudes or anything."

Meyer concurred: "On a certain level, the odds on this movie could be computed on a rather depressing configuration: Mexico for Thailand, a mixed Thai-Mexican crew, three or four different languages on the set, but it's the easiest movie I've ever shot, and certainly the most fun. All my nightmares about not getting the extras to understand me proved wrong. I didn't see the dailies: They were put on cassettes, and sometimes they arrived, and sometimes they didn't."

Hanks was enthused about the film but spoke of the nervousness found on the set of most comedies. Would anyone but those close to the project find it funny? "A movie which is labeled 'comedy' essentially means to the audience to come and see it and laugh ... there's a fine bottom line, a very jagged edge, which you can really get hurt on if you're on the side of it which doesn't make people laugh. People come out of a comedy and may not like it. If you ask them

why not, they'll say it didn't make them laugh. End of critique. There's nothing else to say. And if they did like it, that's also the end of the critique. It did its job. Within those parameters, there's always a huge jeopardy involved for everybody concerned, down to the prop guys and the set dressers. They have to look at something and think, This looks pretty, but is it funny? Does it add to the comedy? So everybody runs around with this horrible glazed look in their eyes, wondering if the movie is funny. . . ."

He needn't have worried. Much of *Volunteers* is indeed funny, although some of the inspired comedy found in the first half degenerates to an all-too-obvious slapstick epic in the second half. Hanks is totally in command as the arrogant but somehow likable Lawrence Bourne III. The movie opens with him hopelessly out of place as he sits in his white dinner jacket like Sean Connery in *Goldfinger*, playing cards with a group of notorious gangsters. Hanks's cool demeanor and ever-present quips make this one of his most watchable comedic performances.

His Lawrence continues to impress when he arrives in Thailand, and although we know he will ultimately redeem himself through heroism, the script, refreshingly, refuses to bow to a corny cop-out end-

ing. The finale actually finds Lawrence as self-centered as ever; only now he appears to have "converted" his new love, Beth. The chemistry between Hanks and Wilson is extremely enjoyable, possibly because we now know there was ultimately more than a professional interest between the two. Wilson's winning performance almost manages to steal some scenes from Hanks, who remains eager to provide his costars with the opportunity to shine.

John Candy is hilarious as Tom Tuttle from Tacoma, and he seldom has been more inspired than in the scene in which he taunts his Commie captors about the uselessness of trying to brainwash him. The scene immediately switches to a few moments later, only to find the would-be John Wayne wearing a Red Chinese army uniform and spouting quotations from Chairman Mao. Like Robin Williams, Candy erupts in so many rapid-fire wisecracks that the film bears watching again just to see how many were missed the first time around. (i.e., just before blowing up his beloved bridge, Candy stares at the detonator and proclaims, "My God, what have I done?"—mimicking Alec Guinness in *The Bridge on the River Kwai*.)

The film also features amusing supporting performances by Tim Thomerson as a Rambo-like

The most significant end product of *Volunteers* was the blossoming romance between Tom Hanks and Rita Wilson. (Tri-Star Pictures)

macho man who has an unnatural relationship with his hunting knife and Gedde Watanabe as Hanks's ever-present Thai sidekick who bears the brunt of his buddy's outrageous schemes. George Plimpton has a brief but funny turn as Hanks's equally snobbish father.

Nicholas Meyer proves to have the capabilities to successfully helm a zany comedy. However, the screenplay meanders through some clichéd situations, and the prolonged climax in which Hanks rescues Wilson from the villains is more manic than funny. The film is aided by an impressive score by James Horner which would probably be more at home in a big-scale action epic.

Volunteers opened in July 1985, exactly one week after the "premiere" of *The Man With One Red Shoe*. The result was the kind of one-two punch Tom Hanks would have rather avoided, for the former film was still being attacked by critics now eager to rake Hanks over the coals in his forthcoming project. While *Volunteers* was not skewered like *Shoe*, the reviews were mixed at best. Hanks was in danger of appearing to be a flash in the pan on the basis of the disappointing box-office results of both movies. In fairness, the movies opened during the traditional summer "bloodbath" in which a handful of megabudget films dominate the marketplace. In the summer of 1985 such epics included *Rambo: First Blood II*, *Back to the Future*, *National Lampoon's European Vacation*, and *A View to a Kill*. Hanks's *Volunteers* played for an abbreviated run before being retired to the "dollar" theaters. Although the movie grossed considerably more than *Red Shoe*, it was still considered a failure. Despite its faults, it deserved a better fate.

"Remember, it was the great *Rambo* summer," Hanks rationalized, "and I think, philosophically, there are aspects of the movie that were not overly popular. It dealt with the Peace Corps during the idealistic sixties, and the subliminal theme of the movie was that just because we're Americans doesn't mean that we have all the answers. That was a gung-ho period in which we thought we were the best and brightest, pure and simple. We had not only the wonders of technology that were developed through the American system, but we also had freedom of thought that went along with the free-enterprise system. But remember, Kennedy's Camelot only lasted nine hundred days, or whatever it was, and I guess in the movie we were kind of hinting that although it didn't all die that November day, there was already some erosion of the ideal."

Years later, he summed up his thoughts on the ill-fated *Volunteers* in an interview in *Playboy*: "A really good idea and maybe sixty percent of it is pretty funny. The last forty percent. . . . What can you say? The audience passed judgment on it and it didn't do that well."

Reviews

"*Take a healthy helping of* Raiders of the Lost Ark, *a dollop of* The Bridge on the River Kwai, *a dash of any Tarzan movie, a soupçon of* Casablanca, *a whiff of* The Wizard of Oz, *and a stunt or two from a favorite Saturday serial, stir frenetically, and*

if you're lucky enough to have snappy dialogue by Ken Levine and David Isaacs, you may end up with as funny a movie as Volunteers. . . . [Hanks is] stylishly droll. He is a center of confidence among the frantic goings-on, turning peril into opportunity with an accent and aplomb that are the birthright of an eight generation Bourne.*"

—Walter Goodman, *New York Times*

"*Aside from a few hootenanny jokes,* Volunteers *has little interest in satirizing the incipient activism of the New Frontier. It's really a yuppie comedy in disguise. . . . Like so many comedies this summer, [it] takes its cues from the pages of* National Lampoon, *displaying all of the influential humor magazine's mean-spirited, preppie insolence without capturing any of its anarchic zeal or corrosive wit.*"

—Patrick Goldstein, *Los Angeles Times*

"*Begins promisingly as a satire of Kennedy-era liberalism but soon collapses into indiscriminate slapstick of almost terrifying desperation.*"

—David Denby, *New York* magazine

"*It's Hanks . . . who gives the movie its seductively sardonic spirit. His character requires both the outsider smirk of a Bill Murray and the debonair inside moves of a Cary Grant, and Hanks has both. His brainy self-interest cuts through the cant. . . .* Volunteers *may not deliver on its wonderful premise, but it's still one of the year's funniest jobs.*"

—David Ansen, *Newsweek*

The Money Pit

Universal, 1986

"As soon as you have a stranger in your house with a tape measure on his belt, you're doomed. You can't get off the operating table and say, 'Doc, you know, don't remove that tendon.' He'd say, 'Shut up, I'm a doctor, I know what I'm doing.' And that's what you have when you have anybody come to do anything at your house."

Cast
Tom Hanks (*Walter Fielding*); Shelley Long (*Anna Crowley*); Alexander Godunov (*Max Beissart*); Maureen Stapleton (*Estelle*); Joe Mantegna (*Art Shirk*); Philip Bosco (*Curly*); Josh Mostel (*Jack Schnittman*); Yakov Smirnoff (*Shatov*); Carmine Caridi (*Brad Shirk*); Jake Steinfeld (*Duke*).

Credits
Director: Richard Benjamin; producers: Frank Marshall, Kathleen Kennedy and Art Levinson; executive producers: Steven Spielberg and David Giler; screenplay: David Giler; director of photography: Gordon Willis; production designer: Patrizia von Brandenstein; editor: Jacqueline Cambas; special effects supervisor: Michael Wood; music: Michel Colombier. Running time: 91 minutes.

Immediately following his work on *Volunteers*, Tom Hanks moved on to *The Money Pit*, a $20 million high-profile farce which was a pet project of Steven Spielberg for his own production company, Amblin. His costar would be Shelley Long, then riding high on TV's *Cheers*. The director would be Richard Benjamin, who had won critical acclaim for *My Favorite Year*. The producers would include Frank Marshall and Kathleen Kennedy, each of whom had an impressive record with box-office hits, including Spielberg's *E.T. The Extra-Terrestrial* and the *Indiana Jones* adventures. Patrizia von Brandenstein, who won the Oscar for her sets for *Amadeus*, would serve as production designer.

All of this heavyweight talent might seem a bit out of place for such a simplistic tale. However, *The Money Pit* was being groomed as Universal's major comedy release for Christmas, 1985, and the Spielberg name as executive producer gave the studio confidence they had a sure winner on their hands. Thus, the steep budget required for the cast and crew was not a major concern for the studio "suits."

Basically *The Money Pit* is a modern-day version of the 1948 comedy *Mr. Blandings Builds His Dream House*, which cast Cary Grant and Myrna Loy as a

couple of big-city sophisticates who try to find paradise in a quaint country home. They soon discover that their "dream house" is actually a cleverly disguised disaster which falls apart at the slightest touch. Almost forty years later, Hanks and Long re-created the Grant-Loy roles with a few contemporary plot variations thrown in. The two are lovers who reside in the Manhattan apartment of Long's ex-husband, Alexander Godunov, a world-famous conductor whose talent is exceeded only by his ego. When he returns to town unexpectedly, the couple must suddenly find other living arrangements.

They opt to buy a palatial country house from sweet, eccentric Maureen Stapleton despite the fact that the deal seems too good to be true. Upon moving in, they realize that is indeed the case. It seems Stapleton and her husband are professional swindlers, and Hanks and Long discover to their horror that the money they have borrowed to finance their dream has been squandered on a house which differs from the *Titanic* only in that the latter was on water and had a band. At every turn, staircases crumble, doors fall off their hinges, faucets ooze sludge, and the roof leaks like Niagara Falls.

Naturally, the house wreaks havoc on the relationship; it also acts like a money sponge, for Hanks and Long must pay disreputable workmen to restore the place to some semblance of a shelter. Throughout the ordeal, Godunov makes relentless attempts to convince Long to return to him, while Hanks tries to cope with the increasing momentum of destruction to his house, his love life, and his mental stability.

The Money Pit was shot in a number of diverse locations. Many of the interiors were filmed at the Kaufman Astoria Studios in Queens, New York, a historic sight once used for comedies starring W. C. Fields and the Marx Brothers. The inside of the "dream house" was created there by production designer Patrizia von Brandenstein and art director Steve Graham. The result was a truly impressive achievement; the set would be turned from a seemingly beautiful mansion to that of a battlefield. The accomplishment of von Brandenstein and Graham is that they illustrate that superior production design need not be limited to high-budget sci-fi films or period pieces.

Exterior sequences were shot around New York City, including Park Avenue, the roof of New York University, Soho, Central Park West, and the elegant Cafe des Artistes near Lincoln Center. Certain scenes were also shot in Miami and on the Universal lot in California. Naturally, the filmmakers required the use of an actual house for many of the exterior scenes. The dilemma was how to find someone who would consent to having their beautiful home partially destroyed. Fortunately, the production company located the Ridder Mansion, on the north shore of Long Island. The house belonged to the family for which the Knight-Ridder news syndicate had been named. As the house was on the market for sale at the time, the owners conceded to let the film crew shoot key sequences there. During the course of filming, the house was virtually destroyed and then rebuilt from scratch.

Walter and Anna meet the strange lady, Estelle (Maureen Stapleton), who sells them her house. (Amblin Entertainment/Universal City Studios)

Richard Benjamin conceded that "*The Money Pit* was the most complex and challenging production" he had ever been associated with. He said he had been attracted to the project because of the "concept of physical comedy played alongside the story of a romantic relationship ... You see dialogue jokes and the like, but we have big action gags that really happen—not faked optically or anything like that. I don't think there was any way to do it than to have Tom Hanks perform many of his own stunts in the film. We made sure it was safe, of course, but it's fun to see him in the midst of things."

For his part, Hanks found that the challenge of doing broad slapstick comedy had its pitfalls—specifically in an ambitious sequence in which a small accident leads to a chain reaction of disastrous occurrences which virtually levels the entire house. He commented at the time: "It's all wonderful physical comedy, which starts very small, just a little broken step and then ... we get into much more serious problems. I knew it was going to be a physical job,

but when you first read the script, it only happens once. To shoot the sequence, though, you have to do it hundreds of times." Referring to the climax of the astonishing scene in which he is covered with plaster, he said, "There are pockmarks on my face from ashes and soot, from bricks and stones, while things hurl at me through pneumatic devices, and blenders implode in my face, as do television sets. I look at it this way: There's an element of danger that you don't find in most professions. I like being the only member on the set who is not wearing a protective face shield during the shot. And that's one of the reasons I'm anxious to take this job."

Despite the rigors of performing so many stunts, Hanks found he had developed a chemistry with Shelley Long. Both had their roots in television sitcoms and could relate to each other on a common ground. Filming of *The Money Pit* had been delayed due to Long's giving birth to her daughter Juliana. When she reported to the set, however, she was more than able to keep up with the furious physical pace of

Walter attempts to lay down the law with two of the less-than-desirable workers who have taken over his home. (Amblin Entertainment/ Universal City Studios)

there and contributes ideas and feelings, and it's always the best. He does take a beating in the film; he's kind of the Esther Williams of plaster. I like Tom a lot."

Despite the happy atmosphere on the set, when the film missed its Christmas, 1985, release date, rumors spread that the production was in trouble. When it was finally released in March 1986, *The Money Pit* was roundly panned as a juvenile farce which relied too heavily on physical comedy at the expense of interesting characterizations. Critics had little good to say about the entire venture, and

the story. Hanks related his feelings about Long as a costar: "We had miniature adventures, great philosophical discussions. We were playing two people who were very much in love, and that requires a certain kind of communication you're not going to invest in anybody else. I'm not saying I have to do this for the sake of the job; it just naturally happens. You end up finishing each other's sentences. It's not sexual, but it's intense, concentrated, packed, dense."

For her part, Long returned the compliment. "Tom Hanks was a problem. He's too nice, just wonderful. He is what you hope for and what you need to create comedy's magic moments. He is

Walter gets an unwelcome makeover. Hanks faced severe physical punishment during the filming. (Amblin Entertainment/Universal City Studios)

"Home, Crap Home": The filmmakers trashed, then rebuilt, a beautiful home on Long Island. (Amblin Entertainment/Universal City Studios)

none of the cast—including Hanks—benefited from strong personal reviews. Cynics began to ponder the Hanks phenomenon. His last three films had been box-office flops, and *The Money Pit* did little to reverse that trend. The movie grossed about $28 million—a modest sum for such a high-profile project—and was listed in the "flop" column at year's end by the industry trade papers.

The harshness of the critical assault on *The Money Pit* is rather puzzling, as such barbs are generally reserved for such "out-of-control" epics as *Cleopatra* and *Waterworld*. Despite a budget that is relatively high for a comedy, there is nothing excessive about the film, and certainly one can see where the money went during the extensive sequences in which the house is demolished and rebuilt. The movie is neither pretentious nor offensive, and screenwriter David Giler wisely followed the old industry adage to "leave the messages to Western Union." In an age in which even the most absurd comedies feel obligated to lecture the audience about the decline of Western civilization, *The Money Pit* is so enjoyable because it refrains from any attempt at social significance and revels unabashedly in its goofiness.

This is one of Tom Hanks's most physically demanding roles, but he brings it off wonderfully. His comic timing is perfect, and his low-key-to-manic reactions to events large and small are textbook examples of how slapstick should be played. His increasing haplessness at dealing with the "house from hell" are among the funniest scenes of his career. Hanks gets first-rate support from Long, who matches his skill in trading wisecracks and practicing "slow burn" reactions to overwhelmingly chaotic mishaps. One is reminded of how unimaginatively Hollywood has thus far used her talents. The relationship between Hanks and Long is a joy to behold, and director Richard Benjamin finds just the right balance. Like any normal couple, these people occasionally blame their desperate plight on each other. There is, however, never any doubt that they are still in love. We come to care about these characters, and that is an essential element if we are to remain emotionally involved with their fate.

53

The strains of homeownership seem to be taking their toll on Anna and Walter. (Amblin Entertainment/Universal City Studios)

The supporting characters aren't nearly as well defined, with the exception of Max, the mad conductor played with wonderful pomposity by the late Alexander Godunov. The former Russian ballet star had recently made his film debut in *Witness* (1984) and seemed to have a promising career in the cinema ahead of him. Watching his skillful comedic turn in *The Money Pit*, one is reminded of how charismatic Godunov could be had he found a screen niche. (Tragically, he died accidentally in 1995.)

There are many sequences in *The Money Pit* that are all too predictable; indeed, there is nary a surprise in the entire film. However, the ability of Hanks and Long to play broad comedy makes for a good number of hilarious moments: Hanks's near-death experience by way of a collapsing staircase; his ridiculous but somehow believable dilemma in which he is suspended for hours in a carpet when a gaping hole opens in the floor; and a truly inspired madcap scene in which a minor mishap results in the wholesale destruction of the semirebuilt house. Throughout all of this insanity, one is constantly aware of the importance that special effects and production design play in the overall film.

The Money Pit never quite caught on with audiences in theaters, although it became a popular title on home video and helped enhance Tom Hanks's reputation as one of the more popular young comedy stars in film. He was philosophical about the box-office failure of three consecutive films and likened it to his frustrations during his early years in acting, when he had to perform Shakespeare for "two thousand completely uninterested public school students who just talked and threw stuff around the theater. . . . I just busted my ass up there for two hours, and they couldn't have cared less. . . . I've been in plays that stank to high heaven. But you've got to shake it off. Most of the actors I know have had periods when they've been shit on, but you learn to take it and get on with life."

Despite the lukewarm reception to *The Money Pit*, Hanks was signed by Columbia Pictures to a lucrative multipicture deal that had the potential to boost his salary to $1 million per film. His reaction was typically low-key and self-deprecating: "The best-case scenario is that I get to do stories and characters that are very interesting to me and Columbia gets to make and distribute movies that make phenomenal amounts of money and go down in the annals of motion-picture history. The worst-case scenario is that everyone sits around and nothing gets done at all, and I go off into the apricot business or something like that. Somewhere in between there is where my deal falls."

Reviews

"If you can imagine a remake of Steven Spielberg's Poltergeist *in which the spirits of the dead have been shoved aside by equally loud, unruly plumbers and carpenters, you'll*

"Instead of a real estate fiasco anybody could roar at in recognition, The Money Pit has been inflated into a noisy destruction derby. . . . The nimble Hanks again proves his delicious way with a double-take."

Newsweek

"The Money Pit is simply the pits. . . . Unofficial remake of Mr. Blandings Builds His Dream House begins promisingly and slides irrevocably downward from there. Most of the scenes in this demolition derby begin with something or other caving in or falling apart, an event which is invariably followed by the two leads yelling and screaming at each other for minutes on end."

—"Cart.," Variety

"We get one monotonous sight gag after another. The most irritating is the one where Hanks falls through the floor and is pinned, halfway down, by a rug. He can't move. All he can do is scream for help, but when Long finally arrives at the house, he screams all the wrong things, until we aren't laughing. Didn't it occur to anybody that the smarter the characters were, the funnier their troubles would be? Make them into idiots, and who cares if their house falls down? . . . There is one sustained Rube Goldberg–type gag that is really funny, as an incredible chain of events unfolds with meticulous precision. But one gag does not a comedy make, and if they'd spent the time on the characters that they spent building the house, they might have had something here."

—Roger Ebert's Video Companion

have some idea of The Money Pit. . . . *The comedy depends entirely on special electrical effects and outlandish physical gags, most of which have to do with heavy objects, including Walter, falling through floors, down staircases and out windows. . . . The film's approach to slapstick comedy recalls Mr. Spielberg's in the director's only outright failure—the monumental 1941. The gags, though elaborately choreographed, are so clumsily broken up in bits and pieces of explanatory 'business' that one never has any sense of overall logic going fatally askew . . . the spectacle is so impressive, that you hesitate to laugh."*

—New York Times

Nothing in Common

Tri-Star, 1986

"It wasn't until Nothing in Common *that I knew enough to tone it down, rein it in, and start trying to tell the truth as opposed to just telling a joke."*

Cast
Tom Hanks (*David Basner*); Jackie Gleason (*Max Basner*); Eva Marie Saint (*Lorraine Basner*); Hector Elizondo (*Charlie Gargas*); Barry Corbin (*Andrew Woolridge*); Bess Armstrong (*Donna Mildred Martin*); Sela Ward (*Cheryl Ann Wayne*); Cindy Harrell (*Shelly the Stewardess*); John Kapelos (*Roger the Commercial Director*); Carol Messing (*David's Secretary*).

Credits
Director: Garry Marshall; producer: Alexandra Rose; executive producer: Roger M. Rothstein; screenplay: Rick Podell and Michael Preminger; director of photography: John A. Alonzo; production designer: Charles Rosen; editor: Glenn Farr; music: Patrick Leonard.
Running time: 118 minutes.

As David Basner, Hanks gets to stretch his dramatic muscles for the first time on-screen. (Tri-Star Pictures)

Despite the modest performances of his post-*Splash* films, Tom Hanks was still perceived as a "hot property" who had only to discover his right niche in the industry. Consequently, Columbia signed him for a multipicture deal beginning with *Nothing in Common*, a seriocomic look at family relationships in the eighties. In addition to making Hanks one of the highest-paid stars in his age bracket, the film was significant in that it offered him the opportunity to portray his most complex and interesting character to date. It also allowed Hanks the opportunity to costar with a boyhood idol: the Great One himself, Jackie Gleason.

Nothing in Common was the brainchild of producer Alexandra Rose, who worked to develop the screenplay with two former stand-up comedians turned television writers, Rick Podell and Michael Preminger. The project started as a TV movie, but when studios proved to be more receptive to the premise than the networks, Rose became determined to bring the story to the big screen.

Simultaneously, Tom Hanks was impatient to try his hand at something other than broad comedy. He commented at the time, "I got the impression I was finally too old for a summer movie" (i.e., sophomoric comedies). He noted that even such high-profile films as *Splash* and *The Money Pit* have "definite beach

mentalities. They were straight comedies, with time in the sack, for God sakes. It's not that I don't think they were good, but it seems that's all Hollywood wants. Despite the fact that I'm in and out of bed in *Nothing in Common*, it was no easy sell. I loved it on first read. . . . Alex [Rose] had to say to the studios, 'Wanna take a big chance? There are no teenagers in this movie.' But the first scene of the script sold them, I guess. At least it sounded like a good sex comedy. If that was the nature of the whole script, I don't think I would have done the movie. But there are puttery, domestic scenes in the kitchen with my mother and a puppy dog, and I cry in it, and hey, there are no guns."

Hanks, who was already receiving more scripts than he could handle, immediately saw the potential in this moving story about David Basner, a workaholic advertising executive who is forced to deal with his estranged, abrasive father, Max, after his mother decides to move out and get a divorce. Both father and son lock horns on virtually every issue imaginable, and the tensions seem to be unsurmountable. However, both men learn to appreciate the other, and a mutual respect arises which allows them to reconcile and develop a loving relationship in the abbreviated time they have left together.

One of Hollywood's most notable producers, Howard W. Koch also found the script to be profoundly moving and, as president of Rastar Productions, decided to finance the project. It was decided that Garry Marshall would direct. Primarily known for his work on popular seventies sitcoms like *The Odd Couple*, *Happy Days*, and *Laverne and Shirley*, Marshall had only recently ventured into feature films with *Young Doctors in Love*. His next, *The Flamingo Kid*, won praise as one of the hippest comedies of recent years. *Nothing in Common* would mark his third motion picture as director. (Earlier he had written and produced James Garner's *How Sweet It Is!*)

The next challenge was to find an actor who could play the extremely demanding role of Max Basner, Hanks's cantankerous on-screen father. The role was reminiscent of Willy Loman, with Max an aging salesman from the old school who finds himself out of his league in the hectic eighties. Faced with failing health and the loss of his treasured career, Max is further devastated by his wife's desire for a divorce. The character needed to be played by someone who could make this outwardly boorish and unlikable man worth caring about. Ray Stark, the chairman of Rastar, knew immediately who would be ideal for the

Hanks theorizes that the reason why he often gets the girl (in this case, Sela Ward, as Cheryl Ann Wayne) is that frustrated screenwriters are living vicariously through him. (Tri-Star Pictures)

role: his old friend Jackie Gleason, who had starred in two of Stark's previous films: the ill-fated *The Toy* and the smash hit *Smokey and the Bandit*. According to Stark, when Gleason read the script, "it was the fastest *yes* I ever received from a star."

Tom Hanks later said: "I was involved from the beginning with the producer, Alex Rose, and the guys who wrote it even before Garry Marshall came in to direct. We were all hungry and wanted to prove something, score a touchdown or whatever. I also thought it was a timely movie—America in 1985. Aging parents, dissatisfaction with one's career, learning that what lasts is not our jobs and what we do with them. In short, a lot of emotion was invested in the movie, and that was the first time it had ever happened to me. So it really changed me and started me looking at my position in moviemaking in a different way."

In a 1986 interview Hanks explained that the movie had personal meaning to him, and he related the script to his own family relationships: "We had no aliens, no mermaids. There weren't even any exploding helicopters. We were playing with certain truths about our generation and our parents. As kids, we swore to ourselves we couldn't make the same mistakes, fall for the same empty promises, go after the same hollow dreams as them. And here we are, in the mid-1980s, discovering we made exactly the same mistakes. In my life, it came to me when I was getting a divorce. I said, 'Jesus Christ, I'm just like my old man.' Sometimes, just when he says something, it hits me—'Holy Cow, I think just the way he does.' Now, how do you show this in a movie without preaching? You've got to sneak it in. Make them laugh, make them cry. It's an emotional tightrope. It's a cerebral battle royal."

Hanks admitted to being a bit nervous over sharing the screen with Jackie Gleason. "Here's a guy I grew up with in my living room, and I get to be in the living room with him. I gotta say that I approached him like my father, really. With love—and a little fear. Of course, the story helped. There were similarities with my own father. He's divorced from my mother, and he's recently been seriously ill." Hanks later said, "There was a certain amount of awe beforehand, but the first day on the set, Jackie came over to me and said, 'Howya doin' kid—let's make

history.' We threw our arms around each other, embraced, and it was easy from then on." Hanks would later add of the Great One: "He's not just the King of Comedy, he's the Pope of Comedy!"

In addition to starring with Gleason, Hanks had the pleasure of playing opposite Eva Marie Saint, as his mother, the long-suffering wife of Max Basner. While the script is very much a story of father and son, Saint is given some wonderful moments. As a woman discovering her individuality and independence after a lifetime serving an ungrateful, self-centered husband, Saint earns the sympathy of the viewer despite the fact that we really can't dislike the Gleason character. Saint found starring opposite these two leading men to be equally rewarding: "I found enormous strength in Tom and Jackie. I could sense what makes (Gleason) special. I had a lot more time with Tom in discussing our scenes and relationships. We almost fell into a mother-son situation. He discussed some very personal things with me and I found myself reacting as I do with my own children."

his father and told him, "You're in this all over the place, Pop. Sorry about that."

He could ill afford to dwell on his personal problems, however, for he was in virtually every scene of *Nothing in Common*. In addition to extensive studio shooting, the production also filmed for three weeks on location in Chicago. On the set, Hanks and Gleason would occasionally argue over the plausibility of a scene or a line of dialogue. Hanks was careful to treat his illustrious costar as a peer, not someone who filled him with awe. "There would be some moments where we'd be sitting together on the set, waiting for things to go, and he would offer a few things, but I made a conscious choice before we went into the movie that I'm not going to ask this guy questions. I'm not going to bother him, because if I do that, I'm not being an actor. I'm being this pesky little fan. 'Remember that scene where you'n Norton got drunk? How'ja do that, huh?'" He later added, "You're dealing with an icon when you talk about Jackie Gleason. And it goes beyond being the comic or the booze hound. He's a much more complex individual than that. And when it came time to stand up in front of the camera,

Hanks had other things on his mind: his pending divorce from his wife, Sam. During the filming, the couple had separated, and Hanks moved in temporarily with David Chambers, an old friend from his *Bosom Buddies* days. He also admitted that the script presented some parallels to his own family relationships, saying, "I had my older brother and sister. I'm not as close with my mom as other kids are, but it doesn't stop the fact that I love her. I say to my mom, 'I love you, but I don't know you because I didn't live with you.'" Hanks said the story also reminded him of his real-life relationship with

he didn't want to be bothered with anything that was going to take away from the concentration of the work. Jackie does not rehearse. He wants to get it right the first time.... He's always, 'Let's do it. C'mon,' which is a great way to work if you're acting for the movies. He's proven he can deliver the goods that way, so it works." The Great One was equally impressed with his costar, saying, "The verdict on Tom Hanks is that he's got it. Anybody can do a line, but Tom has moves. The right moves."

The supporting cast of *Nothing in Common* is uncommonly impressive. The stunning Sela Ward is well cast as Cheryl Ann, the icy beauty whose sexual aggressiveness is nearly more than David can handle. That she happens to be the executive daughter of his biggest client (an amusingly obnoxious Barry Corbin) only complicates matters more. Ward sizzles with her every appearance, and her love scenes with Hanks are both erotic and funny. (Ward was to become a personal friend of Hanks's and would later be a member of the wedding party when Hanks married Rita Wilson.)

Hanks admitted being somewhat self-conscious about playing the on-screen love interest of Sela Ward. He said, "Sela is one of these women who, on first meeting, really does take your breath away, to the point that I didn't know if I could work with a woman who was that beautiful. I felt like a jerk. And I knew that in twenty days we were going to be lying naked together. I would never have the guts to take this woman out. And yet now I'm going to play a guy who is going to hit on this babe repeatedly throughout the course of the movie." Feeling self-conscious about love scenes has long been a facet of Hanks's personality. Asked why such an average-looking guy generally gets the beautiful girls on-screen, he commented modestly, "I think it's because there are a lot of writers who aren't very attractive but who are fair-

ly funny and want to have sex a lot, so I guess I'm the chief beneficiary of that. It's not like I say, 'I'd like to do this movie . . . but I've got to have sex more often!' "

The other notable member of the cast was Hector Elizondo, who has broken some sort of politically incorrect ground in recent films by portraying a boss who is both likable and sympathetic to his employees. When David's personal problems infringe on his job performance, his boss covers for him and ensures that his career is not damaged.

Nothing in Common is very significant in Hanks career in that it proved to be the first mainstream film in which he could extend his talents to drama. The vintage Hanks we all like is certainly present: flirting, being irreverent to stuffed shirts, and joking his way into bed with beautiful women. However, he is equally impressive in the tender sequences between David and his parents. It's easy to be upstaged by the likes of Jackie Gleason and Eva Marie Saint, but Hanks more than holds his own.

The core of the story, of course, centers on the Hanks-Gleason relationship. Gleason is terrific in the role. His character is a complete egotist, yet we cannot help but love and care about him. The subtle method by which Gleason copes with the humiliation

of losing his customers and then his job is wonderfully understated. The intelligent screenplay also refuses to soften his personality for the sake of a feel-good ending. Father and son are reconciled, albeit slowly, but there is no second chance for Gleason and Eva Marie Saint's relationship. Much to Gleason and Hanks's distress, the marriage is over. Praise should be given to director Garry Marshall, who avoids most of the clichés one would expect to find in these types of family dramas.

The film is noteworthy not only because it's a meaningful one filled with genuine laughter and tears. Tragically, it was Jackie Gleason's last movie. He died suddenly in 1987, a year after the release of this film. Given the fact that he had frequently starred in movies which were not worthy of his talents, with *Nothing in Common* he at least went out on "a high note" (as Ralph Kramden might say).

The movie received surprisingly lukewarm reviews and fared only modestly well at the box office, fueling speculation that Hanks's hard-core fans longed to see him in irreverent comedies, not "touchy-feely" domestic dramas. However, he remains proud of his work in the film. "My work in *Nothing in Common* represents the sum total of everything I've learned so far as a human being. It's the sort of role that comes along once every ten years, and if it had come along any earlier, I probably wouldn't have been ready for it." Years later, he would say of the film, "That was the first movie where I *thought* I knew what I was doing, and it turned out I pretty much *did* know what I was doing.

I'm still ludicrously more proud of this movie than I should be, because it didn't do all that great."

Hanks need not apologize. *Nothing* is an *uncommonly* good motion picture which helped pave the way for the challenging roles the future would present.

Reviews

"*The movie is like* Death of a Salesman *as a sitcom, with the father's misery used as a lesson to the swinging yuppie son . . . this Chicago-set comedy-weepie (in the manner of* Terms of Endearment*) is best in its hard-edged parodies of advertising. Its moralizing is insufferable, and so is the way everything is flagged for you. This isn't a movie. It's television on a big screen.*

—Pauline Kael, 5001 *Nights at the Movies*

"*Tom Hanks says the big opening scene in* Nothing in Common *wasn't written out in the screenplay. They had to improvise the series of shots where he walks into the ad agency where he works, and wisecracks his way from one person to another, all the way to his office. He's a high voltage guy, a real character, funny and smart. . . . Hanks gives the sequence all he's got and he's terrific—*

David finds solace with his longtime friend Donna (Bess Armstrong). (Tri-Star Pictures)

but it belongs in another movie. The whole first half of Nothing in Common *belongs in another movie. Either that, or the second half does. The movie splits in two, starting out as a wiseguy comedy and ending up as the heartbreaking story of a yuppie who is trying to understand his bitter, lonely parents. . . . Gleason provides the movie's center of gravity, in a role that has been written with some courage and is not compromised. Here is a man who has lived in silence, with resentment as his constant companion, for years. . . . He is not a curmudgeon with a heart of gold, he's frankly hateful at times and the movie doesn't sentimentalize him. That's why it earns its very effective ending."*

—Roger Ebert's Video Companion

"The picture has both somber and ebullient moods, cut together without much modulation, and only Tom Hanks's virtuoso performance holds the pieces in place."

—David Denby, New York magazine

"The kind of film that tries to be all things to all people and as a result succeeds at none of them. Part youth comedy, part sappy fam- ily drama, pic continually seems to be tripping over itself. Only consistent element is the manic and entertaining performance of Tom Hanks."

—"Jagr.," Variety

"The Tom Hanks turn we've been waiting for. As a hotshot young ad exec, Hanks embodies everything we love and hate about the eighties sense of humor: its lack of conviction, its irreverence, its frank self-interest."

—David Edelstein, Village Voice

"Starts out like another yuppie Tom Hanks comedy—until it takes off in a surprising and unexpectedly rewarding direction. Never has Hanks or Gleason been better . . . by now Hanks could phone in the brash, comical young urban types (to his credit, he doesn't) and it's good to see he's capable of moving beyond this to sustain beautifully a growing seriousness. . . . Nothing in Common may be as rough around the edges as Gleason's crumbling salesman, but it does zero in on some home truths."

—Kevin Thomas, Los Angeles Times

Every Time We Say Goodbye

Tri-Star, 1986

"A period piece, a pure romantic movie, no sex, with this European slant to it. As an actor, I couldn't pass it up."

Cast
Tom Hanks (*David*); Cristina Marsillach (*Sarah*); Benedict Taylor (*Peter*); Anat Atzmon (*Victoria*); Gila Almagor (*Lea*); Monny Moshanov (*Nessim*); Avner Hiskyahu (*Raphael*); Caroline Goodall (*Sally*); Esther Parnass (*Rosa*); Daphne Armony (*Clara*); Orit Weisman (*Mathilda*)

Credits
Director: Moshe Mizrahi; producers: Jacob Kotzky and Sharon Harel; screenplay: Moshe Mizrahi, Rachel Fabien, and Leah Appet; story: Moshe Mizrahi; director of photography: Giuseppe Lanci; editor: Mark Burns; music: Philippe Sarde. Running time: 97 minutes.

The inauspicious first meeting of David and Sarah (Cristina Marsillach), with Victoria (Anat Atzmon, *far left*) and Peter (Benedict Taylor), gave no indication of the love affair to come. (Tri-Star Pictures)

Determined to prove that his acting talents extended beyond the range of comedies, Tom Hanks chose the Israeli-made *Every Time We Say Goodbye* as his first completely dramatic film role. "It was a straight, essentially romantic part," Hanks recalled. "I said, 'This is a movie I haven't made yet. So, without hesitating, I said, 'Sure, you bet.'" He later explained the significance the movie had in relation to his career: "People are going to put more weight on this film because it's a so-called drama and my other movies were so-called comedies. But I'm serious about all my roles. My job is to take a character from the typewritten pages and collaborate with the director to make him come alive. This movie has wit and amusing moments, but it also has sadness, and this combination of humor and warmth and sorrow is the measure of a great work that never ages or bores."

Every Time We Say Goodbye was an offbeat project for Hanks not only because it provided him with an entirely dramatic role but also because of the nature of the story line and the overall feel of the film. Hanks is cast as David, an American in the RAF in the days immediately before the United States entered World War II. While recovering from a leg wound in Jerusalem, he meets Sarah (Cristina Marsillach), a melancholy young Jewish woman who lives very

much under the thumb of her dominating family and reluctantly adheres to the strict rules they have established for her social life. They are insistent that she eventually marry Nessin (Monny Moshanov), a gentle, well-meaning man who adores her but whom she considers only a platonic friend.

When star-crossed Sarah and David meet, she initially finds him rude. However, David is instantly smitten by her and attempts to court her. Her family immediately rejects him because he is a Gentile, but Sarah slowly develops an interest in him. Eventually, the two fall in love. The crux of the story centers on Sarah's trying to cope with honoring her family's demands that she isolate herself from David and David's attempts to make her commit to a relationship. The harsh methods employed by her Orthodox family make Sarah capitulate to their wishes, and she reluctantly prepares to marry Nessim. However, just as David is about to leave on assignment to Egypt, Sarah finds the courage to run to him and promise she will marry him upon his return—knowing it will

sacrifice her relationship with her family.

Hanks found pleasure in working on location in Israel under the direction of Moshe Mizrahi (who had earlier won acclaim for his direction of *Madame Rosa*). Judging by the films credits, Mizrahi was virtually a one-man crew. He contributed to several other key functions, including coauthoring the screenplay from his own original story. Hanks also found it refreshing to star in what would have been a low-budget film by Hollywood standards—$3.7 million. However, that sum made *Every Time We Say Goodbye* the biggest-budgeted film ever shot entirely on location in Israel.

Hanks discovered that the low-key atmosphere on the set was entirely different from the experience of making a film in America. "I was anxious to have the opportunity to work with a small group of people who do a special kind of story—out of the glare of attention. Working in an intimate, nonpressured way is something new for me. We're not going off to a movie studio with parking spaces and commissaries and executives. We're just going out to make a movie where Moshe Mizrahi can concentrate on being a director instead of an executive. And I can concentrate on being an actor and not a movie star. Perhaps European actors are used to making movies this way, but I'm not. What's great about it is that there are no egos like 'This is what I want from this movie.' That's something new and something that doesn't always happen in American movies. There are a number of considerations in accepting a movie role—one, of course, is getting a good part. I'm a selfish actor; I like good roles. Sometimes an actor does a movie because of its story or message. Sometimes it's the people involved; sometimes it's the money. If you're lucky, it's everything rolled into one. And the creative challenge is much more important to me now than running around, having a good time, and making friends. The glamour of making a movie has taken a backseat to that creative aspect. From here on, it's the acting that remains to be seen."

Filming on *Every Time We Say Goodbye* began in February 1986, before the theatrical release of either *The Money Pit* or *Nothing in Common*. Hanks relished seeing the sights and culture of Israel and

David enjoys a traditional dinner with Sarah and her family. (Tri-Star Pictures)

said, "I wouldn't want to rush through a place like Jerusalem. It's a city that you want to roam. And in Tel Aviv I wanted to see how people decorate their apartments, what their political views are, and since there wasn't as many camels as I expected, what kind of cars do they drive. You don't have to be religious to understand the worldwide importance of Israel. This is essentially where all Western societies find their base. And the history here is the greatest story ever told. As an American and a Gentile, I envy the rich Jewish heritage. But what really interests me is how people live today. How they relate to one another and what they do on a Saturday night."

Shooting in the Middle East also gave Hanks the opportunity to escape the glare of the paparazzi, which was becoming an increasingly disturbing by-product of his fame. He commented on how the American media was wreaking havoc on the psyches of actors and entertainers: "It's terrible what they've done to Sean Penn and people like him. They can't walk down the street; they can't go out to dinner. The press, the guys who write the gossip. I hate the way

they attack. They do it to him, they'll do it to somebody else; they'll do it to me. Just look at how it affects a young actor's work.... Look at Tom Cruise, the way he walks, the way he talks. He's losing it as an actor. He's becoming a movie star. He's on the wrong track."

Hanks continued his cynical outlook on fame in an interview with the *Jerusalem Post*: "The sunglasses, the autographs, and limousines are just gossamer. What really counts are the periods of very intense concentration on the film set, when your emotions run at a fever pitch. A movie set is a very exciting place to be, filled with dedicated people doing jobs they're good at. You have to learn discipline and concentration real fast or you're going to get eaten alive. . . . You have all these secretaries. Limos pick you up at the airport, and people bring you diet caffeine-free Cokes all the time and tell you you're fabulous, the show you're working on is great—until it comes out. And then you're yesterday's Danish."

While Hanks deserves credit for appearing in an old-fashioned film like *Every Time We Say Goodbye*,

David soon begins to realize that the bounds of custom and tradition are putting a damper on his feelings for Sarah. (Tri-Star Pictures)

one wonders exactly what it was about the story that he found so appealing. The title alone makes it sound like a film version of those Harlequin romance Xeroxes but is preferable to the two earlier working titles used at various times: *Love Is Ever Young* and *Love Hurts*. The script has its engaging moments but basically moves at a snail's pace. On film, the low budget is apparent. With the exception of a few scenes, the movie is populated almost entirely by a dozen or so characters. At first, the resulting intimacy of the story is refreshing. However, the inability of director Mizrahi to "open up" the movie gives the production a distinctly claustrophobic feeling. The scenic wonders of Jerusalem are only seen sporadically, and it seems as though virtually all of the movie is shot in various apartments, as though Mizrahi were filming a stage production.

It is also puzzling why the plot is set during World War II. To the detriment of the script, virtually no mention is made of the war or its impact on the participants—other than Hanks dreading his pending orders to ship out from Jerusalem and leaving Sarah behind. Considering that the plot centers on Jews whose very existence depends on the outcome of the war, everyone seems to be relatively nonchalant

about the entire conflict. There are a few jokes about Hitler made over dinner, and we see a fighter plane land periodically, but the social and political ramifications of the war are not anywhere to be found. Mitzrahi could have just as easily set the story in contemporary Israel and spared himself the cost of some period costumes.

Every Time We Say Goodbye is basically *Romeo and Juliet* with yarmulkes. Hanks is charming and convincing as David, the good-natured flyboy who finds love at first sight with Sarah. However, his character is never adequately developed, and the script does not allow Hanks to use his many comedic talents. Therefore, David does not appear to be that much different from Nessim (and most of the other characters); he, too, is basically a good-natured bore. Although he stands out like a sore thumb as an American in the RAF in Israel, there is no "edge" to the character, and it becomes abundantly clear that we miss the cynical wit Hanks has brought to his other roles. As Sarah, Cristina Marsillach is beautiful and competent, but her character is so melancholy, one can only wonder what David sees in her. She spends most of the movie pouting behind closed doors or fighting with her well-meaning but strict parents and siblings. If her eyes weren't open, one would swear she was sleepwalking. The best scenes in the film center on the domestic tensions within the household as Sarah tries to fight the authoritative rule to which she has been forced to submit. Her sisters toe the parents' line and are unwilling to side with her. Instead, their idea of fun is sitting in a circle waxing their legs. (No wonder even Hanks's dull character looks like a "catch" to Sarah!)

Every Time We Say Goodbye remains surprisingly engrossing throughout, however, thanks to the appeal of the two stars and a talented supporting cast. Moshe Mizrahi has the chutzpah to make a contemporary film about romance that has the good taste not to descend into gratuitous sex. While he is undeniably talented, though, Mizrahi's obsession with being tasteful also makes for some of the most boring

Sarah and David steal away for a romantic interlude. (Tri-Star Pictures)

love scenes filmed. When Sarah finally comes to her monumental decision to spend the night with David, the sequence should be riveting and erotic. It is neither. While this does not have to be *Last Tango in Jerusalem*, a little steam to the love scenes would have been beneficial. After all, this woman is not only losing her virginity; she is rejecting her family and its customs.

The film also presents one of those maddeningly obtuse endings. While we see Sarah commit to marrying David when he returns from the war, it leaves the most pivotal questions unanswered: How is this woman who is now disowned by her family going to survive? How will she cope with isolation from the only home and lifestyle she has ever known, and

how will she deal with the social pressures and prejudices she will endure? Such minor issues are conveniently swept under the rug while Hanks makes his *Casablanca*-like farewell to Sarah. (Is there one World War II film in which the participants can part without the pressure of having to cope with a plane or train that is departing momentarily?)

Every Time We Say Goodbye did little to further the momentum of Tom Hanks's career. Prior to its release, he remained upbeat about the project, saying, "There are times for tragic peaks and valleys, but you also need the energy sometimes—and it's not roaring laughter but just laughing inside—

David and Sarah's romance grows as they make the most of their limited time together. (Tri-Star Pictures) so the audience can see the tragedy of life together with the comedy of life. And I think that is one of the important elements that make *Every Time We Say Goodbye* special. There's great humor, great warmth, and right next to it, great sadness. I think that's the measure of a great work. That's why such works never get boring or aged. They have that element of wit that makes a classical theme come alive over and over again."

If only the critics had been in agreement. The film had the stigma of box-office poison even before its release. The movie premiered in New York, where theater managers must have been tempted to create their own Wailing Wall when they saw the paltry box-office receipts. Like so many well-intentioned films that dwelled on issues of ethnicity, this one failed to click with audiences. Tri-Star should have considered the disappointing returns from the Neil Diamond version of *The Jazz Singer*, which also examined the problems faced by parents and children in a Jewish family. Whereas that film had the redeeming value of having the esteemed Sir Laurence Olivier delivering lines like "Isn't it tough enough bean-kachoo" (translation: "Isn't it tough enough being a Jew") and a hit soundtrack album, the Hanks movie did not even have those marketing angles. The film was never shown theatrically in Los Angeles despite the presence of Hanks's name above the title.

Hanks looked back on the film in a 1988 interview, saying, "I've really only done two films that disappeared without a trace. So I guess if you want me to answer from a crass monetary point of view, yeah, I've done *pretty well*. One of [the bombs], it's on cable now, was a drama [*Every Time We Say Goodbye*]. And actually that was a no-lose situation. We were trying to make a sweet little movie. No one expected that it would be a blockbuster." Hanks then placed the film's financial failure in context with a previous flop which was an artistic failure, saying, "But *The Man With One Red Shoe*? That was an absolute *dog!*"

Unlike that film, *Every Time We Say Goodbye* was still an effort of which Hanks could be proud. Many other rising young stars would prefer to play it safe in popular, genre-type films, but Hanks placed his need to master a dramatic role above box-office receipts. While this project was not a critical or financial success, it did succeed in being the "sweet little movie" Hanks set out to make.

Reviews

"Tom Hanks is utterly out of place in this Israeli romance for at least two reasons: because there's something so innately comic about him, even in solemn surroundings, and because he has so much more energy than the film does. . . . What might have made the film more interesting is some attention to the feelings of Jews in Palestine about the ongoing war. There are brief complaints about British rule and curses directed at Hitler, but aside from that the film doesn't attempt a broader perspective. Instead, it concentrates on Sarah, her large and boisterous family, and her and David's lukewarm love affair. Not even the film's pointed attempts to explain various Jewish customs, as in the lengthy Sabbath dinner scene, have any real verve. Of more interest, though it goes unexplained, is the sequence in which the women in Sarah's family sit together around a warm cauldron, communally waxing their legs."

—Janet Maslin, *New York Times*

"Love stories come and go, but every once in a while there's one with such a sense of urgency that it seems as if nobody was ever in love before. Such freshness can be found in [this movie]."

—William Wolf, Gannett News Service

"A straight romance, it's Hanks's least likely film—and not half bad. B-"

—Ty Burr, *Entertainment Weekly*

"The lead performances are equally lukewarm, Tom Hanks's relying on a noncommittal blankness enlivened by a twitch of something that may be charm, or perhaps an attempt to emulate his idol James Stewart."

—Verina Glaessner, *Monthly Film Bulletin* (U.K.)

Caught in a swirling family tempest, the two soon realize that their passion cannot be denied. (Tri-Star Pictures)

"[The film's primary interest for the audience] will be watching an effective Hanks in this warm, though slow-paced film . . . the movie is not devoid of humor. Early scenes when Hanks is accepted to dinner by the family as a friend and not yet a suitor are funny and believable. Culturally rich story is aided throughout by the pic's all-Israel shoot, nicely highlighting the different worlds these two lovers come from."

— "Roy.," *Variety*

···10

Dragnet

Universal, 1987

"I went to the guys at Universal and said, 'Okay, here's why I want the job: one, because I don't have to win the girl at the end of this movie and I'm tired of that; two, because I get to play a cop who does things like slug people; and three, because I want to work with Dan Aykroyd. If those are the reasons you want me, then make the deal."

Cast

Dan Aykroyd (*Joe Friday*); Tom Hanks (*Pep Streebek*); Christopher Plummer (*Reverend Whirley*); Dabney Coleman (*Jerry Caesar*); Alexandra Paul (*Connie Swail*); Harry Morgan (*Capt. Bill Gannon*); Elizabeth Ashley (*Commissioner Kirkpatrick*); Jack O'Halloran (*Emil Muzz*); Kathleen Freeman (*Enid Borden*); Bruce Gray (*Mayor Parvin*); Lenka Peterson (*Granny Mundy*).

Credits

Director: Tom Mankiewicz; producers: David Permut and Robert K. Weiss; executive producer: Bernie Brillstein; screenplay: Dan Aykroyd, Alan Zweibel, and Tom Mankiewicz; director of photography: Matthew F. Leonetti; production designer: Robert F. Boyle; editors: Richard Halsey and William D. Gordean; music: Ira Newborn. Running time: 110 minutes.

Joe Friday (Dan Aykroyd) and Pep Streebek (Hanks), dedicated to protect and serve (Universal City Studios)

Among the great comedy shows of all time, *Dragnet* must certainly rank alongside *The Honeymooners*, *The Dick Van Dyke Show*, and *The Andy Griffith Show*. This is not meant to be disrespectful to the series' beloved star, creator and director, Jack Webb. Webb was a truly innovative force in TV's early days, and when he first introduced the show in January 1952 (following a long run on radio), the series was an immediate hit and ran for a remarkable seven-and-one-half years. In 1967, Webb brought the show back, presumably to rally against the counterculture movement, which was at its peak. The frustrated members of the Silent Majority could console themselves that Webb was back and putting those hippies and drug pushers in their place. Critics scoffed that Webb's staccato, robotic delivery of lines, coupled with bit players from the Home for the Criminally Untalented, would be laughable in the late sixties. However, Webb's audience rallied, and the new show ran for three years. Hard as it is to believe in these days of *COPS* and other cinema verité shows, *Dragnet* was as close as TV got to portraying the real-life stories behind the day-to-day duties of the L.A.P.D.

By 1986, *Dragnet* was remembered as a bit of

DRAGNET

The stars of the original *Dragnet* TV series, Harry Morgan and Jack Webb

nostalgia, primarily because of its famed "*dum-de-dum-dum*" theme song. Producer David Permut envisioned yet another resurrection of *Dragnet*—this time as an *intentionally* funny big-screen comedy. He approached Dan Aykroyd, who considered the project manna from heaven, saying, "I've had a fascination with Joe Friday since I was a kid. Next to Clouseau, he's the most famous cop in the world. I've studied his speech inflections, his mannerisms, his walk. . . . If there was ever a character I'd always wanted to play, it was this one."

Permut and coproducer Robert K. Weiss signed Aykroyd for the lead role of Joe Friday, the nephew of the famed L.A. detective. Aykroyd would also coauthor the screenplay, along with *Saturday Night Live* writer Alan Zweibel and veteran screenwriter Tom Mankiewicz, who would also make his directorial debut with this film.

With the project taking shape, the key missing ingredient was casting the pivotal role of Joe Friday's partner. In the sixties TV version, Harry Morgan was Jack Webb's sidekick, Officer Bill Gannon. Morgan's performance was generally the most enjoyable element of the show; his laid-back, natural acting style was in direct contrast to Webb's "stiff-as-a-board" characterization. Although the age difference made it unfeasible to cast Morgan as Dan Aykroyd's foil in

the cinematic *Dragnet*, the producers nevertheless wisely signed him to portray Capt. Bill Gannon, now serving as the younger Joe Friday's boss.

The script for the film called for Friday's partner, Pep Streebek, to be the antithesis of the by-the book cop which Friday represented. Streebek is a sloppy, unorthodox undercover officer who is instantly at odds with his hopelessly square partner—the only man under age eighty who still wears a fedora. John Candy was considered for the Streebek role, but a commitment elsewhere prevented him from participating. Ultimately, an enthusiastic Tom Hanks was signed for the part. Coming off two very dramatic films, *Every Time We Say Goodbye* and *Nothing in Common*, Hanks was eager to take on a role which would represent pure fun. He recalled, "Those two films required a lot of not just concentration but also emotional investment, which is very, very exhausting. I don't think it's particularly good for your psyche, because you find yourself analyzing so many things. Eventually, you can drive yourself crazy."

Despite his enthusiasm for the role of Pep, Hanks confessed to having some concerns about taking on what was very much a supporting role to Dan Aykroyd: "I just took the job as a hired gun, and it makes me nervous. Dan has his Joe Friday that he's doing that is set in stone. Next to that, if I so much as raise an eyebrow, it's like screaming at the top of my lungs. Dan is Joe Friday all the time; he's got that kind of analytical mind. It's very much Dan's movie, so much so that I wonder where I fit in."

Having heard that Aykroyd shared his disdain for egotistical behavior, Hanks was happy about the opportunity to work with him. "I just have a wonderful time working. I took *Dragnet* because I thought it would be a gas to do. I knew it would be invigorating to work with a comedic actor as good as Dan Aykroyd. There's no competition, none of the 'star' stuff. In fact, he even told me once, 'Ya know, "star" is "rats" spelled backwards.' I think that's a pretty good way of putting it."

Friday and Streebek do whatever it takes to uphold the law. . . . Like we said, *whatever* it takes! (Universal City Studios)

Hanks found that the chemistry he shared with Aykroyd was every bit as genuine as he had hoped: "I've always been lucky in being matched up with first-rate actors throughout my career. Dan and I met each other and instantly knew we were going to have a blast making this movie. It was great working again with someone from Second City. I'd worked with both Jim Belushi and John Candy, so I've always felt real comfortable around folks from that group."

He also worked with Aykroyd in developing his character: "In this movie, audiences will be seeing two of the world's most famous fictional cops, Joe Friday and his partner. . . . Who was his partner, anyway? You've got to have some kind of spin going in. Sometimes there's a little more written out about the guy, but in this case there wasn't. So, between talking with Dan and making up a bunch of stuff myself, we managed to put the guy together. I always figured he was in the air force or something and came really close to being thrown out. He's someone who likes being a cop, but he's easily bored by what he perceives as the trivialities of the job: filling out forms, following proper procedure. The sort of things that Friday thrives on."

Coproducer Robert K. Weiss gave his own interpretation of Hanks's character: "He's a pretty wild individual. He's been transferred out of vice for practicing exotic police techniques. He also has a major problem with authority and rebels against the establishment. So we take him and put him with a straight arrow like Friday, and that's where we have some fun. These two try to get along, and during the course of the investigation they not only become buddies but actually start to take on some of each other's characteristics."

A key inspiration to the cast and crew was Harry Morgan, who delighted in reprising his role of Bill Gannon. Morgan said, "I first heard from my agent that they were doing this movie takeoff on the show and they wanted me to play my old role of Gannon. I was pleased they had elevated me to captain. I would have felt a little foolish back on the streets after all those years. When he said, 'Dan Aykroyd, Tom Hanks, and Tom Mankiewicz, I said "yes" without reading the script.'" Morgan kept his costars amused with anecdotes about filming the old *Dragnet*. Hanks noted at the time, "He told us stories about Webb, that he was a gracious host but a taskmaster on the set who put people through hell. The shows were done in two days, and they did everything off a TelePrompTer. You always have the same actors because a lot of them couldn't handle working off cue cards. If an actor memorized his lines, he would never be used again. Webb felt that if you memorized the script, you'd take pauses, and he wanted a staccato quality. He didn't want any emotional aspect brought

right comedy. Aykroyd declared, "We've done our research and taken great pains to re-create and revitalize the form that Jack Webb created for TV. The essence of the film is consistent with what he believed in, the speeches are speeches he could have written himself, and the delivery is the way he would have done it. It's all in the spirit of affection for a piece of American pop culture that my generation grew up on that's also had a significant impact on kids of today. I hope people who recognize the old show will get a laugh from the recognition. And I think those who are too young to remember will quickly discover the humor and pathos in these characters and, hopefully, leave the theater wanting to see some of those old programs. Then maybe they'll come back and find a whole other level of things to laugh about."

into it; he literally wanted just the facts. It was dialogue right on top of dialogue."

The filmmakers tried to keep the spirit of Webb's *Dragnet* in the big-screen version, making obvious concessions to the fact that they were filming an out-

The movie was shot almost entirely on the streets of Los Angeles, plus Venice Beach, Bel Air, a barrio in the San Fernando Valley, inside Pasadena's newly renovated Brown Derby Restaurant, and in the below-freezing winds of the Mojave Desert. One of the more unusual sites was the Angel's Cultural Center in San Pedro, a World War II munitions bunker that was partially excavated and restored for the film.

If ever a television property seemed appropriate for adaption to a big-screen comedy, *Dragnet* was it. Given the talents of the cast, it would have appeared as

It's either lunchtime or they're searching for evidence! (Universal City Studios)

Hanks relished the opportunity to play second fiddle to Aykroyd, a veteran of The Second City comedy troupe. (Universal City Studios)

though this project were as much of a sure thing as one could imagine. And yet the film rarely generates any genuine laughs and is so sloppily constructed that one suspects the people in charge thought that the sight of Aykroyd's uncanny Jack Webb impersonation would sustain the audience for the entire length of the movie. The fault can be laid at the feet of Tom Mankiewicz, who coauthored the screenplay and made his directorial debut here. Mankiewicz has had a checkered past in terms of his accomplishments. While he is credited with making significant contributions to the first two *Superman* films (undoubtedly the best of the series), Mankiewicz was far less successful with his work on three 007 films. His screenplays for *Diamonds Are Forever* and *The Man With the Golden Gun* are arguably the worst in the Bond canon. For *Live and Let Die*, Mankiewicz indulged in unspeakable script padding by creating a protracted boat chase that dominates the entire middle of the film without significantly advancing the plot whatsoever.

He shows the same flaws as director of *Dragnet*: when in doubt, just stage some long, pointless car chases. The cliché of the mismatched police partners has enough moss on it to grow penicillin and is boring even with the likes of Aykroyd and Hanks in the roles. The movie can't decide whether it wants to be a blatant send-up of the detective genre or a quasi-comedy sandwiched between some extravagant action sequences. The result is an unsatisfying mishmash that is never exciting and only sporadically funny.

Whatever value there is to the movie can be attributed to Aykroyd's dead-on performance as Joe Friday. A virtual clone of Jack Webb, he re-creates that actor's mannerisms so perfectly that you have to

keep reminding yourself that you are seeing an impersonation. However, Aykroyd's respect and reverence for Webb prevent him from making the character a total boob. Instead, he comes across as an extremely competent square. In the context of a broad comedy, however, the idea of the hero-detective being *competent* is virtually mutually exclusive to the premise that he will be *funny*. Can one imagine the *Pink Panther* films with Inspector Clouseau solving the case in any manner other than by accident? How amusing would those films have been if he were simply a master detective with a strange accent and a few eccentricities?

Hanks fares even worse, however. Despite all the effort put into fleshing out the character of Pep Streebek, the role is still boring and superficial.

Police work ain't all bad! (Universal City Studios)

Director Mankiewicz fails to utilize Hanks's natural comedic skills in any meaningful way. Hanks just ambles through the proceedings, yelling occasionally and looking seedy. We *want* to laugh at some of his smarmy wisecracks, but the situations are too lame and the writing too uninspired for this to happen. The role is far below his capabilities, and it appears as though he realizes it.

The supporting cast is impressive and provides some of the few inspired moments in the film. Christopher Plummer as a corrupt television evangelist with megalomaniac goals is wonderfully funny, playing against type as an effete, prissy snob. Dabney Coleman has little more than an extended cameo as a pornographer with a speech impediment, but he, too, manages to add enough eccentricities to provide a couple of laughs. Like his costars, Harry Morgan is not given much too work with, but it still is wonderful to see him back as Bill Gannon.

Dragnet is not without a few other merits. Aykroyd's Jack Webb–inspired, seemingly endless lecture about law and order given to Plummer in a men's room is superbly played, and the film has a few good gags in the last few minutes: the best being the re-creation of the old epilogue from the TV show in which we learn the fate of the criminal. It's a brief but very funny moment. Incredibly, as critic Roger Ebert

pointed out, the filmmakers neglect to use Walter Schumann's famous *Dragnet* theme song. True, there is a variation on the theme from the sixties show complete with Aykroyd and Hanks "rapping," but the familiar strains of "*dum-de-dum-dum*" are not capitalized on except for a fleeting moment. It's another indication of the sloppiness of the production.

Dragnet met with mixed reviews but generated enough interest among the public to be labeled a hit for Universal. If the film did not provide Tom Hanks with a challenging role, it at least helped reverse his disappointing trend of late at the box office. *Dragnet* earned more than twice the amount of film rentals as *Nothing in Common* despite the fact that the earlier was far superior in every way.

As for the *Dragnet* legacy, the film surprisingly never spawned a sequel, although it would have been unlikely that Hanks would have taken the second-banana role again.

Jack Webb had died before this incarnation was planned, and one can only wonder what his reaction to it might have been. He was not above spoofing his own image and may have given the project his blessing. His real legacy, however, is that he was so identified with playing Sgt. Joe Friday that police departments nationwide considered him an honorary police officer. Upon his death, the flags at Los Angeles police stations were flown at half mast. The recent revival of *Dragnet* in reruns has ensured that the show will be enjoyed by a new generation—a tribute far more appropriate than the mediocre feature film. For those who relish a genuinely hilarious police spoof, look no further than *The Naked Gun*. Now *that's* funny!

Reviews

"[The movie] is great for an hour, good for about twenty-five minutes, and then heads doggedly for the standard 1980s High Tech Hollywood Ending, which means an expensive chase scene and a shoot-out. God, I'm tired of chases and shoot-outs. . . . Aykroyd's performance is the centerpiece of the film. He must have practiced for hours, even days, to perfect the rapid-fire delivery he uses to rattle off polysyllabic utterances of impenetrable but kaleidoscopic complexity. Listening to him talk in this movie is a joy. . . . Hanks and Aykroyd have an easy, unforced chemistry, growing out of their laconic delivery and opposite personalities, and the movie is filled with nice supporting turns, especially from Elizabeth Ashley and Dabney Coleman. This would have been a great movie if they'd bothered to think of an ending for it. And used the original Dragnet *theme. The end of the film cries out—cries out, mind you—for the simple, stark, authority of dum-de-dum-dum. I wanted to hear it so badly I walked out of the screening singing the notes out loud to drown out the disco Drano from the screen."*

—*Roger Ebert's Movie Home Companion*

Dabney Coleman stealing scenes (as usual) as soft-porn king Jerry Caesar (Universal City Studios)

"Overlong parody with some obnoxious amusements before the whole thing becomes tiresome."

—*Halliwell's Film Guide*

"The surprise about Dragnet *is not that it's less than an alloyed delight, but that it manages to be funny at all. The new, updated parody has some real laughs, though they don't come in clusters. They're as isolated and lonely as stoplights in the suburbs. Considering the age of the material, as well as its relentless recycling, it's some sort of wonder there's anything left to which to pay a comedic homage. . . . This new* Dragnet *is actually sloppier in its initial conception than in its execution."*

—Vincent Canby, *New York Times*

Big

20th Century-Fox, 1988

"I think the most convincing performance I've given was in Big
—I look at that now and say, 'How'd I do that?'"

Cast

Tom Hanks (*Josh Baskin*); Elizabeth Perkins (*Susan Lawrence*); John Heard (*Paul Davenport*); Jared Rushton (*Billy Kopeche*); Robert Loggia (*"Mac" MacMillan*); David Moscow (*Young Josh*); Jon Lovitz (*Scotty Brennen*); Mercedes Ruehl (*Mrs. Baskin*); Josh Clark (*Mr. Baskin*); Kimberlee M. Davis (*Cynthia Benson*); Oliver Block (*Freddie Benson*).

Credits

Director: Penny Marshall; producers: James L. Brooks and Robert Greenhut; coproducers and screenplay: Gary Ross and Anne Spielberg; director of photography: Barry Sonnenfeld; production designer: Santo Loquasto; art directors: Tom Warren and Speed Hopkins; editor: Barry Malkin; music: Howard Shore. Running time: 104 minutes.

While working with director Penny Marshall may have been exasperating to Hanks at times, the result of their collaboration is magnificent. (20th Century-Fox)

Tom Hanks's "second fiddle" role to Dan Aykroyd in *Dragnet* did not capitalize on the acting strengths so apparent in *Nothing in Common*. While *Dragnet* was a financial success, it was a decidedly backward step in terms of breaking the momentum Hanks was gaining as an innovative presence in contemporary cinema. His next film, however, would be the highlight of his career to date, with one of the most inspired comedic performances of recent years.

Big was originally regarded as anything but the high-concept comedy it proved to be. Screenwriters Gary Ross and Anne Spielberg (the sister of *the* Steven Spielberg) collaborated for the first time on this engaging tale in which twelve-year-old Josh Baskin—frustrated over the "burdens" of being a kid—attends a local carnival and encounters a fortune-telling machine inhabited by a frightening mechanical genie. He makes a wish to be "big," and upon awakening the following morning, finds that he is now a thirty-something grown man. The imaginative script finds Josh unable to convince his mother of what has happened. She believes the man is her son's kidnapper. With the help of his one confidant—pal Billy Koepeche—Josh hides out in a sleazy Manhattan hotel. Through a quirk of fate, the boy/man lands a job with a major toy company, where his enthusiasm

for the product line enables him to become an inadvertent marketing genius. Along the way he also falls in love, and his girlfriend must try to comprehend why Josh seems so naive and inexperienced when it comes to romance. The story's bittersweet but sentimental conclusion reminds one of the old adage "Be careful what you wish for. You just may get it."

Ross and Spielberg devised the idea for the plot in one hour. However, the final script would take almost three years to complete, with the writers doing the project "on spec"—i.e., without being commissioned by a film studio. Their patience was to be rewarded quickly, however. The script was barely out of the word processor when director James L. Brooks (*Terms of Endearment*, *Broadcast News*) agreed to produce the film.

The saga of *Big*'s journey to the screen became even more intriguing. No sooner had the agreement with Brooks and 20th Century-Fox been reached than it was learned that any number of similarly themed films were in the works at other studios. Brooks later said, "There were not other projects like this out there when we started, but we moved at a very deliberate pace, and then, about six months after we started, we became aware that there were other projects. At that point, the decision was whether to hurry and make a race out of it or to do it in our own time. We decided to do that, and now, despite the obvious problems of the delay, it does feel a little bit like destiny that the picture got made this way."

As it turned out, the other "age reversal" films—*18 Again!*, *Vice-Versa*, and *Like Father, Like Son*—were unsuccessful, thus making the *Big* project about as promising to industry talent as *Ishtar II*. Steven Spielberg had enough chutzpah to reject the offer of directing the film despite it being based on his own sister's screenplay. Harrison Ford considered playing the role of Josh, but he and James L. Brooks could not agree on a suitable director. Warren Beatty wanted an unacceptably high salary ($7.5 million) to star in *Big*, and Robert De Niro's interest was also dampened by failure to agree on financial compensation.

Faced with these dilemmas, Brooks concentrated on finding a director, with the hope that a lead actor could be found later. Although her feature-film directorial career consisted solely of the mediocre 1986 Whoopi Goldberg comedy *Jumping Jack Flash*, Penny Marshall was signed for *Big*. Known primarily as a comedic actress, Marshall, from TV's *Laverne and Shirley*, seemed like a long shot to helm a film as complex and challenging as *Big*. Both Marshall and Brooks agreed that Tom Hanks would be the ideal choice to portray Josh. When the deal with De Niro fell through, it was decided to halt preproduction on the project until Hanks could be persuaded to accept the role.

While Hanks was certainly eager to play characters which were well defined and outside the range of the cynical wise guy with which he was so identified, he had concerns about the *Big* project. Penny Marshall said, "I think that he was worried that it might be a Jerry Lewis–type film instead of more serious. So it was a matter of meeting to discuss the tone of the film. I usually approach comedies as dramas and dramas as comedies, so our visions of the film were the same." Hanks felt comfortable with the notion of working with Marshall, commenting, "Penny and I are good friends, so when we started talking about the movie, it wasn't like dealing with a stranger. I knew from the start what she was saying wasn't ego or fluff or diatribe." (Hanks earlier had worked with her director-brother Garry on *Nothing in Common*.)

Hanks discovered that the script was unlike anything which had been offered to him before: "What I dug about it was there was no car chases, no bad guys, no guns. A massive amount of the movie is just two people sitting around talking." Hanks also saw the premise of the film as an insight into human nature. He told the *Chicago Tribune*, "As adults, we can all probably pinpoint that single moment or month or year when we became adults, the last time of our youth. When it's gone, it's gone, and you wish you could go back sometimes to when you were a kid and you could sleep in the back of the car while Dad did the driving. None of us would ever really want to, unless maybe just for a day. But that, to me, is what the film is about, and it's a tough line to walk, to do a comedy with a capital C, one that you hope they laugh at but find endearing and are enriched by as well."

The greatest challenge was to be able to convincingly portray a twelve-year-old and keep the character and mannerisms consistent with his adult alter ego. "For me, it required a lot of paring back of the stuff I'd done before and done with some success. This is a guy who isn't very verbal or aggressive. I've played guys who were verbal, aggressive, sarcastic, and caustic. In this case, I had to play someone who is literally innocent." He later added, "You have to forget a lot of worldly knowledge you have about the way things work, the societal disciplines of living as an adult, and still show up on time for work. At the same time, the parameters that were described by the script, the individual scenes and the fact that he's almost thirteen years old, dictated a very specific path for me to take. We made Josh a not very verbal guy—he doesn't talk a lot.

There's a lot of nodding and shrugging of shoulders in order for him to communicate."

To successfully identify with his character, Tom Hanks spent a good deal of time with David Moscow, the boy who was cast as young Josh. Hanks reviewed videotapes of Moscow's actions and mannerisms and incorporated those into his own portrayal. He also called upon memories of his own childhood—both positive and negative: "If there's any age that I had gone back and analyzed, even before preparing for the movie, it was those junior high years, when you can't figure anything out. You're cranky all the time [because] the chemicals in your body are out of whack. . . . When I was thirteen, I was younger than my years. I could still *play* really well. I can remember things I loved to do, the way you could have, you know, toy soldiers or a plane and you could sit on the couch for hours and have incredible adventures." Among the negative memories: "I was a geek and a real spaz. Junior high was hell. I was the type of kid who, while the class was watching slides like 'Bushmen of the Kalahari Desert,' would be the one who screamed out, 'Hey, it's Craig Gammelgard!' That was *my* sense of humor."

Hanks also found inspiration in watching his

Josh frantically tries to make sense of what happened to him, but the carnival has left town. (20th Century-Fox)

own children's behavior: "What I gleaned from watching my own kids was a sense of play that exists in children until they start coping with stress. It's an eye-opening experience when you pay particular attention to them, because more often than not, you're telling them to shut up. Then with Jared [Rushton, the actor who played Billy] and David [Moscow] I found myself part of a Three Musketeers group in which I was the adult with these two kids. And it was nice to be in junior high for a while. It was

Scrambling to get to school, Josh discovers his pants are a tad too tight. (20th Century-Fox)

a release from the responsibility of being an adult human being."

The Hanks-Marshall collaboration went swimmingly, although at first his director's insistence on seemingly endless rehearsals almost caused friction. He would later remember, "One thing she did that drove me crazy was to test over and over and over again with all sorts of actors. There were scenes that I must have done two hundred times on videotape and then two hundred more in the rehearsal process. Penny just wanted to see all *sorts* of things. I would say, 'I can't do this scene one more time. I don't care

who it is. I cannot read these same goddamn words one more time or by the time we get finished I'm going to hate it so much that I'm not going to do it well at all.' Well, what happened instead was, I knew all of the material so well that by the time we shot it, it turned out to be the best rehearsed of all the movies that I've done. There are only certain people I would accept that from. Penny is one. To most others I would say, 'Look, you either tell me exactly what is wrong or what is right about this or I'm going to strangle you.' "

Filming began on *Big* in August 1987 in Cliffside Park, New Jersey, an upper-middle-class neighborhood in the shadow of the George Washington Bridge. Here the exterior sequences of Josh's house were shot. The carnival seen in the opening of the movie was an actual traveling show which was hired for three days by the filmmakers for location shooting on the shores of the Hudson River. There was also extensive location filming in Times Square, Greenwich Village, Central Park, and Rye Playland, all in New York. Most of the interiors—including those inside Josh's house—were filmed at Camera Mart Studios in Manhattan. The sequences in the MacMillan Toy Company, where Josh is employed, were actually filmed at an advertising agency. Hanks said at the time, "Making the movie wasn't very easy because almost every location was an actual building, so there was none of the comfort and ease that go with making a movie in a studio. We were always going into a building—always dragging a cable in—and having to deal with the problems that you don't normally encounter."

A full two days were spent in Manhattan's famed FAO Schwarz, perhaps the most famous toy store in the world. Here Hanks and costar Robert Loggia shot their now-famous dance on the giant piano keyboard. Loggia would comment later, "This was perhaps the single most enjoyable scene I've done in a film in a very long time. That scene in FAO

Schwarz on the piano has the chance to become a screen classic." However, the sequence proved to be anything but enjoyable to Tom Hanks, who said, "It was exhausting. We rehearsed until we dropped. Robert [Loggia] plays three sets of tennis every day, so he was in shape for it. It was like jumping rope for three-and-one-half hours every time we did the scene. It was *really* hard work."

Despite the more grueling aspects of the filming, Hanks enjoyed working with Elizabeth Perkins, who plays Susan, the power-obsessed executive who rediscovers the joy of life through her relationship with Josh. Perkins recalled some of the more delightful sequences to shoot: "There were so many childlike facets to it. I remember when we were shooting a scene on a roller coaster and they said to us, 'Oh, we're going around a couple of times.' And Tom and I said, 'Well, we don't mind six or seven times on the roller coaster—that's fine with us.' . . . We had a very good time!"

If *Big* proved to be an enjoyable experience for those involved with the production, it is all the more so a delight for the audience. Although filmed with little fanfare, the movie proved to be one of the most original comedies in decades. Released in the sequel-saturated summer of 1988, *Big* wiped such competition as *Rambo III*, *Crocodile Dundee II*, and *Poltergeist III* off the box-office charts, not to mention the other "big" movies of that year: *Big Business*, *Big Bad Mama II*, *The Big Blue*, and *Big Top Pee-wee*. Within its first week of release, the movie was being called the sleeper hit of the year. It established Penny Marshall as a director of great skill and—more important by Hollywood standards—bankability. *Big* would make her the first woman to direct a film which grossed over $100 million.

Critics and audiences agreed it was *the* breakaway film for Tom Hanks in terms of proving once and for all the extent of his talents. Hanks's performance as Josh is a remarkable achievement, comparable only to Steve Martin's earlier performance in the gender-splitting "out-of-body" comedy *All of Me*. Hanks is absolutely convincing as the man-child Josh, and the performance never resorts to the over-the-top gimmickry other actors might have employed. Hanks does more with a nuance and a grin than most actors can accomplish with two pages of dialogue. His total naïveté in coping with the adult world is both hilarious and touching, and he benefits from a wonderful supporting cast. Elizabeth Perkins and Hanks display a terrific on-screen chemistry, and her fascination with her bizarre new lover is remindful of Hanks enduring the weird social habits of "mermaid" Daryl Hannah in *Splash*. Equally good is Robert Loggia, whose brief but refreshing appearances are capped by the aforementioned sequence in which Hanks inadvertently reminds him of all that is fun in life by inviting him to join him in the piano dance. As Loggia had hoped, the sequence is considered a classic, and the keyboard now proudly resides on the wall of Planet Hollywood in London. It should also be mentioned that young thespians David Moscow and Jared Rushton are every

As all expected, the piano dance remains one of the most delightful scenes in film history. (Brian Hamill, 20th Century-Fox)

bit as good as their adult counterparts, and add immeasurably to the success of the film.

By the end of 1988, *Big* was still being highly touted as one of the best films of the year. Tom Hanks would go on to win the Los Angeles Film Critics Award for Best Actor (for both *Big* and the subsequent *Punchline*) and the Golden Globe Award for Best Actor in a Comedy. The ultimate triumph was an Oscar nomination for Best Actor at the 1989 Academy Awards. (Dustin Hoffman ultimately won the award for *Rain Man*.)

Hanks seemed overwhelmed by the success *Big* had brought him, and told the *Detroit Free Press*: "In all honesty, let's reserve this type of exposure for rocket scientists and guys who are running for office. It's not anything I ever thought would happen. Then, when it does and they ask you to be a *Newsweek* cover, you think, 'Fine.' And then you say, 'Wait a minute. . . . If Hurricane Gilbert slams into Galveston, who's more important?" In an interview with *Rolling Stone*, he expressed concern with his workaholic ways: "*Big* is my tenth movie. That's almost too many. I made *Splash* in '83. In five years that's a lotta work. For a while there I made movies in an absolute flurry of activity. But the opportunity was there. And I had a great desire to be working. You do get those feelings

that you're never, ever, going to work again. . . . There are other things that are just more important than being a hotshot celebrity movie actor. I simply want to pay attention to those other things for a while, things like life and love and going to the bank and organizing your garage. When I'm on film sets, so much of my life is completely put on hold. Eventually you realize, 'When this work is done, I have to go home to a place I've had so little personal investment in that it might as well be just another hotel room.' Which is just no way to live."

There was an afterlife for *Big*: It was turned into a Broadway musical that opened in the spring of 1996.

Josh makes a positive impression on his employer "Mac" Macmillan (Robert Loggia), much to the chagrin of Susan (Elizabeth Perkins) and Paul (John Heard). (Brian Hamill, 20th Century-Fox)

never been better. Unable to employ his usual wise-guy irony, he reveals new depths to his comic technique, creating an adolescent body language that's as funny as it is accurate—he's infantilism incarnate. Even with its last act lapse, Big *remains one of the year's most charming entertainments."*

—David Denby, *New York* magazine

"Wide-eyed, excited, and wonderfully guileless, Mr. Hanks is an absolute delight, and the film is shrewd in relieving him of the responsibility to behave furtively and hide his altered condition. . . . Features believable young teen-age mannerisms from the two real boys in its cast, and this only makes Mr. Hanks's funny, flawless impression that much more adorable. For any other fullgrown actors who try their hands at fidgeting, squirming, throwing water balloons, and wolfing down food in a huge variety of comically disgusting ways, this is really the performance to beat."

—Janet Maslin, *New York Times*

Reviews

"The casting is just about perfect. For an adult to play a child is probably more difficult than for an actor with 20/20 vision to play a blind man. It requires a whole new way of looking, talking and thinking. But Hanks, who emerges from this film as one of Hollywood's top comic actors, is both believable and touching as a boy lost in a grownup world."

—Gerald Clark, *Time*

"Don't hold Big's *premise against it—[it] is hilarious because this is indeed how a boy would react to being trapped in an adult body in a grown-up world. The laughs start rolling the minute Hanks swings his large, hairy legs over the edge of his bunk bed and crashes like a giant to the floor. Hanks has*

Susan suddenly realizes she is socializing with a man wearing the weirdest tuxedo in history. (20th Century-Fox)

···12

Punchline

Columbia, 1988

"I always regarded being a stand-up as one of the hardest jobs in show business. Now, I think it's one of the hardest jobs in America. It's a dangerous combination of power and weakness to stand up there and control people."

Cast
Sally Field (*Lilah Krytsick*); Tom Hanks (*Steven Gold*); John Goodman (*John Krytsick*); Mary Rydell (*Romeo*); Kim Greist (*Madeline Urie*); Paul Mazursky (*Arnold*).

Credits
Director: David Seltzer; producers: David Melnick and Michael Rachmil; screenplay: David Seltzer; director of photography: Reynaldo Villalobos; production designer: Jack DeGovia; editor: Bruce Green; music: Charles Gross. Running time: 128 minutes.

At the time, Hanks referred to Steven Gold as "the closest I've come to playing an unredeemable character." (Columbia Pictures)

Filmed prior to *Big* but released on the heels of that breakaway hit *Punchline* was one of Tom Hanks's most challenging projects. Playing his most complex character to date, Hanks was able to draw upon all of his experiences as an actor to create a personality that was never less than fascinating. It also marked the first time in which he played a leading role that was not entirely sympathetic. Just as *Nothing in Common* earned praise for not watering down or sentimentalizing the Jackie Gleason character, *Punchline* presented audiences with an image of Hanks heretofore unseen: a self-indulgent perfectionist whose superiority complex alienates most of the people he should be the closest to. He would later say of the role, "I think the closest I've come to playing an unredeemable character was the stand-up comic in *Punchline*. He had a psychosis to him that was not particularly personable, but you were still pulling for him. That was the most complex I've been in films, and I don't know who that guy is."

In fact, Hanks is not the focal point of the story. The central character is Lilah Krytsick (Sally Field), an aspiring stand-up comic who is frustrated by having to juggle her responsibilities as a wife and mother with the extraordinary and draining demands of honing her comedic skills in front of largely unappreciative audiences. While performing at a nightclub which

89

Comedienne wannabe/housewife Lilah Krytsick (Sally Field) is awestruck at her initial meeting with Steven. (Columbia Pictures)

specializes in giving amateur comedians a forum, Lilah is awestruck by the brilliant routine played out by Steven Gold (Tom Hanks), generally regarded as the club's most promising talent.

Lilah's attempts to win advice and encouragement from Steven fall on deaf ears, and she quickly realizes he is an egotist who is willing to sell his soul for the one big shot at fame which all aspiring comics dream of. As time goes on, however, Lilah realizes that Steven is a man who is haunted by demons from his past, including memories of a strict upbringing in a cold, unloving family environment. Steven is determined to show his estranged relatives that he can be successful as a comedian despite his failed attempts to succeed at medical school.

Ultimately, Lilah's frustrations with a husband (John Goodman) opposed to her moonlighting and the problems caused by Steven's inner demons form the basis of a relationship between the two comic wannabes. Steven's advice and tips about comedic timing help Lilah become one of the most prominent stand-ups on the amateur scene. When Steven admits

he has fallen in love with Lilah, she is forced to choose between her husband and children and the soul mate she has found in Steven. The complex situation reaches a climax during a nationally televised contest in which the two must compete for a shot on a major entertainment program. It is a night of glorious highs and miserable lows for all involved, and Lilah is forced to make the most important decisions of her life.

Punchline was in development as far back as 1979, when writer David Seltzer approached producer David Melnick with the property. The script, which Seltzer originally had written as a possible television movie, was eventually shuffled to various studios, and at one time Howard Zeiff was considering directing it as a feature film for Columbia. That deal fell through, however, and the script gathered dust for years until Melnick once again tried to market it. He recalled why there was trouble securing studio financing: "The major trouble with *Punchline* was that it wasn't conventional material. It was either a comedy with a seriously dramatic story or a drama with an outrageously funny background."

Melnick's original intention was to make the film with a modest budget of $8 million and no major stars. However, when he brought the script to Sally Field's attention, she was immediately enthused and felt the property would be an excellent follow-up to her well-received film *Murphy's Romance*. Said Field at the time, "I saw the potential for interesting personalities interacting with each other in a fascinating drama."

Now the idea of making *Punchline* a low-budget film was no longer practical. Columbia had allocated a production budget of $15 million—almost twice the original estimate. This allowed David Seltzer, who was now signed as director of his "pet project," to consider a bankable leading man for the role of Steven Gold. There was no hesitation about his first choice. "I really wanted Tom Hanks from the outset, and when we heard he was interested, we didn't even consider anyone else. Tom has the quick-wittedness and unpredictability that is believable in all facets of this role, and like Sally, he has a vulnerability that makes for a truly interesting human being."

Hanks did not have to be strong-armed into signing for the role. He explained, "I read it and I got it. I sought out the powers that be, the writer David Seltzer. I sat down with him and essentially said, 'What do I have to do to get this part? You tell me.' I was even bodacious, kind of bold, because I said to him, 'You must know what you've written, for this guy's comedy routine is not funny. You realize, then, that whoever plays this role is going to have to construct a stand-up comedy act.' He agreed. He told me, 'Whoever does this is going to have to go out and figure this all out.' That's why I say *Punchline* was a very important experience for me as an actor, because I realized that the scope of an actor's true influence doesn't go beyond his part. That sounds like a very simple thing to say, but it's very true. I knew that I would have to go off and begin

Hanks won the L.A. Film Critics Best Actor Award, but Oscar would once again elude him. (Columbia Pictures)

this stand-up process and that I would not be any good at all. But by not being good at it, I would be gaining insights about how to do the part. . . . Eventually, after the entire course of shooting, I had a forty-minute act. We had a bona fide stand-up comedy presentation that was funny unto itself. So in doing that, it was more preparatory activity than just research. This was a life experience."

The filming of *Punchline* began in March 1987, on location in New York City. Within twenty-four hours, the crew was facing a major logistical problem: The balmy and unseasonably warm weather had suddenly changed, and temperatures dropped dramatically. The wind chill made for a temperature difference of over one hundred degrees. The weather would remain cold and miserable for the entire two-week location shoot. David Melnick admitted: "Filming on location in New York isn't the most economical way to make a movie, but it provides authenticity, and that makes a big difference in the film." Interiors were filmed over an eight-week period at the Burbank Studios near L.A. Here the set for the Gas Station—the fictitious "Improv"-like nightclub in which much of the action takes place—was constructed on a soundstage with props brought in from old time service stations to add to the ambience. (The exteriors of the Gas Station were actually shot at a Harlem jazz club.)

To research their roles, Hanks and Field sought advice from professional stand-up comics. Hanks received "training" from comedians Barry Sobel and Randy Fechter (an old college friend of his). The two helped Hanks create a full-blown stand-up act of his own which he was to perform in front of live audiences. Fechter found humor in everday situations, and this formed the basis of Hanks' "act." ("Doctors look

at our wives' breasts; why can't we look at *theirs?*") Fechter was impressed by his student's abilities: "Tom is such a natural talent, that it wasn't like training a noncomic to be funny; it was like working with a talented stand-up comedian to sharpen his act." Barry Sobel echoed the praise: "It's so easy and fun to work with Tom. By the end, he was as good as any stand-up comic I know." Ultimately, professional comedy writers Scott Rubin and Douglas Kor also contributed jokes to Hanks's stand-up act.

For her part, Sally Field was also deadly serious about learning the fine art of comedy. Studying with real-life stand-up comic and housewife Dottie Archibald and Susie Essman, another aspiring comedienne, Field admitted the task of being funny was not always fun: "In my last film, I had to learn to ride a horse, but this is harder. . . . I don't know how they do it, the comics . . . It is so high, it is dangerous."

After Hanks received his "training," it was time for his coaches to send him in front of live audiences to hone his act. He made surprise appearances at both Igby's and the Comedy Store in L.A., before

Lilah attempts to gain knowledge from Steven but soon finds him to be a troubled soul. (Columbia Pictures)

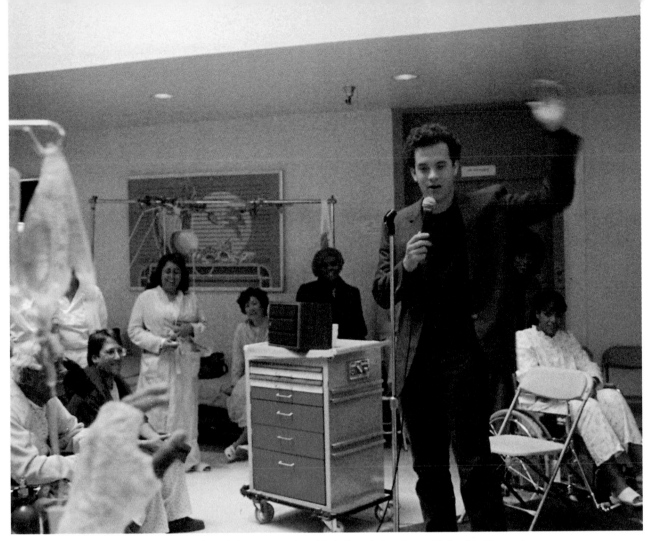

The usually arrogant Steve shows a tender side by entertaining elderly hospital patients. (Columbia Pictures)

audiences which included such comedic regulars as Gallagher, Howie Mandel, and Jimmie Walker. In New York he interned at the Comic Strip, where he did two nights of twenty-five-minute sets. Hanks said at the time, "I wanted my character to be authentic, so I decided to try out my material in real comedy clubs. At first I bombed terribly. In fact, one of the most important lessons I learned was how much it hurt to be really bad." He later expanded his feelings on his stand-up act, telling the *New York Post* "Sometimes it went well, other times it was, 'Well, that was very nice, Mr. Hanks. Now when are you gonna be funny for us?' On occasions, I died like a dog, but that's part of the process. On the surface, being a comic seems like a pleasant lifestyle, but it is actually very hard and sometimes tragic. Coal mining, police work, and stand-up comedy are, I believe, the three hardest jobs to have. All I have to do now is find a coal-mining picture."

Like real professional stand-up comics, Hanks found that by perseverance and hard work he could eventually win the audience over. Having the audi-

ence in the palm of his hand on the good nights gave Hanks a feeling of power and satisfaction: "It is incredibly exciting when you have a good twenty-minute set. If you do well, nobody else did well; all the glory is yours, and you don't have to share it with anybody else. The adrenaline is pumping, and you do honestly feel on top of the world." Still, Hanks found the downside of the comic's lifestyle depressing. "It's a very, very solitary kind of existence," he said. "Lonely and also late. I would do a set at eleven-thirty or midnight, and I would be up until four in the morning waiting for the buzz to wear off. I can't do that." He also found fear onstage, saying, "When you get up there for what is supposed to be seven minutes and run out of material in two and a half and you continue thinking you can make stuff up but you can't get any laughs, it's terrible."

The supporting cast of *Punchline* relied heavily on people who would feel at home in the world of amateur comedians. David Seltzer decided, appropriately enough, to cast actual aspiring comics in many roles. He auditioned over 150 individuals and found

Although Hanks jokingly referring to Field as "his boss," theirs was an enjoyable working relationship. (Columbia Pictures)

duced by her company.) Field returned the compliments: "It would be one thing if he was just this great, goofy guy. But that lasts for about thirty seconds, and then you want to meet somebody real. The reason he's a movie star and is going to stay one is that he's much more complicated than that. Yes, he's very entertaining and funny and easy to be around. But you know there's somebody else underneath, somebody dark. There's a sad side, a dark side. And that's what makes him so compelling on the screen."

Hanks found it creatively stimulating working with Seltzer, who had directed only one previous film—the 1986 sleeper *Lucas*. "For me, he's the best kind of director,

he had more talent than he had parts to cast them in. Rather than turn away the talent, Seltzer shoehorned them into minor parts. He said, "I'm casting some in roles that have nothing to do with comedy, i.e., a minister, a patient in the hospital, a hairdresser, a heckler, and a coffee-shop waiter." Among those cast in the film: Damon Wayans and Max Alexander. The key role of Romeo, the owner of the Gas Station nightclub, was played in manic style by film director Mark Rydell (*On Golden Pond, The Cowboys*). Veteran writer-director Paul Mazursky also shows up in a supporting role.

Hanks said of his costar, "She was great, supportive, and always there." (He jokingly referred to Field as his "boss" because the film was being pro-

Discouraging Lilah (Sally Field) from entering show biz (Columbia Pictures)

because he allows you the freedom to work with the script and the characterization until it feels completely natural." Seltzer had similar feelings about Hanks, and said, "Tom has acting muscles like no one else has. He's sexy and he's funny and he's strong, but it's his vulnerability that makes Steven work. He would have come off as nothing but an unlikable lout if you couldn't see a man who's scared and in pain beneath it all. It's that mix of messages that Tom can send out that makes him a charismatic actor."

Punchline is an ambitious film which succeeds in blending both humor and pathos into an engrossing story line. This is clearly an actor's movie, and both Hanks and Field perform naked—at least in the figurative sense. This is a small-scale, character-driven film which does not allow the actors to hide behind elaborate sets or state-of-the-art special effects. At its best, it conveys the masochistic world of the stand-up comic in a way that no other film has done. When Hanks and Field's on-screen acts bomb, we lost sight of the fact that these are actors portraying fictitious characters. Instead, we feel their humiliation, desperation, and pain. Conversely, when they win over the audience, the feeling of triumph is felt by the viewer.

Hanks is perfect as Steven Gold; indeed, it would be difficult to imagine anyone else in the role. While the character may be the epitome of the self-centered egotist, Hanks's charm and wit make it impossible not to care about him and empathize with his moments of shame and glory. One of the flaws in the script is that the character of Steven is never fully developed. The climactic moment in which he breaks down onstage when he sees his dominating father in the audience rings somewhat hollow despite Hanks's bravura acting. We have not been given enough background on Steven to make us relate to the pain he is feeling at this encounter. However, Hanks handles the stand-up acts with such flair and professionalism, one finds it difficult to imagine he was not weaned on this type of comedy. His performance in *Punchline* (and in *Big*) would ultimately win him the Los Angeles Film Critics Award for Best Performance by an Actor.

Sally Field is as engaging as ever but seems a bit out of place in the atmosphere of the nightclub setting. She is wonderfully convincing in the sequences in which she tries to cope with the marital problems her "career" has placed between herself and her husband (John Goodman), but somehow onstage Field just doesn't have the edge that Hanks brings to his role. Much of this may be due to the material in the script. Hanks's nightclub act suits his well-established personality. It seems natural to see him tossing off irreverent or tasteless one-liners to gain a laugh. Field, however, just seems far too wholesome to make it in the cutthroat world of stand-up comedy. On top of which, her on-screen gags are never sharp enough to merit the kind of acclaim she receives from audiences. It's not so much the fault of the actress as it is the script. Still, she exudes a good chemistry with Hanks, and their freshingly chaste love affair rings with conviction.

The film also benefits from some nice supporting turns. John Goodman is a standout in a role that could have been a cliché: the unsympathetic husband who berates his wife for having a career. The script, though, allows a fresh twist on the relationship by showing Goodman to be, well, a good man. He is seen coping with the trauma of working hard in his career, only to have the kids thrown at him in the evening while his wife plays nightclub gigs all night. The scenes between Goodman and Field are wonderfully written and enacted, and when Goodman finally gives Field his support, it's a truly satisfying moment on an emotional level.

Mark Rydell is surprisingly good as Romeo, the Danny Rose–like manager of the Gas Station who has seen numerous acts go on to fame and fortune, only to forget that he gave them their start. The other supporting players are well cast but not seen enough to make any real impact. The script could have used a few more minutes exploring the ambiguous relationships between these comics, who ostensibly wish each other well but go into fits of jealousy when someone else gets more attention than they do.

Punchline was originally intended to be a Christmas 1987 release. However, production delays forced the film to open in the summer of 1988, after *Big* had already established itself as a box-office smash. Yet the film did not benefit significantly from Hanks's success in *Big*, and *Punchline*'s grosses were disappointing. Critics called the film pretentious and too sentimental to be a truly satisfying experience. Hanks received the lion's share of praise—mostly at the expense of Sally Field, who was unjustly criticized for being miscast. While it is true that a more earthy actress could have brought greater realism to the role, Field did not deserve most of the brickbats she received.

Despite lukewarm reception at the box office, Tom Hanks remains proud of his work in the film. He told *Playboy* in 1989, "The movie didn't do that well, which was really disappointing. If I were going to figure out why, I would end up taking a bunch of cheap shots at an awful lot of people who tried real hard, and that's not fair. What can you say? But it's the best work I've ever done. We were talking some real naked truths about the characters and, in a lot of ways, about myself. I was too close. . . . The guy in *Punchline* probably has the worst aspects of my worst aspects. He is extremely competitive, for one thing. Competitive to a fault. He is unable to balance his daily existence so that real life and what he does for a living have an equal weight. I've certainly had those problems; I think any actor has. The only time you really feel alive is when you're working."

The relative failure of *Punchline* on a commercial level was more than offset by the continuing praise Hanks was receiving for his performance in the film as well as his work in *Big*. On the basis of the two roles, Hanks was very much in the spotlight in the summer of 1988.

Steven makes a futile attempt to charm Lilah into becoming his lover. (Columbia Pictures)

Reviews

"Hanks is hilarious and horrifying as a stand-up comic with an ego on overdrive. A brilliant performance in a half-baked movie."

—Ty Burr, *Entertainment Weekly*

"Hanks lets rip with a performance of dazzling complexity, vertiginous mood swings and dangerous edges. . . . The beauty of Hanks's performance is its transparency. You feel for Steven because Hanks understands him so completely and allows us to peer inside this brilliant s.o.b's stunted soul. You never catch him wallowing in the part. Steven may grandstand, but Hanks doesn't. His acting has wit, velocity, relaxation and the extraordinarily physical dexterity he demonstrated in Big. This guy may give you the creeps, but he holds you spellbound."

—David Ansen, *Newsweek*

"A tepid romantic comedy . . . As he demonstrated in his breakthrough film Big, Mr. Hanks is a fine comic actor. He is full of nervous energy and has the talent to channel is properly. When Mr. Seltzer gives him good material, he's very funny and affecting here. Miss Field also has a sense of humor, though it has nothing to do with stand-up comedy. A big Punchline problem is that it's impossible to tell the difference

"Steven is God of his universe as long as he's got a microphone in his hand." (Columbia Pictures)

between Miss Field's routines that are supposed to be awful and the awful ones that are supposed to be funny."

—Vincent Canby, *New York Times*

"Tom Hanks exhibits flashes of brilliance as a caustically tongued stand-up comic in a strange, undefinable romance with protégé comedienne Sally Field. Hanks is the real reason to see [this] film and those who enjoyed watching him in Big *will find a different, more realized comedian in* Punchline.*"*

—"Brit.," *Variety*

The 'burbs

Universal Pictures, 1989

"An ensemble piece . . . weird neighbors move into a dead-end street in the suburbs. It sounds like one kind of movie, but because Joe Dante directed it and Bruce Dern and Carrie Fisher are in it, it ends up taking a whole different spin."

Cast:
Tom Hanks (*Ray Peterson*); Bruce Dern (*Mark Runsfield*); Carrie Fisher (*Carol Peterson*); Rick Ducommun (*Art Weingartner*); Corey Feldman (*Ricky Butler*); Wendy Schaal (*Bonnie Rumsfield*); Henry Gibson (*Dr. Warner Klopek*); Brother Theodore (*Uncle Reuben Klopek*); Courtney Gains (*Hans Klopek*); Gale Gordon (*Walter*); Dick Miller and Robert Picardo (*Garbagemen*).

Credits:
Director: Joe Dante; producers: Michael Finnell and Larry Brezner; screenplay: Dana Olsen; director of photography: Robert Stevens; production designer: James Spencer; editor: Marshall Harvey; music: Jerry Goldsmith. Running time: 103 minutes.

Carol (Carrie Fisher) and Ray (Hanks) enjoy another beautiful morning in suburbia until those weird neighbors move in. (Imagine Entertainment/Universal City Studios)

With critical accolades from *Punchline* still fresh, Tom Hanks returned to more familiar turf—the theater of the absurd—with his next cinematic vehicle, *The 'burbs*, for Ron Howard and Brian Grazer's production company, Imagine Films. It proved to be offbeat even by Hanks's standards and certainly ranks high among the more unusual comedies made in the eighties.

Hanks plays Ray Peterson, a hopelessly dull executive who resides with his wife, Carol (Carrie Fisher), in a stereotypical "white bread" suburban neighborhood. Disenchanted with the mediocrity of his own life, Ray begins to take notice of the frustrating habits of his neighbors during a weeklong vacation he has decided to spend at home. There is Rumsfield (Bruce Dern), a would-be Rambo with a penchant for fatigues, camouflage, and hi-tech weaponry; Art (Rick Ducommun), a nosy buffoon who is obsessed with spying on his neighbors; Ricky (Corey Feldman), a teenage burn-out who holds seemingly endless wild parties in which the attendees' main recreation is observing the often absurd habits of the neighborhood residents; and Walter (Gale Gordon), an elderly widower over whom Ray keeps a watchful eye.

When the Klopeks, a strange new family, move into the midst of this group, they become the objects

ble but unorthodox man of medicine; and Hans Klopek (Courtney Gains), a bizarre and mostly silent young man who makes the hillbillies in *Deliverance* look like Mel Gibson.

Ultimately, Ray and his friends sneak into the Klopek house while the family is away on a rare outing. During the search for evidence of a murder, the Klopeks return home and catch the group in the act. The "victim," Walter, also shows up safe and sound, having merely been out of town without Ray's knowledge. Ray accidentally ignites a gas line and destroys the Klopek house and almost the entire neighborhood. As he is arrested, Ray gives a heartfelt speech about how people should not be suspicious of others simply because they do not conform to what society deems "normal." He berates himself and his friends for destroying the home and reputations of a family that was totally innocent. However, the story has a twist which leads to a manic and somewhat surprising conclusion.

The 'burbs screenwriter, Dana Olsen, based the script on experiences in his own past: "I had an ultranormal middle-class upbringing, but our town had its share of psychos. There was a legendary hatchet murder in the thirties, and every once in awhile, you'd pick up the local paper and read something like LIBRARIAN KILLS FAMILY, SELF. As a kid, it was fascinating to think that Mr. Flanagan down the street could turn out to be Jack the Ripper. And where there's fear, there's comedy. So I approached *The 'burbs* as "Ozzie and Harriet Meet Charles Manson."

Olsen's script attracted producer Larry Brezner, who brought the script to Imagine Films and found an enthusiastic reception from Brian Grazer. "I liked the concept of a regular guy taking a vacation in his own neighborhood, plus it was funny and well writ-

of everyone's suspicion. Noisy explosions can be heard coming from their basement, and the group rarely wanders outside in the daylight. When Walter seems to have disappeared without a trace, Rumsfield and Art engage a reluctant Ray into investigating whether the Klopeks are guilty of murdering him in a satanic ritual. Before long, the neighbors become convinced this is the case, and along with Carol and Rumsfield's wife, Bonnie (Wendy Schaal), they pay a "social visit" to the Klopeks' to try to find evidence of a murder.

Once inside the spooky domain, they meet family patriarch Reuben Klopek (Brother Theodore), a humorless, sinister-looking man who barely tolerates their presence. The other Klopeks consist of Reuben's brother Dr. Werner Klopek (Henry Gibson), a socia-

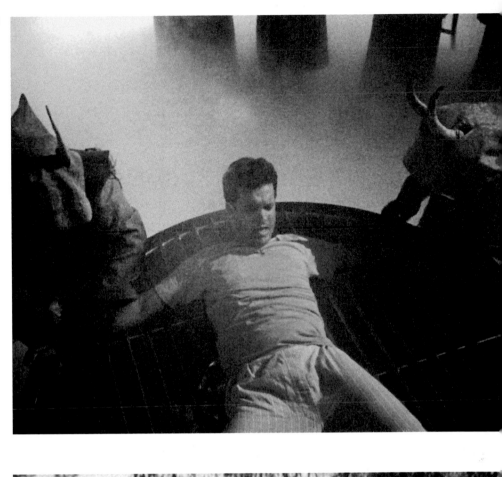

In a bizarre nightmare, Ray is barbecued by the new neighbors. (Imagine Entertainment/ Universal City Studios)

ten . . . It suddenly dawned on me that Joe Dante would be fantastic [as a director], because it's a mixture of comedy, horror, and reality."

Genre hero Joe Dante, the innovative director of *Gremlins* and *Innerspace*, and his partner, Michael Finnell, were immediately impressed by the concept of *The 'burbs*. Dante, who specializes in offbeat subject matters, was intrigued by the blending of real-life situations with elements of the supernatural. "When I tell people about the story, a remarkable number say, 'On my grandmother's block there were people like that. They never mowed their lawn, and they never came out, and they let their mail stack up, and nobody ever knew where they were.' And I must confess that in my own neighborhood there's a house like that, falling to wrack and ruin. I think this is perhaps a more common event than most people are aware of."

Dante, Brezner, and Finnell agreed that Tom Hanks would be the most suitable actor to portray the harried Ray Peterson, a conservative man who tries to introduce excitement into his life by investigating the activities of his strange neighbors. Dante referred to Hanks as "the reigning Everyman, a guy that everybody can identify with" and went on to give the umpteenth comparison between Hanks and Jimmy Stewart. Brezner echoed the sentiments, saying, "Hanks is an actor capable of acting funny rather than funny acting. He also has no problem with transition from comedy to pathos, as he showed in *Nothing in Common*, and

Ray gets a laugh at Art's (Rick Ducommun) expense. (Imagine Entertainment/Universal City Studios)

he's now proving himself as one of the country's most versatile actors."

Hanks accepted the role of Ray with enthusiasm. "What's so bizarrely interesting about this black psychocomedy is that the stuff that goes on in real life in a regular neighborhood will make your hair stand up on the back of your neck." He was also intrigued by his character and saw in him the challenge of creating a totally unique character with distinctive personality traits. "Sometimes there's more of an opportunity to create than others. Here's a guy with a great life—a nice house, a wife, a beautiful tree, a nice neighborhood—and he's happy. Next day, he hates it all. I thought something must've happened to him offstage.

The three men devise an elaborate scheme to get to the bottom of the mystery of the Klopeks. (Imagine Entertainment/Universal City Studios)

... And that's the challenge for me of the part, to communicate Ray's offscreen dilemma. One of the reasons Ray doesn't go away on vacation is because it's another extension of the normalcy he's fallen into. So he thinks he'll try a more Bohemian thing, which is to just hang around the house. With a week's worth of free time on his hands, Ray is drawn into the preoccupations of his neighbors, who always seem to be at home. . . . But what I did is just back-story embellishment that any actor will do. Perhaps from my repertory experience. I don't ask a director for motivation. If he says, 'Go over to the window,' I find the reason myself."

Hanks found admiration for Joe Dante's directorial style, saying "Joe has a stylized, visionary way of looking at the entire movie. It's pure filmmaking—the story is told from the camera's point of view, and that's a type of movie I haven't made." Dante, in turn, praised his star. "The most impressive thing about Tom Hanks as a comic actor is how effortless he makes it seem. He actually is very diligent about his acting, but his comic sense of what is going to work—and what isn't—is really unparalleled."

Filmed entirely at Universal Studios, *The 'burbs* presented technical and logistical problems for Dante and the crew. "I can't think of many pictures since *Lifeboat* that all take place in the same area," Dante said as production was under way. "There was a lot of temptation to broaden it and go outside the neighborhood, but it seemed to violate the spirit of the piece. It's almost the kind of thing that could be a stage play except that you could never do onstage what we've done in this movie."

Dante used the "Colonial Street" set on the back lot. The set was being used at the time as the location for the *Still the Beaver* television series—the eighties follow-up to *Leave It to Beaver*, so the entire area "reeked" of normalcy. Dante said, "I asked [production designer James Spencer, a veteran of *Poltergeist* and *Gremlins*] if he thought he could turn that street into the neighborhood we needed in that period of time." Spencer rose to the challenge, and within a few days they began work on sketching the proposed designs for sets. Spencer observed, "We had to be on the spot. Due to the lack of time, it would have been ludicrous to do our drawing elsewhere." The "sacred" Beaver household had to be carted away to make room for the dilapidated Klopek home. By the time Spencer was through, the entire street had been reconfigured.

The ten-week shoot took place during the summer of 1988, with Dante directing Hanks and the high-profile supporting cast. Dante's laid-back, casual style encouraged improvisation among the actors. He noted, "Tom doesn't like to do scenes the way they're always done. He goes out of his way to put a different spin on everything and his being good as he is and as open as he is encouraged the other actors to do the same. It set a tone for the movie that made it a lot of fun to make."

A writers' strike was imminent and forced the production to work at a rapid pace, thereby eliminating the opportunity for revisions to the script as the shooting proceeded. Indeed, Dante was filming a scant seven weeks after receiving the script. He recalled after shooting was completed, "Nobody was ever happy with the script the way it was. On this picture, we just had to smooth out the rough edges ourselves. Luckily, Tom has a very good sense of what works for him."

Despite its seemingly promising premise and its ambitious aspirations, *The 'burbs*—an uneasy blend of social satire and horror spoof—never finds its niche. It's offbeat but not original enough; manic but not consistently funny. And the intriguing premise of the story—that we never truly know those who live so near to us—is not explored in anything but the most juvenile way. Had the script stuck to one genre, the result might have been successful. *The 'burbs* remains, however, too much of each genre and not enough of either. One can easily envision Tom Hanks in a nose-thumbing spoof of modern suburbia—in the same manner in which Jack Lemmon made *Good Neighbor Sam* the ultimate sixties suburban satire. Hanks though, is left to look perplexed, bewildered, and wild-eyed. *The 'burbs* is not the place to relish Hanks's inimitable, subtle comedic talents.

The supporting cast does not fare much better. Bruce Dern is given an uninspired and clichéd role as the gun-crazed Vietnam vet determined to protect his neighbors from themselves; Carrie Fisher has an even less interesting role as Hanks's exasperated wife; Rick Ducommun shows promise as Hanks's sidekick in a role that has "John Candy" written all over it, but he, too, is restricted to juvenile sight gags. The biggest laughs come when the Klopek family is on-screen—which, unfortunately, is not nearly enough. Henry Gibson, Brother Theodore, and Courtney Gains give wonderfully eccentric characterizations; and make their "normal" neighbors seem boring by comparison. The highlight of the film is the "social visit" paid to the Klopeks by Hanks, Dern, Fisher, and Schaal.

Ray and Art make a startling discovery about their new neighbors. (Imagine Entertainment/Universal City Studios)

Production designer James Spencer makes the inside of the Klopek mansion as foreboding and intriguing as we hoped it would be, and Hanks and Dern's strained attempts at conversation with the Klopeks generate the movie's only sustained laughs.

The ending of *The 'burbs* is a shambles, and one wishes Dante merely threw up his hands and let the pieces fall where they may, à la the finale of Mel Brooks's, *Blazing Saddles*. Instead, aside from a refreshingly creative twist concerning family, the script consists of endless explosions, screaming and clichéd jokes. (e.g., the hospital gurney falls from the ambulance and races downhill as Ray and Dr. Klopek struggle atop it—a gag that was stale in Mack Sennett's day.)

Although *The 'burbs* is anything but inspired, it does fulfill one basic rule of any comedy: It is never dull, and watching it is an amusing enough experience if one can forget the fact that a great deal of talent is being wasted on a B haunted-house spoof. The

103

film opened with huge grosses but quickly faded when negative reviews and bad word of mouth began to take their toll. The ad campaign, which insinuated this would be Tom Hanks in a reality-based comedy, made audiences feel disappointed when confronted with a pseudo–horror film. Small wonder that Tom Hanks would remark years later, "There's no question that the movie is not all that great."

For the ultimate haunted-house spoof, no one has ever topped Don Knotts in *The Ghost and Mr. Chicken*. Now *that* was funny!

Reviews

"The best thing that can be said for Joe Dante and Dana Olsen is that they don't try to stuff The 'burbs *with a worthy message. The movie is as empty as something can be without creating a vacuum. . . . So little goes on that it might be argued that* The 'burbs *means to be a comment on the vacuity of popular entertainment in the television age, though it's much more an example of it. The film does nothing for the reputation of any-*

one connected with it, including Mr. Hanks, who deserves the Oscar nomination he just received for his work in Big. *This time, he's attempting to act a role in a screenplay whose pages are blank."*

—Vincent Canby, *New York Times*

"It's sort of a lynch-mob movie for laughs—laughs that are meant to catch in the back of your throat like movie-house popcorn that turns out to be all kernels. One of the new neighbors is described as 'about a nine on the tension scale.' And so is this smart, crafty, off-putting movie. Well, satire was never meant to ingratiate and The 'burbs *is unsparing in its cauterizing of provincialism. . . . Hanks throws himself into this antiaudience movie with such suave energy that he seems determined to torpedo his hard-won rep as Hollywood's most comfortable new star."*

—Richard Corliss, *Time*

"Mostly the stars look like appealing people waiting around for a neat thing to happen. . . . There is no serious effort to send up the eminently satirizable life of the American suburbs and this lampooning of horror films (and maybe the old Twilight Zone*) doesn't go far. Any episode of* The Addams Family *or* The Munsters *is sharper and funnier, not to mention an hour shorter."*

—Ralph Novak, *People*

14

Turner & Hooch

Touchstone, 1989

"Turner's a man who is compulsively neat and organized. He thinks he can only be happy if he has all these walls of protection around him. In almost one night, Hooch breaks down his barriers and destroys all those preconceived notions. It's a story of this man's life being completely rendered asunder by this dog. In some ways, it's the ordinary man in an extraordinary circumstance. He's not the usual type that I've played."

Cast:

Tom Hanks (*Scott Turner*); Mare Winningham (*Emily Carson*); Beasley (*Hooch*); Craig T. Nelson (*Chief Hyde*); Reginald VelJohnson (*David Sutton*); Scott Paulin (*Zack Gregory*); J. C. Quinn (*Walter Boyett*); John McIntire (*Amos Reed*); David Knell (*Ernie*).

Credits:

Director: Rodger Spottiswoode; producer: Raymond Wagner; executive producer: Daniel Petrie Jr.; screenplay: Dennis Shryack and Michael Blodgett, Daniel Petrie Jr., Jim Cash, and Jack Epps Jr.; story by: Shryack and Blodgett; director of photography: Adam Greenberg; production designer: John DeCuir Jr.; editor: Garth Craven; Music: Charles Gross.
Running time: 98 minutes.

Although *The 'burbs* fell short of its ambitious aspirations, it was at least a somewhat original comedic concept. This was not the case with Tom Hanks's next venture, *Turner & Hooch*, the umpteenth variation of *The Odd Couple*—this time with an anal-retentive, neatness-obsessed detective (Hanks in the "Felix" role) teamed with an ugly mutt (Beasley, playing the part of "Oscar"). The film rested entirely on Hanks's considerable skill at physical comedy (as well as his canine costar's). Fortunately, that's enough to make *Turner & Hooch* a passable timekiller, although a rather benign project for the star of *Big*.

Hanks plays Scott Turner, a small-town detective who is bored with the lack of challenging police work. He is transferring to San Francisco's police department and is in the process of training his replacement, David Sutton (Reginald VelJohnson), when the first murder in many years occurs. The victim is Amos (John McIntire), an amiable eccentric whom Turner has watched over in recent years. When Amos observes suspicious goings-on at a fish-packing plant next door, he is whacked by thugs who are using the plant as a cover for a money-laundering

Hanks and Beasley, the stars of the latest odd-couple/cop-buddy picture (Touchstone Pictures)

operation. The only witness to the murder is Hooch, Amos's mangy and viscious mutt. Despite his hatred for the dog, Turner temporarily adopts him in the hope that Hooch can "shed" some light on the crime.

The relationship proves to be a trying experience for both man and beast. Hooch cannot warm to his ill-tempered new master, and Turner finds that his pristine apartment now resembles Hiroshima after the blast, courtesy of his canine roommate's slobbery habits. Ultimately, however, both Turner and Hooch develop a mutual love and respect when the two must depend on each other to escape the killers.

Turner & Hooch was Tom Hanks first film in a multi-picture deal with Disney. Released by Touchstone Pictures, Disney's recently formed subsidiary, the film would be marketed toward adults and not to younger audiences—a surprising strategy considering the undeniable appeal of Hanks's jowelly costar. Hanks confessed to having mixed emotions

about the new picture deal, saying, "I have a relationship with Disney that will last for a number of films that I bring to them or they to me. I don't know if I have the acumen for this or if I like the process. I did it once before at another studio, and the timing was not correct for either of us. But here, these guys are entrenched. They have a philosophy of making movies . . . it's like a huge juggernaut . . . But it's more imposing than somebody else's style of making movies." Still, Hanks knew that despite the autocratic reputation of Touchstone, it was considered one of the great contemporary studio success stories, producing hits from the very instant it was formed (e.g. *Splash*).

Originally, Henry Winkler had been signed as director of *Turner & Hooch*. However, Winkler left after only twelve days, attributing the reason to "creative differences" with Tom Hanks. Winkler's replacement was Roger Spottiswoode, who got off to a better start with his star. He observed of Hanks,

"Above all, Tom is a consummate professional and gifted performer. Tom has the intelligent instinct to create a character grounded in reality. He doesn't make the mistake of being too overblown. He plays Turner with great honesty, and out of the honestly portrayed situations comes the comedy."

The biggest challenge to have faced the studio was the casting of the perfect canine. The script called for an animal who looked so pathetically ugly that the audience could not help but love him. The dog explained why Beasley got the "gig": "Everyone immediately agreed that Beasley was the dog. You see this dog and you know why. The way the dog holds his face on the screen, it's funnier than any line I could ever write." So strong was the conviction that Beasley was "the man for the job" that he was hired despite the fact that he was untrained. Consequently, Rowe and his new student embarked on an aggressive five-month training period.

To prepare for his own role, Tom Hanks decided

Turner is left with no choice but to take in the mangy Hooch when his master, Amos, is brutally murdered. (Touchstone Pictures)

would also be required to perform many complicated actions on cue (with the help of a stunt-double mutt to perform the more dangerous assignments). Producer Raymond Wagner spoke about the dilemma in finding such an animal: "The dog needed to be an animal that could start out as a junkyard beast, a monster . . . dirty, horrible, snarling, happy to chew up anything and anyone. But he also has to grow on you so that over the course of the film you come to realize that this isn't a bad dog."

Wagner enlisted the services of veteran animal trainer Clint Rowe. Through Rowe, the filmmakers decided to cast Beasley, a Dogue de Bordeaux with an irresistible, sad-eyed look, not to mention a penchant for gross drooling. Screenwriter Daniel Petrie Jr.

it would make sense to "bond" with Beasley. He spent a good deal of time at Clint Rowe's training facility in Southern California. Hanks was initially uncomfortable working with Beasley and his stunt double, Igor: "It wasn't just a matter of getting used to working with a very intimidating physical being right next to me, but multiple physical intimidating beings. It was a long-haul process. . . . Clint wanted me to understand that he was always going to be right there. He reassured me that there would never be a circumstance where I was going to have to control the dog."

Filming of *Turner & Hooch* began in February 1989 on L.A.'s Terminal Island. After twenty-two days of shooting, the company relocated to Disney

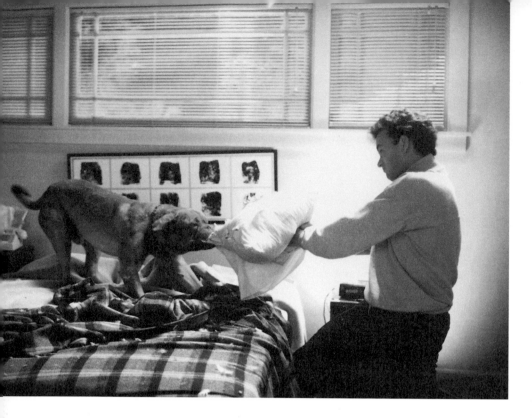

Studios in Burbank, where they occupied two sound-stages for several weeks. Other exteriors and certain interior shots were filmed in San Pedro and on the Monterey Peninsula. A ten-day shoot was done at Pacific Grove, California. The entire production wrapped in fifty-nine days, and because Touchstone was anxious to release the film quickly, director Roger Spottiswoode had a very lean postproduction schedule. Hanks admired his director's ability to remain calm in the face of pressure: "Roger brought clarity to the project right from the very beginning. He knew exactly what he wanted and how to visually tell the story. His strength as a filmmaker lies in the fact that he's not satisfied until each scene plays with a completely natural flow. Making this movie turned out to be a very invigorating, exciting process.

Daniel Petrie Jr. recalls of Hanks: "I never worked with an actor who is as much a filmmaker, who takes a great deal of responsibility for the film without being an interferer. Tom writes notes that are more intelligent than the studio notes." Petrie credits Hanks with equating Hooch to a frustrating girlfriend of Turner's—someone he can't wait to get rid of but finds he is miserable without. "I hadn't really thought of Hooch

in the same way as some crazy girlfriend coming into your life," confessed Petrie. "The minute I had that image in mind, a lot of things really fell into place."

Despite all this, *Turner & Hooch* is little more than a big-screen version of a weekly sitcom. It's *Cheers* with fleas. That isn't necessarily a knock, but the project seems rather lightweight for Hanks. The film does give him the opportunity to create some truly inspired moments of comedy, but most of the situations in which the script places him were stale when Rin Tin Tin was a pup. It also continues the politically correct trend of ensuring that the hero is paired with a black partner. In this case, it is the very watchable Reginald VelJohnson. Here Hanks gets all the good scenes, while VelJohnson guards the squad car.

With Mare Winningham, who plays Turner's requisite love interest, vet Emily Carson (Marcia Reed, Touchstone Pictures)

The script's pretentiousness is also apparent in the way a beautiful female veterinarian (Mare Winningham) is shoehorned into the story, as if to assure us that Turner isn't quite *that* much in love with Hooch. Hanks and Winningham share a few nice moments, but the relationship is never developed to any degree. What is incredible is that the script for this film required more writers than *The Bridge on the River Kwai*. Yet there is hardly a single original thought among them. Maybe they needed enough guys around a table to get a poker game going.

The movie became a minor cause célèbre upon its release due to the rather odd decision to kill off the lovable Hooch despite the fact that such an action does nothing to advance the plot. When Hooch is wounded saving Turner's life, the script cruelly sets us up for an uplifting ending as we watch Turner give a pep talk to his dog during an operation to remove the bullets. Suddenly and shockingly, we watch the lovable canine die before our eyes. This allows Hanks the opportunity to break down like Ricky Schroder in *The Champ*, but it leaves the audience stunned and disappointed.

The studio defended the decision to have Hooch meet his demise, explaining that in test screenings audiences preferred this version of the film to one in which the dog survives. Touchstone was aware that Hooch's death not only would exclude children from the core audience but also would negate the very viable merchandising deals that could be made from the film. (Consider the future licensing success of *Beethoven*.) Consequently, it was only with great reluctance that they allowed Roger Spottiswoode to maintain the downbeat ending. Hanks would make light of the decision years later, telling David Letterman: "We made a fatal mistake. . . . It cost us twenty-five million at the boxoffice. . . . They now have that written in topiary hedges in the front of the Disney studio: 'Don't Kill the Dog!' The merchandis-

Turner tries in vain to convince Hooch that he is a dog and that dogs should sleep outside. (Touchstone Pictures)

ing alone would have been mammoth. And I had a piece of that. I had a piece of those little Hooch dogs!"

In fact, the film's climax was to have been even grimmer. When Turner confronts the mysterious criminal mastermind (in a plot device that is telegraphed seemingly right after the opening credits roll), the character played by Reginald VelJohnson was to have been killed off as well. Audiences failed to respond positively to this scene, however, and VelJohnson was spared in the final cut, albeit at the price of making his role less interesting. The decision was also made to soften the last scene by showing Turner and the vet now married, with a litter of puppies and a mutt who is obviously the offspring of Hooch. This fails to cheer up the viewer, however, as it appears to be exactly what it is—a tacked-on afterthought.

Despite lukewarm reviews, *Turner & Hooch* was deemed to be superior to the other cop-and-canine

who rises to the level of his best material, as he did in Big, *and who has the intelligence and charm to rise above his weaker roles. He is the best part of this film. . . . It isn't his fault that the five writers don't come up with five funny lines or one exciting scene.*"

—Caryn James, *New York Times*

"*This is obviously not* Lassie Come Home. . . . *Hanks, a wonderfully natural and unpretentious actor, may be the only star capable of holding his own against [Hooch], even stealing a scene or two from his furry friend. This little nothing of a movie—sweeter and smarter than it has a right to be—may cheer you on through the, uh, dog days.*"

—Richard Schickel, *Time*

"*In the race for 1989's best crime comedy about a cop who inherits a mangy dog,* Turner & Hooch *leads* K-9 *by a muzzle. Most of this has to do with Hanks, who—with all due respect to W. C. Fields—is way too appealing to be in any danger of being overshadowed by Beasley. . . . Not that Beasley doesn't try. . . . One of the film's shortcomings, in fact, is that while it took five people to write its screenplay, it depends mostly on jokes involving Beasley slobbering, biting, or indulging in flatulent behavior. The film has a friendly feel, though, and encourages a rewarding number of smiles. If there were a canine branch of* At the Movies, *this film would rate about a paw and a half with a small tail wag for good measure.*"

—Ralph Novak, *People*

caper in release at the time, *K-9.* (We *told* you there was nothing original here.) Critics *did* enthusiastically cite Tom Hanks's performance. *Turner & Hooch* became a box-office hit and helped erase memories of the disappointing grosses for *Punchline* and *The 'burbs.* Hanks would have to savor this moment.

Reviews

"*Clearly goes in for excess. It at least has three plots credited to five writers. . . . Hanks is a brilliant understated comedian,*

15

Joe Versus the Volcano

Warner Bros., 1990

"Volcano is one of those movies that is going to age better than it played originally. When it came out, some people just plain didn't get it. That's okay—The same thing happened with The Wizard of Oz. *But I don't think you're going to see any ads saying, 'You loved them in* Joe Versus the Volcano. *You'll adore them in* Sleepless in Seattle.'"*

Cast

Tom Hanks (*Joe*); Meg Ryan (*De De/Angelica/Patricia*); Lloyd Bridges (*Graynamore*); Robert Stack (*Dr. Ellison*); Abe Vigoda (*Chief of the Waponis*); Dan Hedaya (*Mr. Waturi*); Amanda Plummer (*Dagmar*); Ossie Davis (*Marshall*); Carol Kane (*Hairdresser*).

Credits:

Writer-director: John Patrick Shanley; producer: Teri Schwartz; executive producers: Steven Spielberg, Kathleen Kennedy, and Frank Marshall; director of photography: Stephen Goldblatt; production designer: Bo Welch; editor: Richard Halsey; music: Georges Delerue. Running time: 102 minutes.

If *Turner & Hooch* was not a significant artistic success, Tom Hanks could at least console himself with the fact that it had proved to be a *popular* success. No such fate awaited the offbeat modern fantasy *Joe Versus the Volcano*. The ambitious production certainly fit in with Hanks's determination to do films which were original in their concepts. However, this awkwardly titled, high-budget comedy was probably *too* original to appeal to mainstream audiences.

The film's message is that people have the ability to change their lives if they only have the courage to do so. The script is the creation of John Patrick Shanley, an off-Broadway producer who became the sensation du jour in Hollywood following his Oscar-winning screenplay for *Moonstruck* in 1987. Shanley immediately fell victim to "the Orson Welles Syndrome." That is, his first major work was so well received that it became difficult to live up to expectations on subsequent projects. Shanley wrote the screenplays for some low-profile films that sank even on the art-house circuit. *Joe Versus the Volcano* was to be his "comeback" film—a $50 million production for a major studio. Steven Spielberg and Warner Bros. had enough confidence in the unusual story to allow

producers. With such illustrious names attached to the project, Shanley knew the property was sure to attract major stars.

The role of Joe was challenging enough to appeal to any number of comedic actors. The character is a meek clerical worker whose miserable life consists of dragging his body to the most depressing office environment imaginable (can *anything* be worse than working in a rectal probe factory?) and being constantly degraded by his "boss from hell." A self-professed hypochondriac, Joe is startled to learn from a doctor (Robert Stack) that he is actually dying of a rare disorder called a "brain cloud," which will allow him to live normally for six months, before total brain failure and sudden death occur. In a rare, uncharacteristic burst of courage, Joe humiliates his boss, quits his job, and decides to "live it up" for six months and discover what joy there is in life. His goal is unattainable, however, due to his impoverished state.

Joe's fortunes change when he meets a millionaire named Graynamore (Lloyd Bridges), who offers him an unusual proposition. Graynamore wants to mine rare minerals from a South Pacific island inhabited by wild natives known as the Waponis. In order to do so, he must provide a volunteer to be sacrificed to a live volcano. Graynamore convinces Joe that since he is going to die, anyway, he may as well go out in style and become a legend among the tribesmen. In return, he can spend the next few weeks as a millionaire, courtesy of Graynamore's credit cards. Feeling he has nothing to lose, Joe accepts.

He is escorted to the South Pacific atoll by one of Graynamore's daughters, Patricia (Meg Ryan), a cynical, hard-bitten woman who eventually falls in love with Joe. Arriving on the island, he is treated by the natives (under the rule of Jewish Abe Vigoda) like a

Shanley to make his directorial debut with this feature.

Prior to scripting *Moonstruck*, Shanley was suffering from depression due to his inability to interest Hollywood in his rather eccentric style of scriptwriting. When *Moonstruck* hit pay dirt, he understandably felt more confident, claiming he "no longer had to worry about making a living and paying the rent." He finally had time to indulge in one of his favorite pastimes—theorizing about the meaning of life through such questions as "What am I doing on this planet, and what do I do with my limited time here?" Such questions inspired the screenplay for *Joe Versus the Volcano*, which Shanley enthusiastically completed in a little over six weeks. Luck would smile on him again, when he convinced Steven Spielberg, Kathleen Kennedy, and Frank Marshall to serve as executive

New York version of Kurtz in *Apocalypse Now* and is regaled as a god because of his willingness to sacrifice himself to appease the raging volcano. Joe and Patricia are married in a brief ceremony atop the volcano and then decide to take the plunge together. At that precise moment, the volcano erupts, and a burst of steam sends them flying into the ocean. Saved by this "miracle," Joe confesses he has only a few months to live. Patricia informs him that he is in perfect health and has been duped by her father and the doctor in order to pacify the natives and gain the mineral rights to the island. Feeling he has been born again, Joe and Patricia sail off to a new life—atop his floatable luggage—as the end titles assure us: "And they lived happily ever after."

Joe gets a makover while chauffeur-mentor Marshall (Ossie Davis) looks on. (Warner Bros.)

The wacky story was not without its charms, and Shanley met with Tom Hanks to offer him the starring role of Joe. They discussed the character and Shanley's anticipated use of camera work and sets to illustrate the difference between Joe's miserable existence in an office and the joy he finds on his way to becoming a sacrificial lamb in the Pacific. Shanley recalled: "I talked about the palette, from desaturated, extreme blues and grays to very saturated color as Joe comes back to life. . . . [I] told him what he'd be wearing, what he'd look like [in the final jump scene]. And I played him the music, stuff from Borodin, Tchaikovsky, Grieg . . . that 'Sunrise' music from *Peer Gynt*. The story moves to a more and more splendid environment, from Long Island City to the South Pacific under a canopy of stars, when Joe comes fully back to life. It's a movie about people leaping from apparent safety to apparent doom, and by leaping, saving themselves."

Tom Hanks bought "the pitch" and signed on as Joe. This delighted Shanley, who said, "The life force burns brightly in Tom. And he's smart, and he's sensitive, and he's very serious about his work. You *see* that look in his eyes—there's a lot of life there. There's really somebody at home. That's inexplicable, incandescing with the life force." For those who don't speak in hokey New Age jargon, Shanley added, "That's great!"

Meg Ryan was cast in the role of Patricia, but the part would prove to be a tour de force. She gets to play two other prominent roles as well: as an office worker who almost has an affair with the newly "liberated" Joe and as Graynamore's other daughter, an air-headed, gun moll type who escorts Joe to the yacht which will take him and Patricia to the South Pacific. Ryan immediately felt a bond with Hanks: Like him, she was intrigued by the hidden meanings of Shanley's script. "When you feel your little foot going over the edge of the volcano, that's the *most* exciting time in our life. . . . This is about life, about love, and the fact that it's scary but so-o-o good! It's just been so liberating . . . we felt let loose and free [on the shoot], sailing in this huge yacht with the wind, the sky, the billowing white sails on the high seas."

For his part, Hanks found working with the new director stimulating but demanding: "Shanley can tear you a new asshole if you don't know what you're doing. He gives you the goods and expects them right back from you. A lot of people in this town would call that ego. I call it honesty." Hanks described how he would psyche himself up to play key scenes: "You have big red-letter days circled. You begin to strip down for the big game. Tuesday you start thinking about it; Wednesday you start carrying it around with you; Thursday you wake up and don't listen to the radio on the way to work, don't talk to your buddy on the set. . . . It's stupid to say, but there are people *born* with the ability to act. On the emotional level, it's really weird, very strange. That's why not everybody can do it. You feel graceful and powerful and intelligent and wise. People like Shanley have written this for you to seem that way, allowing you to do this. And so much is relying on it—money, for one, but also the integrity of everybody involved."

For all the money spent on *Joe Versus the Volcano*, it is somewhat ironic that it was not filmed on location in the South Pacific but rather on some enormous sets on two Hollywood soundstages (including the one which the Yellow Brick Road was constructed for *The Wizard of Oz*). The sets are somewhat of a triumph for production designer Bo Welch (he also did the ones for *Beetlejuice*). In particular, the sequences at the horrid factory/office environment in which Joe works are enormously creative and oppressive, making those found in *1984* look like Club Med. The environment fits perfectly with the mundane job Joe has to do. The most brain-dead

occupation imaginable (aside from being a toll taker). The rest of the film takes place largely on a plastic Polynesian paradise that is all the more charming because it is so patently—and intentionally—phony.

The film itself is difficult to analyze. Most of the elements don't jell, largely because it may have been crystal clear to Shanley about what messages he hoped to convey, but to those not among the enlightened, the entire affair seems like a lot of work to suggest a simple theory: Don't let your job overwhelm the everyday joys in life. The film is filled with life and good intentions, but one suspects that it meant more to those involved than to the general audience. The script doesn't have many belly laughs, but it doesn't appear to aspire to them.

Patricia (Meg Ryan) falls in love with Joe, and the two agree to take the plunge together. (Warner Bros.)

In a scene cut from the final film, Patricia and Joe are confronted by the evil Dr. Ellison (Robert Stack). (Warner Bros.)

and condescending tactics of his manager (a wonderfully mean Dan Hedaya). Stuck in a concentration camp–like factory, where morale building is limited to signs like Home of the Rectal Probe and 50 Years of Petroleum Jelly, Hanks is remarkable to watch, turning from a helpless worm into Superman upon learning he has nothing to lose. His diatribe against Hedaya is worthy of a standing ovation. The rest of the film does not give him any distinctly memorable scenes, although the Hanks charisma makes all of this nonsense appear more interesting than it actually is.

The real value of *Joe Versus the Volcano* is in the first pairing of Tom Hanks and Meg Ryan, who has emerged in recent years as one of the most natural actresses working in films. She is particularly good playing two of the three prominent female roles in the movie, both of which render her almost unrecognizable. Three years later, Hanks and Ryan would team again for *Sleepless in Seattle*.

Joe Versus the Volcano was a critical and box-office disappointment, although it was hardly an unmitigated disaster. The presence of Tom Hanks ensured that grosses would be higher than one might expect for such an offbeat tale. Still, there was no disputing that *Volcano* was an overall money loser and a career setback for John Patrick Shanley, who continues to write for films, awaiting his next big opportunity to exploit his individualistic, original style of moviemaking.

Reviews

"Not since Howard the Duck *has there been a big-budget comedy with feet as flat as [this movie]. Many gifted people contributed to it, but there's no disbelieving the grim evidence on the screen. There appears to be no stinting on sets, costumes, and special effects. The consumption is conspicuous. Yet, nothing works. . . . Mr. Hanks gives a carefully thought-out performance that never manages to be more than theoretically comic, since the material is so muddled—a mixture of comedy, fantasy and rock-dirge. Miss*

Shanley seems to want to convey a moralizing, gentle comedy rather than a "roll-in-the-aisles" farce. This isn't necessarily wrong, but the end result is an unsatisfying mishmash of pretentious lessons about life, gooey love interludes, and scenes that fall short of their potential.

Yet, for all its faults, *Joe Versus the Volcano* is impossible not to like and admire on certain levels. For one, it dares to be original and is unlike virtually any other comedy. While Shanley often flounders as director, he has an ability to write some clever scenes and dialogue. Especially amusing are the sequences with Robert Stack, playing his stoic, Mount Rushmore image to the hilt, and the charismatic Lloyd Bridges, an actor who has never received enough acclaim for his contributions to so many films. Sadly, both Bridges and Stack make only token appearances. Abe Vigoda turns up in a brief but amusing performance as the native chieftain with a Brooklyn accent.

Tom Hanks gives a delightful performance as Joe, the Everyman who fulfills the dream of the common worker seeking to regain his dignity by telling the boss to go to hell. He is at his best in early sequences in which he must cope with the abusive

Joe finds the native rituals include having a baby octopus attached to his face! (Warner Bros.)

Ryan plays with equal distinction the three women with whom Joe becomes involved, though no point is made by having one actress do the three parts."

—Vincent Canby, *New York Times*

"Shanley's wildest, most ambitious movie yet. Partly because of this, it's also his least realized. . . . Even on it's own playfully unrealistic terms, the plot doesn't quite work . . . an actor who can be very, very good (in Big

Preparing to go out with a bang (Warner Bros.)

With Meg Ryan (Warner Bros.)

and Punchline*), [Hanks] also can be very, very bad (*The 'burbs, The Money Pit*). Here, he is not much of either. Except for the scene when he dances to a transistor radio on a raft, he never gets a handle on the sweet loser he is playing. But as imperfect as the whole is, the parts are often marvelous."*

—Us magazine

"A fiasco made by an extremely talented man. . . . Hanks, as ever, turns a comic line with effortless grace. . . . The catch is that Shanley, making his debut as director, simply can't do the job. There's no sense of pacing or forethought; scenes seem thrown together. Individually, the actors are fine, but Shanley can't blend their divergent styles. . . . Somewhere along the line, Shanley let his gentle fable about the fear of love, responsibility and commitment degenerate into crude farce. And he has only himself to blame."

—Peter Travers, *Rolling Stone*

"Gradually, through the opening scenes of Joe Versus the Volcano, *my heart began to quicken until finally I realized a wondrous thing: I had not seen this movie before. Most movies, I have seen before. Most movies are constructed out of bits and pieces of other movies, like little engines built from the cinematic erector sets. But not* Joe Versus the Volcano. *It is not an entirely successful movie, but it is new and fresh and not shy of taking chances, and the dialogue in it is actually worth listening to because it is written with wit and romance. . . . Tom Hanks and Meg Ryan are the right actors to inhabit it, because you never catch them going for a gag that isn't there. . . .Hanks is endearing in the title role because in the midst of these astonishing sets and unbridled flights of fancy, he underplays. Like a Jacques Tati, he is an island of curiosity in a sea of mystery."*

—Roger Ebert, *Chicago Sun Times*

16

The Bonfire of the Vanities

Warner Bros., 1990

"I did everything I could to make it work. The fallout from it was that it makes you reflect for a while. You question yourself. But what can you do? You take your shots, and you swing away. You can't go back and correct it or change it. You wish it had been different, but it's not. It just solidified what William Goldman said a long time ago, that there's only one commandment in Hollywood: Nobody knows anything. And that includes me."

Cast

Tom Hanks (*Sherman McCoy*); Bruce Willis (*Peter Fallow*); Melanie Griffith (*Maria Ruskin*); Kim Cattrall (*Judy McCoy*); Saul Rubinek (*Jed Kramer*); Morgan Freeman (*Judge White*); John Hancock (*Reverend Bacon*); Kevin Dunn (*Tom Killian*); F. Murray Abraham (*D.A. Weiss*); Donald Moffat (*Mr. McCoy*); Robert Stephens (*Sir Gerald Moore*); Alan King (*Arthur Ruskin*); Beth Broderick (*Caroline Heftshank*); Mary Alice (*Annie Lamb*); Rita Wilson (*PR woman*).

Credits

Producer and director: Brian DePalma; executive producers: Peter Guber and Jon Peters; coproducer: Fred Caruso; screenplay: Michael Cristofer, based on the novel by Tom Wolfe; director of photography: Vilmos Zsigmond; production designer: Richard Sylbert; editors: David Ray and Bill Pankow; music: Dave Grusin.
Running time: 125 minutes.

Many questioned the casting of Hanks as Sherman, Melanie Griffith as his mistress Maria Ruskin, and Bruce Willis as reporter Peter Fallow. (Warner Bros.)

Tom Hanks's enviable string of films which were either critical or box-office hits (usually both) came to a screeching halt with the ill-fated *The Bonfire of the Vanities*. Producer-director Brian De Palma's screen version of Tom Wolfe's bitchy satirical novel seemed to be destined for failure before the cameras even began to roll. But common sense is not in great abundance in the industry that produced *Ishtar* earlier and *Waterworld* later. Like the Light Brigade, the filmmakers ignored even their own misgivings and proceeded half a league onward—toward inevitable disaster.

How could a film which boasted so much top talent, both in front of and behind the cameras, go wrong? How could a film based on a source novel which was *the* sensation of the publishing world be so totally misguided? The answers are too contrived and complicated to adequately sum up here. Suffice it to say that despite the best of intentions, virtually every wrong decision was made. In the old days, megabudget films went out of control due to unforeseen circumstances and unpredictable events. In today's ego-driven industry, inevitable disaster is not reason enough to place a high-profile clunker on the back

Steven Spielberg were all considered at one time or another to helm the most high profile comedy in years. To the amazement of virtually everyone, Brian De Palma was chosen as director. De Palma is best known for directing slice-and-dice thrillers that, according to his admirers, are tributes to Hitchcock, and, according to his detractor's, are merely rip-offs of the master director's best films. De Palma's most highly acclaimed film—the 1987 big-screen version of *The Untouchables*—hardly qualified him as the man to be entrusted with a big-budget comedy.

Playwright Michael Cristofer, who had adapted *The Witches of Eastwick* for the screen, was hired to write a screenplay that was to capture the essence of Tom Wolfe's massive novel while at the same time taking certain artistic licenses to ensure that the story played in Peoria. De Palma began to get cold feet when he read Cristofer's first draft. Complaining that it deviated too much from the source novel, De Palma told his agent, "This movie's going to be an endless talk fest. I'm having real second thoughts about this," but was assured that his fears were groundless and that the project was "the best thing around." De Palma stayed aboard even after Peter Guber resigned as the film's producer in order to move to Columbia (although his name remains on the credits). De Palma found himself not only directing but now producing as well.

De Palma became intrigued by *Bonfire* when he read the book while filming *Casualties of War* in Thailand. He wanted to follow that grim movie with something of a lighter nature and felt that Wolfe's novel, considered by many to be unfilmable, represented a suitable challenge. He saw the opportunity to make something along the lines of Kubrick's *Dr. Strangelove*. After signing on as director of *Bonfire*, he immediately began to consider who would play the

burner. With all the talent that would have to be paid off anyway, it becomes virtually impossible *not* to make the movie.

The genesis of the screen version of *Bonfire* began shortly after the book became a media sensation. Tom Wolfe's politically incorrect barbecuing of New York's intellectual elite, as well as its underprivileged, made for a frantic bidding war among the major studios for the screen rights. Ultimately, Warner Bros. was the winner, although there would certainly be irony in classifying anyone associated with the project as a "winner." Originally the film was budgeted at $29 million, but the cost began to escalate once the high-powered talent began to sign on.

Directors Adrian Lyne, Norman Jewison, Mike Nichols, James L. Brooks, Martin Scorsese, and even

Sherman's wrong turn would change his life forever. (Warner Bros.)

role of Sherman McCoy, the snooty, spoiled Wall Street financier whose life becomes a shambles when he and his mistress, Maria, take a wrong turn one night and end up in the South Bronx. They find themselves in an encounter with two black thugs, which results in one of the punks being severely injured and McCoy and Maria fleeing the scene of the crime. When his car is tracked down, McCoy is arrested and becomes the magnet for a media maelstrom in which virtually every special interest group in New York stands to benefit by framing him and seeing him crucified.

William Hurt was widely considered to be the shoo-in choice for McCoy. However, De Palma had other ideas: "As when Kubrick cast Peter Sellers as Strangelove and Quilty in *Lolita*, I was basically looking for a movie star who could play comedy. I think Tom Hanks is the best comedic actor around who can convey a serious side. And there's no doubt in my mind that it's easier to play drama than it is to get that precise comic timing." Yes, Hanks was the man—despite earlier considerations Steve Martin and Michael Douglas.

"When I first heard that Brian De Palma wanted me for this job, my immediate reaction was total intimidation," Hanks admitted. "Among other things, the novel itself was revered, and it captured the image of an entire decade. Sherman is the main figure in this work. Everyone who's read the book has his or her own idea about what Sherman should look like, how he talks, what his attitude is. I was going to have to be the walking embodiment of this guy about whom people had already formulated their own specific image and opinions."

Hanks had reason to be nervous. Not since *The Godfather* had there been so much speculation regarding who would play a leading role. When it was announced that the choice was Tom Hanks, the actor began to get bad vibes from the public: "I knew I was not the physical embodiment of Sherman McCoy. But I wasn't able to say 'Well, gee, I can't do the role.' I'm not gonna turn down that any more than I'd turn down a chance to do *Richard III*. I had people at a play leaning over and examining me saying, 'No, I don't see it. I just don't see it.'" Hanks admitted that casting him as McCoy represented a "huge, massive crapshoot," but he could soothe himself with the fact that he would be compensated with a $5 million salary.

Based on his personal interpretation of the character from the novel, Hanks had specific ideas as to how he would play McCoy: "Most people focused on whether Sherman was the manifestation of the worst aspects of American society or whether he was just trying to play by the rules as he understood them. Some people were glad to see what happened to him, and some felt sorry for him getting caught up in this merciless machine. I had my feelings about those things, too, the first time I read the book. The second time, I began to explore other qualities that Wolfe infused into this character. On the surface, McCoy thinks of himself as Master of the Universe, so he should have this strength and sense of control over his environment. But I didn't think so. I saw him as a guy who thought he could control his environment and *thought* he was Master of the Universe. But he's not. He's a pretender to the title."

If the casting of Hanks was controversial, he would not have to endure the pressure alone. Equally strange casting decisions were to follow. The character of Peter Fallow, as depicted in the novel, was a brash, cynical Australian journalist, of late an alcoholic has-been in search of one last career-saving story. His exploitation of the McCoy case leads him to sell out his journalistic integrity, but it does revive his sagging reputation and make him a celebrity. Although John Cleese was considered for the role, De Palma decided that because the character narrates the story, an Englishman might alienate the audience. He then promptly cast Bruce Willis, to the further dismay of fans of the novel.

The next bizarre casting revolved around the character of Maria, Sherman McCoy's air-headed, nymphomaniac girlfriend whose presence in his car on the night of the fateful wrong turn leads to the destruction of his marriage. Michelle Pfeiffer passed on the part, but Uma Thurman gave a credible performance in a screen test. Tom Hanks, however, felt the chemistry between him and Thurman just wasn't there, so De Palma continued to search until he came up with a choice that represented something less than a brainstorm: Melanie Griffith, the reigning Queen Bee of dizzy-blonde roles who had starred in De Palma's *Body Double*. The decision was about as inspired and original as casting John Wayne as a sheriff.

Griffith arrived on the set fresh from filming *Pacific Heights*, but the shooting of her *Bonfire* scenes had been delayed, resulting in her hanging around the set for nine full days before her first take. Her patience began to wear thin. When the camera finally rolled, Griffith's frightfully inept southern accent proved to be incomprehensible. Nearly one-hundred lines of dialogue would have to be rerecorded. (Why De Palma continued to insist she play the role of a *southern* dizzbrain as opposed to Griffith's by-the-numbers *Brooklyn* dizzbrain remains a mystery. The southern angle adds nothing vital to the story, and Griffith's accent is so phony, not to mention the fact that it comes and goes, that it distracts the audience.) Griffith also had another big surprise in store—or rather *two* big surprises. Midway through filming of her scenes, she underwent breast-enhancement surgery without notifying the production company. Fortunately, Griffith had not yet filmed her seminude scenes, so continuity was not the insurmountable problem De Palma feared it might be. As lovely as Griffith's newfound assets are to behold, one wishes she had spent the time and money on a few sessions at the Actor's Studio, as *Bonfire* would be just another in the long line of less than illustrious performances with which she has graced high-profile films.

The casting controversy did not end there. The pivotal supporting role of Justice Myron Kovitsky was still undecided. De Palma had auditioned a real-life Bronx judge, Burton Bennett Roberts, with good result, but it was decided he was not likable enough to win the sympathy of the audience. Walter Matthau agreed to take the part but outpriced himself at $1 million for eight days work. Alan Arkin was then cast but dropped before he even reached the set. (He was still paid his full $120,000 salary.) De Palma then went with the most logical choice to fill the role of the feisty Jewish Judge—Morgan Freeman! Yes, the distinguished black actor was hired for the job, and fast

Kim Catrall gives an all-too-brief performance as Sherman's spoiled wife, Judy. (Warner Bros.)

McCoy is arrested as the scandal unfolds (Warner Bros.)

rewrites had to be done to accommodate the change in race. (De Palma probably would have cast Woody Allen as "Malcolm X.")

Critics immediately jumped on De Palma for softening the screenplay by making the character, who plays an important role in the climactic, racially divisive trial, more sympathetic to blacks. Blacks don't fare well in Wolfe's novel, but that would be no problem; neither does anyone else. De Palma kept a straight face and answered his accusers: "I felt that visually it gave the story more balance. Having a black judge go after a black character like Reverend Bacon would eliminate a racial conflict that an audience might focus on if the judge were white, Jewish, Italian, or whatever." Cast at the last minute, however, Freeman barely had time to prepare for the role. He was scheduled to star in a live production of *The Taming of the Shrew* at the New York Shakespeare Festival in the very near future and seemed distracted by having to prepare for the play and the film. The

Sherman's worst nightmare comes true: incarcerated with the "commoners" (Warner Bros.)

vigorous speech Freeman gives at the end of the film was considered so weak that it was originally cut. It was later restored after test audiences seemed to think it enhanced the flow of the story.

If De Palma had problems dealing with Morgan Freeman's distractions, virtually everyone else on the set had to deal with Bruce Willis's ego. He traveled with an entourage, including *two* bodyguards to keep the unwashed public from his presence. Willis's plate was full, and he had to complete his scenes on schedule because he was due in Europe to begin filming *Hudson Hawk*, the bloated big-budget disaster-in-the-making that would make *Bonfire* look like *Citizen Kane*. Willis's voice-over had to be recorded in Rome, where production had already begun on *Hawk*. Then a crew had to be sent over a second time when the first recordings were deemed unusable.

Other troubles also plagued the production. A judge in New Jersey caused a legal hassle when he refused to let filmmakers shoot at the Essex County Courthouse in Newark for fear of offending the predominantly black community. Local officials filed suit, claiming the judge had no constitutional right to deprive the city of the $250,000 Warners offered to use the facility. Ultimately, most of the courtroom scenes were filmed in the Queens County Courthouse in New York. Ironically, the one ambitious sequence filmed at the Essex County Courthouse—an elaborate scene, which didn't appear in the novel, in which Sherman literally duels with the paparazzi and an unruly mob—ended up on the cutting-room floor.

Shooting began in April 1990 in New York City. While the film includes location shots of many Manhattan landmarks, certain places were verboten to De Palma because of the bashing they received in the novel—among them, the Metropolitan Museum of Art. The seventy-five day shooting schedule included lavish interiors constructed on soundstages in L.A. The stunning panoramic view of Manhattan which opens the film was shot by De Palma's protégé, Eric Schwab, from atop the Chrysler Building at a cost of

Melanie Griffith is miscast—but stunningly so—as Maria (Warner Bros.)

$150,000. Not all sections of New York fared as well. True to the novel, the film's depiction of the South Bronx is that of Dante's Inferno—a wretched wasteland in which human life is valued less than an old tire. Bronx politicians demanded that the film carry a disclaimer, complete with a featurette showing the advancement of the community in recent years. In a rare display of political incorrectness, the producers and studio compromised with a generic one-sentence disclaimer buried at the end of the film and a $10,000 donation to a Bronx charity.

Throughout all of this chaos, Tom Hanks tried mightily to perfect his characterization of Sherman McCoy. He visited the bond trading room at Merrill Lynch and had lunch with the company's most successful trader in order to gain a better understanding of the business. Hanks strove to retain a personal aspect to the story amid the sweeping production values. He recalled, "The only thing about *Bonfire* was how huge it was. Every day there was something massive about it—the set, the number of people, the number of script pages you were doing, the shot itself. You weren't intimidated by the size of it all. But sometimes you wondered. Is this stuff all going to fit together?"

Hanks began to become distressed by the logistics of the film: "From the very first moment when anything was announced about the movie, we couldn't make a decision without it being second-guessed and pulled apart. We couldn't go in a direction that wasn't analyzed every step of the way. But without question, I don't think we did the best condensed version of Mr. Wolfe's thousand-page novel. . . ."

The Bonfire of the Vanities is in its own way a unique achievement. One would think that consider-

can be said is that his Sherman McCoy is one of the least interesting characters he has ever portrayed, serving only as a catalyst for events involving the eccentrics around him. The inept performance of Melanie Griffith makes Hanks's look like Olivier doing King Lear. With her previously mentioned Southern accent and squeaky voice, one can say that the only redeeming quality of Griffith's screen time is the ample display of her store-bought breasts.

Bruce Willis comes off almost as badly. Although the role of Fallow was originally slated to be a periph-

Judge White (Morgan Freeman) delivers one of his moral diatribes to Sherman, prosecutor Larry Kramer (Saul Rubinek), and defense attorney Tom Killian (Kevin Dunn). (Warner Bros.)

ing the amount of talent and money involved, there had to be many redeeming values. Alas, there are some, but they are few and far between. This makes it one of those films that is so bad that the story behind the making of the production is far more interesting than anything on-screen. Virtually everyone is at his or her worst here, although some escape with a bit more dignity than others.

Tom Hanks emerges unscathed. Although the consensus was that he was miscast, he has no embarrassing sequences to suffer through. The worst that

eral one, upon Willis's casting the script was quickly rewritten to expand his sequences. Big mistake, considering his limited acting chops. Alas, he is on-screen a good deal of the time but is given absolutely nothing to do except stumble around and mumble. His few scenes with Hanks look pretentious because they appear to be exactly what they are—last-minute attempts to at least get the two stars in a few frames together. Willis does not help matters by giving one of the worst performances as a drunk ever committed to film. He's like Foster Brooks with a lampshade on his head. The intelligence level of *Bonfire* is demonstrated by the fact that—lest we don't get the point that his staggering on-screen indicates he is a down-and-out alcoholic—Willis gets to wear a lumpy old hat.

Willis's somnambulistic performance contrasts with the overacting of the supporting cast. F. Murray Abraham, usually one of the best actors around, gives an embarrassingly manic portrayal as a power-hungry D.A. (a thinly disguised Rudy Giuliani). The man who won an Oscar for *Amadeus* is here forced to scream an endless barrage of obscenities that are nei-

John Hurt delivers at the beginning of *Heaven's Gate*. With all this ham on-screen, the premiere should have been held at Hickory Farms. Only John Hancock as the Reverend Bacon delivers any sense of genuine fun. His impersonation of that real-life publicity hound Rev. Al Sharpton generates the film's only laughs, but he is on view only fleetingly.

Technically, *Bonfire* is a joy to behold. The magnificent sets and production design almost make the film look better than it is, and Vilmos Zsigmond's superb cinematography far outclasses anything that

Sherman loses his cool and waves a rifle at his party, only to be mocked by the partygoers. (Warner Bros.)

ther inspired, funny, or even necessary. Abraham had the good sense to have his name taken off the credits due to a billing dispute. The move turned out to be a blessing in disguise for him, as he is the only perpetrator of this mess not identified on-screen. Canadian actor Saul Rubinek—so good in *Unforgiven* and other films—is equally annoying as Abraham's assistant D.A. Morgan Freeman is powerful in the film's final moments, but his corny tirade about moral responsibility ranks as the most boring and least effective cinematic speech since that rambling talk

happens in the story. On the other side of the technical spectrum is Dave Grusin's surprisingly inappropriate musical score, which resembles that of a sixties sitcom.

On the eve of its release, Warner executive Mark Canton boasted, "In my ten years at Warner Brothers, *Batman* was my big commercial hit, and this will be my big artistic hit. . . . It's a great movie, and I'm proud to be involved in it." Not exactly a clairvoyant, Canton is probably still sporting a Mondale for President button. When *Bonfire* opened

127

in December 1990 the grosses were soft. From there, the decline was rapid and irreversible. Word of mouth was uniformly negative, and the film gained the distinction of being cited as the biggest box-office bomb in years. No one in the cast would put *Bonfire* high on their resumés, and although Hanks emerged relatively unscathed compared to his costars, he still had to endure stinging comments from those critics who usually praised his work. Only Tom Wolfe could be philosophical, telling the press, "The great thing about selling a book to the movies is that nobody blames the author." By April of 1991, the film was already on home video—an astonishingly short time frame for such a major production. Surprisingly, it fared well in this medium.

In the wake of the *Bonfire* disaster, Hanks made an important career decision: He severed relations with his longtime representative, the William Morris Agency, and jumped aboard the Creative Artists Agency (CAA) bandwagon. Headed by legendary dealmaker Mike Ovitz, CAA had become *the* agency for the hottest talent. Hanks insisted the move had nothing to do with the *Bonfire* fiasco and that he had

been contemplating switching to the superagency for quite some time. Despite the change in representation, for once work was the last thing on Hanks's mind. He took a nineteen-month hiatus from filmmaking to spend time with wife Rita Wilson. The couple had their first child together, Chester, during this period. Hanks told the press, "I've made fifteen movies since 1983, and that's too much." He later added, "I needed a break from the industry. And the industry needed a little less of me for a while. How many times can you see somebody on yet another magazine cover? Plus, with me its always the same story: I'm an average guy, down to earth, kinda quirky, blah, blah, blah. Please destroy that myth. Please feel free. That's why I grew this goatee—so people would fear me."

Over the years, *Bonfire*—like all megabudget bombs—has become the subject of much interest in film circles. Just as *Heaven's Gate* spawned the best-selling *Final Cut*, detailing the road to ruin initiated by the filmmakers and studio brass, so, too, did *Bonfire* with *The Devil's Candy*, a well-received chronicle of the *Bonfire* debacle that is must reading for anyone with interest in how a well-intentioned project can go so hopelessly wrong.

In a 1995 interview, Hanks admitted, "I probably get asked about *Bonfire of the Vanities* more than any other film because it was so expensive and such a disaster for everyone involved in

Director-producer Brian DePalma (*second from right*) sets up a shot with Hanks. (Warner Bros.)

what I like to remember as 'that highly anticipated motion picture event.' The natural pattern for anybody in any creative industry or art is that the commercial successes come and go, and the emotional successes do, too."

Reviews

"A misfire of a thousand manities. A strained social farce in which the gap between intent and achievement is yawningly apparent. Ultralavish production has the money, cast and best-seller name value to attract a crowd initially, but down-beat reviews and word-of-mouth will surely put a damper on box-office prospects of Warner Brothers' $45 million-plus project. . . . *The satire is about as socially incisive as a* Police Academy *entry . . . Seeing the normally adept and appealing [Hanks] put through the wringer here will prove few people's idea of fun."*

—"Cart.," *Variety*

"While De Palma has stoked a broad and billowing comedy—one which coughs up a lot of belly laughs—it's one that will leave fans of Wolfe's scathing social satire choking and heaving with disapproval. Bonfire will be quickly extinguished at the box office."

—Duane Byrge, *Hollywood Reporter*

"[A] gross, unfunny movie. . . . Mr. De Palma and Michael Cristofer . . . have made a series of wrong decisions that have the effect of both softening the satire and making it seem more uncomfortably racist than the Wolfe original. . . . The casting isn't ideal. Mr. Hanks comes off best as the bewildered

A fabricated scene which would afford the two lead actors more screen time together (Warner Bros.)

victim. He's nobody's idea of a prototypical Yale man, which is the way he's described in the novel, but he's a good comic actor. . . . More surprising is what seems to be the film's technical flaws. There are times when dialogue sounds disconnected from the speaker, as if post-synchronized. Some scenes are awkwardly staged, including the initial confrontation in the Bronx. In one brief love scene, Miss Griffith's body appears to be so perfect as to look surgically reconstructed. Perhaps not, but The Bonfire of the Vanities *is so wildly uneven that everything in it seems open to question."*

—Vincent Canby, *New York Times*

"De Palma's high-decibel burlesque wipes out the sets and the actors. Instead of satire, he gives us rabid lampoon, each actor mugging wildly as the camera spins, circles, dips, climbs, and ducks, trying desperately to find an unusual angle to shoot from. Nothing is observed, everything is hyped."

—David Denby, *New York* magazine

17

Radio Flyer

Columbia, 1992

"I always thought Radio Flyer *walked a dangerous line and if they did it right they'd touch on something grander than just a period piece about child abuse. But I don't think anybody could get past that. Of all the movies I've done that didn't do well, I was surprised at the vehemence of critics who said, 'You can't do that. You can't make a movie like that on this subject matter. You have to present it in a constantly hideous fashion.'"*

Cast
Lorraine Bracco (*Mary*); John Heard (*Daugherty*); Adam Baldwin (*The King*); Elijah Wood (*Mike*); Joseph Mazzello (*Bobby*); Ben Johnson (*Geronimo Bill*); Tom Hanks (Unbilled, *Mike as adult*).

Credits:
Director: Richard Donner; producer: Lauren Shuler-Donner; executive producers: Michael Douglas, Rich Beieber, and David Mickey Evans; screenplay: David Mickey Evans; director of photography: Laszlo Kovacs; production designer: J. Michael Riva; art director: David Frederick Klassen; editor: Stuart Baird; music: Hans Zimmer. Running time: 114 minutes.

Director Richard Donner between takes with his stars (Columbia Pictures)

Of all the films with which Tom Hanks has been associated, none has been as disastrously received as *Radio Flyer*, with the possible exception of course, of *Bonfire of the Vanities*. Ironically, like *Bonfire,* this movie was considered one of the hottest properties in Hollywood. During the course of development and production, however, it would gain a reputation—still intact today—as one of the most excessive and misguided motion pictures of recent years. Few films have been as savaged by the critical establishment; and yet, seen from an objective vantage point, *Radio Flyer* has much to recommend it.

The much publicized story behind this project appeared to be one of the entertainment industry's true overnight successes. Writer David Mickey Evans wrote the script for *Radio Flyer* "on spec," meaning he had not been commissioned by a studio. From the moment it began to circulate among the "players" in Tinseltown, the buzz was that this was the hottest script around. The story is an offbeat combination of fantasy and ugliness as reflected in the eyes of a man named Mike (Tom Hanks), who is seen in the opening sequence telling a story about his childhood to his

The opening scene in which an adult Mike reveals to his sons the fate of their uncle Bobby (Columbia Pictures)

young sons. The strange tale begins when Mike (played as a boy by Elijah Wood) and his brother Bobby (Joseph Mazzello) are in grade school. Their father deserts their mother, Mary (Lorraine Bracco), and the family heads west to make a new life.

Upon arriving in a small town in northern California, the family settles in for a spartan but

A young Mike (Elijah Wood), his little brother, Bobby (Joseph Mazzello), and best friend Shane in happier times, before the King arrives (Columbia Pictures)

happy existence—until Mary marries her new beau, nicknamed "the King" (Adam Baldwin). The King is a man of violent mood swings and, unbeknownst to Mary, ends his daily drinking bouts by habitually beating little Bobby. Not wanting to worry their mother, who works day and night to help support the family, the boys find solace in their fantasy world. Inseparable, and unaccepted by the other kids in the community, they have a bond necessitated by their mutual need for survival. When Bobby's beatings become intolerable, the boys plan a daring course of action. Bobby, who is obsessed with his dream of someday becoming a great pilot, begins to construct a fantastic flying machine with the aid of his brother. The boys work for weeks on the contraption, which is constructed from a Radio Flyer red wagon and common household items. Their strategy is for Bobby to launch his "plane" from atop a towering precipice on a nearby hill in the belief that he will be able to fly away from his miserable situation at home. The brothers are inspired by a local lad who attempted the same many years ago and ended up crippled but became a legend. The film builds to a chaotic climax when Bobby narrowly escapes the pursuing King by launching his craft and successfully flying away. In a brief epilogue, however, Mike informs his sons that all history takes on the prejudices of the person telling it. Did Bobby indeed fly away and roam the world, sending postcards to his famliy from exotic locations? Or do the tears in Mike's eyes reveal a more sobering truth that he is trying to convince himself never occurred?

The unconventional screenplay became the subject of a bidding war in Hollywood. Eventually, Stonebridge Entertainment—owned in part by actor-producer Michael Douglas—paid David Mickey Evans the (then) staggering sum of $1.1 million, along with a promise to let the

The boys keep the news of Bobby's being abused from their hard-working mom, Mary (Lorraine Bracco). (Columbia Pictures)

unknown writer make his directorial debut with this film. The terms raised eyebrows, even in an industry which makes huge gambles on a daily basis. Yet, for Evans, *Radio Flyer* seemed to be the vehicle to establish him as the biggest symbol of the Horatio Alger syndrome since Sylvester Stallone rose from being an unknown to a major industry force with *Rocky* in 1976.

However, at this point, the tale of *Radio Flyer* would become almost as disheartening as the events depicted in Evans's screenplay. After seeing a few days' footage which director Evans had shot, Michael Douglas showed his displeasure by summarily firing him. Production was halted until Richard Donner took over the director's chair. While Donner was a well-known talent, having helmed such action/adventure hits as *Superman* and *Lethal Weapon*, his being placed in charge of a sensitive drama was also a major gamble. Donner's enthusiasm for the story was unmistakable, however. He had urged Warner Bros. to bid on the script and had initially been disappointed when Stonebridge and Columbia Pictures won the rights to the story and hired Evans to direct.

Donner, who received a guarantee of $5 million to direct, also had the clout to have his wife, Lauren Shuler-Donner, named as producer. He explained his interest in the project: "The first time I read the script, it was obviously a very special story. I saw it through the eyes of a child, from a point of view way down there close to the ground. I realized that to children the world still has magic, and if I could see a film through their eyes, I could live their magic, and I could make it work. From that moment on, I knew I had to direct this picture."

The Donners succeeded in casting two remarkable child actors as Mike and Bobby, Elijah Wood and Joseph Mazzello, both under ten years old. Richard Donner said of their screen test "When we got Elijah and Joey together, I just looked at Lauren and said, 'Stop right now,' because we'd found what we were looking for. The chemistry was simply phenomenal. It grew and developed throughout the picture. They became like real brothers—the teasing, the loving, the pain, the happiness."

Shooting began in October 1990 in the town of Novato, California, a suburban location that would have to look as it had in 1970. (Donner had opted to move the story's location from Los Angeles for obvious logistical reasons.) Production designer J. Michael Riva (grandson of Marlene Dietrich) explained that the background and atmosphere were not as important as the events happening in the household of Mike and Bobby. "The neighborhood shouldn't be something that stands out. There should be a sameness, a kind of uniformity that conveys the haziness of detail in memory. The story is told in a reflective narrative. In trying to visually set that tone, you want only the most important elements to be prominent, just like they are in memory. The background is unexceptional, the people, the pets, the clubhouse in the backyard—those are the things that stand out in childhood."

After six weeks of shooting, production moved to Sonora, heart of the gold rush country and the site of many western films. For nearly two weeks, Donner shot at night on a hill overlooking the town's tiny airport. Here the giant rock (called the Wishing Spot by the boys in the film) was constructed for several key sequences. It was also here that a ramp was constructed from which Bobby takes off on his death-defying flight on the Radio Flyer. The distance from the base of the ramp to the landing area was one-hundred-thirty feet, including a jump of fifty feet over the top of a barn. Cushions had to be placed all over the ground when stuntman Doc Charbonneau took the ride of his life, peddling at a speed of twenty-five miles an hour.

Production then moved to Sony Studios in Culver City, where the Novato neighborhood and the interior of the boy's home were re-created. Here a replica of the Wishing Spot was also built for special effects and close-ups. Donner used an F/X process called Zor Optics, which he first utilized in directing *Superman* (1978). Due to production delays, the firing of Evans as director, and budgetary excesses, the film finally crawled to completion, at a cost of $45 million—an astonishing $31 million over the original estimate.

The industry was abuzz with speculation as to how such a modest story could have ended up costing more than *Apocalypse Now*. The anonymous chairman of a major studio told the *New York Times*, "The argument really is not so much about the making of the movie; it's an important subject that television handles well. The argument is really about its cost. It's one thing if you have a $10 million movie that doesn't work. It's another thing if you have a $40 million movie that's a disaster. There won't be any foreign sales on this. The video market is zilch for this kind of film. It's very sad and very frightening how everyone misjudged." Compounding the problem was that the film did not boast a single bankable star, since Tom Hanks insisted on no billing.

By the time *Radio Flyer* was released in early 1992, its failure was all but assured. The movie was virtually impossible to market—should the studio stress the social problem angle of child abuse or the whimsical fantasy element? The movie was too tragic to sell to family audiences and too fantastic to be a successful tearjerker. The result was an ad campaign that stressed nothing. There were some indications that the film was a tale about two boys growing up, but that was about the only clue to the story line save for the incomprehensible image of Bobby's fantastic flying machine in the clouds. *Radio Flyer* did not even receive the dignity of being a high-profile flop, like *Howard the Duck*. It opened to little fanfare, and the studio itself seemed to give the film little more than a cursory publicity campaign. By the time the first weekend's virtually nonexistent grosses were reported, *Radio Flyer* had crash-landed. After a brief run in theaters, the film proved the naysayers right by becoming a similar "nonevent" on video. Coincidentally or not, Columbia Studios head Frank Price was fired after production on *Radio Flyer* had staggered to completion.

How, then, does the movie fare on its own terms? Well, this is a problematic film from a number of different standpoints. The combination of child abuse with a fantasy element never quite jells. Since most of Bobby's beatings take place off camera, we can never truly relate to his dilemma. It is also inconceivable that two boys subjected to these daily horrors would opt not to tell their mom simply because they don't want to upset her. Adding to the problem is Donner's decision to make the King little more than a shadowy presence with no personality. He is filmed in brief glimpses and through fast cuts. Only the beginning scene, in which he takes the boys fishing and turns from a friendly sort of guy into a sadistic brute, do we have any interest in him as a person. There are also some heavy-handed attempts to link the King's excesses with his drinking. Donner shows us the King reaching into a refrigerator for a cold brew so many times that we think subtitles will appear saying, "He's drinking beer again. This will make him drunk and violent. Drunkenness, violence. Get it?"

Yet the film has many merits which the critics completely overlooked. Both Elijah Wood and Joseph Mazzello give amazing performances that should have received far more recognition than they did. Whatever flaws are apparent in the rest of the film, the boys' acting skills are not among them. The adult cast is basically window dressing, although Lorraine Bracco is convincingly loving but naive in her concern for the boys. (Rosanna Arquette was originally scheduled to play the role.) There is also a brief appearance by the late Ben Johnson, looking as fit as he did in those old John Ford westerns, and he gives his sequence a sense of dignity and fascination which the rest of the film lacks.

The main problem with *Radio Flyer* is the uneasy blending of fantasy and real-life drama. This is never more apparent than in the scene in which Mike imagines he is talking with a buffalo the boys had seen previously at a remote tourist attraction. The pathetic and lonely animal haunts the boys in a moving sequence in which they first encounter him. However, when the beast returns in Mike's dream, the film depicts it as a gigantic animal that speaks English like John Houseman. The scene is meant to be inspiring and touching but comes off looking goofy and unintentionally hilarious. Likewise, the climax of the film initially seems out of place. We watch Bobby successfully fly off atop his weird contraption. Taken at face value, it seems as though the film has deteriorated into a totally unbelievable fantasy. At second glance, however, we begin to suspect that in reality he suffered a more tragic fate. This ends the story on an intriguing and thought-provoking note, since the script refuses to tie up all the loose ends in a neat package. If only the rest of the film had been so bold.

Tom Hanks appears briefly in the first few minutes of the film and again in the movie's epilogue. However, his narration runs throughout the course of the entire movie.

Radio Flyer is a misguided, wholly uncommercial film whose intentions are far more impressive than its execution. However, the movie has its moments and can at least lay claim to being something that most contemporary films are not—a completely original concept.

To help Bobby escape, the boys begin fashioning a fantastic flying machine. (Columbia Pictures)

Bobby and Mike ready the Radio Flyer for launching. (Columbia Pictures)

135

Reviews

"One of those infrequent and embarrassing efforts of a perfectly adequate Hollyood director to make the kind of offbeat movie for which he has no aptitude at all. That's the only way to explain why this tale of childhood magic winds up being so bleak and gross. . . . [The film] is both too literal and too fanciful. There may have been a good film in David Mickey Evans's screenplay, but it is unrealized by Mr. Donner. . . . Dealing with this delicate material, he is like someone trying to thread a needle while wearing boxing gloves."

—Vincent Canby, *New York Times*

"A film one would like to like more. David Mickey Evans' screenplay about two boys' fantasy of escape from an abusive stepfather is sometimes moving but too often distant and literal-minded. Richard Donner's direction of a difficult subject matter is sensitive but lacks the delicacy François Truffaut brought to such material. . . . Pic, however, has a feeling of distance reinforced by some major screenplay gaps and by heavy-handed narration by Tom Hanks. As the grown-up

Does the tear in Mike's eye hint at what really became of his brother? (Columbia Pictures)

Wood, Hanks bookends the film by telling his own sons what happened to their uncle. But Hanks's crushingly literal voiceover undermines the children's point of view the film strives for, and it seems like a crutch for filmmakers all too aware of narrative problems in their film. . . . Hanks' presence finally pays off at the end, as his mournful expression suggests that his fantastic tale is his way of dealing with the unspeakable truth of what actually happened to his brother. If all of [the film] had been as good as the last, it really could have soared."

—Joseph McBride, *Variety*

A League of Their Own

Columbia, 1992

"It was brand-new turf for me. Because it wasn't the romantic lead of the movie. It was a big fat guy in the back, which actually was a blast to do. And it opened up a lot of avenues for me."

Cast

Tom Hanks (*Jimmy Dugan*); Geena Davis (*Dottie Hanson*); Madonna (*Mae Mordabito*); Lori Petty (*Kit Keller*); Jon Lovitz (*Ernie Capadino*); David Strathairn (*Ira Lowenstein*); Garry Marshall (*Walter Harvey*); Megan Cavanaugh (*Marla Hooch*); Rosie O'Donnell (*Doris Murphy*); Bill Pullman (*Bob Hinson*).

Credits

Executive producer/director: Penny Marshall; producers: Robert Greenhut and Elliot Abbott; coproducers: William Pace, Ronnie Clemmer, and Joseph Hartwick; screenplay: Lowell Ganz and Babaloo Mandel, based on a story by Kim Wilson and Kelly Candaele; director of photography: Miroslav Ondricek; production designer: Bill Groom; editor: George Bowers; music: Hans Zimmer.
Running time: 128 minutes.

Ever since his first taste of success, Tom Hanks had mentioned in virtually every interview that his primary goal as an actor was to expand his horizons, playing complicated and challenging roles. By 1991, the "good guy" image which had originally served him so well seemed to be waning. Hanks had experienced at least one box-office disaster (*The Bonfire of the Vanities*) and the relatively disappointing performances of *Punchline*, *The 'burbs*, and *Joe Versus the Volcano*. Only *Turner & Hooch* was an unqualified hit, and it cast Hanks in the typical guy-next-door image he was trying to lose. Following *Bonfire*, Hanks took a nineteen-month sabbatical from the motion-picture business. "I had worked myself into a hole, and I also think there was a chance that the American public was gonna get so sick of looking at me. I'd been out there with a movie every spring and summer for a lot of years, and you can easily overstay your welcome. So it's good to go away for a while."

When Hanks did come back, it was in a dream role, portraying a character so unlike any other he had played that he could overlook the fact that it was a decidedly supporting part. The film was *A League of Their Own*, and it would elevate him back into the major leagues of top box-office performers. It covered one of the most fascinating, though lesser known,

Hanks's costars: Geena Davis (Dottie, *upper left*), Jon Lovitz (Ernie Capadino, *upper right*), and Madonna (Mae Mordabito, *lower left*) (Columbia Pictures)

chapters in American sports—the All-American Girls Professional Baseball League (AAGPBL). During World War II, so many baseball stars dropped their bats and mitts to enlist in the service that the team owners worried that the sport would be irreparably damaged by the time the war finally ended. They wanted to find a way to keep the public interested in baseball until the leagues could be brought back to full strength at war's end.

The solution was a league of women players. Initially scoffed at by sportswriters and the public, the owners persevered and began to develop professional teams. Scouts canvassed America looking for young women with exceptional athletic ability to pitch, catch, and swing a bat. Even the most seasoned scouts were impressed with the talent they found. The women were quickly organized into teams, and intense training periods were planned. For many of the ladies, this represented the first time they had left home. In those times it was considered shocking for women to live on the road, and the chosen few of the baseball league were initially the objects of scorn and

derision. Their games initially drew so few fans that the league was nearly disbanded.

Gradually, however, word got out that there was more than a bit of excitement to be found at the games. The public began to attend—out of curiosity at first and then, later, out of genuine interest. The ladies' teams began to develop their own stars with loyal followings. The fans admired their dedication. Just like their male counterparts, the women often traveled all night to play a doubleheader in excruciating heat on only a few hour's sleep. The league, which was originally supposed to be disbanded immediately after the war, lasted through 1954. It wasn't diminished interest which eventually killed the league: it was the lack of new players to replace those who retired. In the postwar years women returned to the more traditional place in the home and raised the generation that became known as the Baby Boomers.

The league remained virtually forgotten until 1988, when the Baseball Hall of Fame inducted the women players. The event received a good deal of media attention and spawned a reunion of the original players the following year, which was the subject of a documentary eventually seen by director Penny Marshall. Marshall was so fascinated by the subject that she began to explore the feasibility of making a film based on the league. She learned that a company called Longbow Productions was simultaneously developing its own film and had acquired the rights to the AAGPBL Players Association. Marshall and Longbow partners Bill Pace and Ronnie Clemmer decided to join forces on a film to be released through Columbia.

Marshall explained her motivation for pursuing the project. "It's a subject nobody knew about. A baseball league existed, but *nobody knew about it!* I felt I owed it to the league's real players to get this movie done. And because of my situation, I'm the only person who could do it. I didn't know what I was getting into. They say I work great under pressure. Well, no, I don't!"

Ironically, while Penny Marshall had succeeded in getting approval to do a film which would give the neglected women of baseball their due, there was an unspoken understanding among all of those involved that for the movie to be a commercial success, it needed the presence of a male star. This is one of the unfortunate situations in today's Hollywood. Despite all the lip service given to equality among actors and actresses, the bottom line is that few women have the box-office clout of their male counterparts. Screenwriters Lowell Ganz and Babaloo Mandell fashioned a script with a prominent but distinctly supporting role: the male manager of the Rockford Peaches team. The role would be that of a boozy, obnoxious, out-of-shape former big leaguer named Jimmy Dugan whose last chance in baseball is to manage the women's team. Against all expectations, the most enthusiastic candidate for the role was Tom Hanks.

Penny Marshall had worked with Hanks before on *Big*, one of the highlights of both their careers. Since then, Marshall had gained a reputation as a world-class director, and had recently won acclaim for the Robin Williams/Robert De Niro drama *Awakenings*. Although she had great respect for Hanks, she was not certain he was the man to play Jimmy Dugan. "He wanted the role, but I wasn't sure he could do it. Not because of his acting ability but

because the character wasn't supposed to be cute. We had to make him less attractive, and he ended up eating his way through half of Louisiana." She later added, "My only concern was making him look not so cute so that a whole team of girls didn't have a crush on their coach. I think he saw it as a role that, although it wasn't a lead, you were happy every time you saw him. There was no ego involved with him. It was never: 'I need more scenes.' It was: 'Do you need me anymore?' And he would go off and amuse the extras, trying to hit the ball through the hole in the scoreboard. He was happy every day just to go out and have batting practice. I think he liked what the role was about."

Indeed, Hanks was ecstatic with the role, for it represented a character not only based on an actual person but someone who was the antithesis of his usual image: "The character was written much older, but then there's got to be a better explanation of why he is where he is. I'm not that old. I should be in the war— what happened? That's when we worked up the concept of him blowing his knee out. That's why he's a 4-F, why he should still be playing and isn't. Then it made sense for me to do it. . . . My character is based

Team photo of the Rockford Peaches and their manager (Columbia Pictures)

140

"I wanted to be able to play a guy who had his entire life right there on his shirtsleeve, and you saw it as soon as you walked in the room." (Louise Goldman, Columbia Pictures)

on Jimmy Fox. He was a behemoth of a man who hit fifty-eight home runs, should have played longer than he did, drank himself out of the game, and was one of the first managers in the women's league. I talked to 'Pepper' Paire Davis, who was one of our advisers, and she says he wasn't as angry as my character. He was actually very friendly and treated the women well. He just slept through the games and drank on the bus rides, that's all. . . . It's the kind of role they never, ever give me. They just want me to be charming and youthful and naive. I don't want to go to the charm bank too many times. That likable thing gets to be a drag after a while because you have to be likable in every aspect of the movie. How do you have a fight with your wife in a movie and still be likable?"

Another rewarding aspect of the role was that it required Hanks to put on twenty pounds. He was delighted at playing "the heavy"—both literally and figuratively. "They put me in this really boxy suit for the first scene, and I looked like a behemoth. I had rolls of fat on my neck. And my fingers—I looked ham-fisted. When I saw it, I was *really* pleased. . . . the reason I got as heavy as I did was to give the audience a sense that this guy, when he was in shape, had really been an athlete. I don't want to have my skinny little wrists and pipe-cleaner neck. I didn't want him to look like me."

As for Hanks's working relationship with Marshall, he was quickly reminded that her penchant for endless retakes on *Big* exasperated him. "She can drive me crazy," he admitted, "making you do things one-hundred thousand times. But Penny's passive personality gives a collective feeling on the set instead of the idea that the director is God." Marshall admitted her methods could be frustrating to her actors: "My personality is, I whine. It's how I feel inside. I guess it's how I use being female, too. I touch a lot to get my way and say, 'Pleeaase, do it over here.' So it can be an advantage, the antidirector."

The most prominent characters in *A League of Their Own* are the fictitious sisters, Dottie and Kit, who leave the farm to pursue big league baseball. Dottie, the gorgeous model of femininity, frustrates her tomboyish younger sister, who is tired of living in her shadow. Their hostilities increase when they are separated by a trade and have to compete against each other in the league's World Series. The pivotal roles had to be played by strong actresses since—despite Hanks's top billing—they take up the lion's share of the screen time. Debra Winger and Lori Petty were signed to play Dottie and Kit, respectively. However, when Madonna joined the cast in a supporting role as a player with whom it was easy to get to first base, contractual problems developed with

Winger. One month before filming, she left the production.

Marshall found herself desperately in need of a lead actress. Ultimately, she approached Oscar winner Geena Davis to take the part of Dottie. Davis recalled: "I got this call, 'Can you come like *tomorrow* to Chicago and start this movie?'" When she arrived at the location, she discovered that the role would require an enormous amount of skill actually playing baseball. The other actresses had already been well into their training sessions. "The others had an advantage over me, but in the end I *slaughtered* them." In fact, Davis—like most of the other actresses—had never picked up a baseball bat in her life.

Like his female costars, Hanks endured months of extensive training on professional ball fields, which came somewhat easier to him. He also studied the L.A. Dodger coaches during actual games. The women seemed to be everywhere, trying desperately to learn America's favorite pastime before principal photography began. Lori Petty remembers: "You couldn't get into a batting cage in L.A. for two weeks. Famous, famous women were out there putting their quarters in." Petty explained the appeal of appearing in *A League of Their Own*: "These were fully developed female characters in a major motion picture. You didn't have to take your clothes off. You didn't have to wear some tiny little dress and hang on the arm of an action hero who's going out to kill a million people but you love him, anyway." (Ironically, Petty would soon accept the role of an action hero in the offbeat film *Tank Girl*.) Marshall was determined that her cast resemble baseball pros no matter how strenuous the training might be: "Batting was the easy part of it. They really had to look as if they could play ball. You can act attitude, but you can't act certain skills."

The training field knew no favorites. Rising comedic actress Rosie O'Donnell, not known for her svelte figure, laughingly remembers the first workout session: "The first time we got to the field, they said, 'Okay, two times around.' I said, 'Around what? Are you kidding me?' They were coaching me, holding doughnuts, saying, 'Come on, Rosie, you can do it!' It was a nightmare." O'Donnell's costar, "bad girl" Madonna, was also not to be pampered. She, like her fellow actresses, was training under the guidance of two of the actual players from the women's league. Terry Donohue and Pepper Davis. Donohue complained, "When we saw Madonna, we said, 'She throws like a girl,' Madonna tried sliding into second

base but just laid there. She did it all wrong, but you have to give her credit for trying. She batted until she had blisters on her hands."

Rounding out the cast were some talented relatives and friends of Marshall. Her brother Garry, the comedy director, gives a very good performance as the millionaire who funds the women's teams. Penny's daughter Tracy Reiner appears as Betty "Spaghetti" Horn, one of the players; her niece, Kathleen Marshall, plays "Mumbles Brockman;" David Lander, her former costar as "Squiggy" on *Laverne and Shirley*, has a supporting role, and old friend Jon Lovitz (Hanks's costar in *Big*) makes a hilarious appearance as a lowlife New York baseball scout.

Filming took place between July and October 1991, with most scenes shot in Chicago's Wrigley Field and in Evansville, Indiana, at Bosse Field. At the

latter location, there was so much interest by the locals in participating as extras that four-thousand people had to be turned away. Filming was anything but fun. Producer Elliot Abbott recalled some of the pitfalls experienced by the cast and crew and why the film went considerably over budget to a $50 million cost: "When you watch [baseball] on TV you've got about eight cameras and see what happens. If you want something specific to happen, if you want a ground ball to go up the middle, it may take a little while." Thousands of baseballs were ultimately utilized in the quest to get the right takes. Many cast members suffered minor injuries from getting "beaned" with balls, and several others passed out from playing in temperatures of up to 110 degrees. Hanks explained how the damage to actors was kept to a minimum: "Making the movie, there was stuff that we had to fake, and that was a drag. You had to use these sponge balls sometimes because they didn't

want some cameraman to get whacked on the head and conked out by a real ball." Still, Hanks kept his sense of humor and in the dugout would entertain the extras with impromptu puppet shows.

Off the set, Hanks enjoyed the atmosphere of Evansville. Unlike Madonna, who bad-mouthed the place as hopelessly dull, Hanks found the small-town surroundings a refreshing change of pace. "I've made movies in the equivalent of damp airplane hangars for three months at a time, so it was a pleasure to be out on the grass, with the open air, a place to sit down and diet root beer always handy. There was always somebody to talk to, always someplace to go play catch. It was a pleasure. I was there with my wife and my kids. We stayed in a beautiful house on five gorgeous acres with a pond. We loved the place, loved going to the Dairy Queen and getting a chocolate cone on Thursday nights."

About the only controversy Hanks caused were his comments which contradicted studio press releases that most of his female costars were now excellent baseball players in their own right. "No more than Superman could really fly," he quipped. "This absolutely required the magic of motion-picture making." However, he did concede that there were exceptions: "Rosie O'Donnell? Excellent player. Lori Petty became a fierce pitcher. Robin Knight is a baseball player, pure and simple. And Freddie Simpson is so authentic a player that she dipped Skoal."

A League of Their Own broke the standard rule in Hollywood that baseball-oriented films could not be major box-office successes. Mixed critical notices not withstanding, audiences embraced the movie immediately, and with good reason. This is a superb film on every level—filled with gentle comedy, wonderful atmosphere (you will swear it was actually filmed in the 1940s), and plenty of sentimentality. Penny Marshall may be a pain in the neck on the set, but few could argue that she is a director with terrific instincts. As she has proved time and again, she is also an actor's director and has the ability to showcase her cast at their very best.

Tom Hanks very much underplays his role as drunken Jimmy Dugan. Initially feeling that coaching a women's team is demeaning, Dugan gradually takes pride in his team and becomes a coach in every sense of the word. The role itself is a cliché, but Hanks is a joy to watch, and his periodic appearances inspire a good deal of anticipation. Refreshingly, there is no attempt to soft-pedal the character too much, and the growing affection between him and Dottie is all the more appealing because the script never takes the obvious road by providing the inevitable bed scene. Instead, Dottie remains devoted to her trusting husband, who ultimately returns from the service and joins her on the road. Hanks admitted that a love scene was planned for him and Geena Davis but was later cut: "I thought it was great that [the film] did nothing to adhere to the usual formulaic relationship between a guy and a woman. We actually did have a sexual relationship at one point, but they cut it out of the movie because they found it was much better without it. The story of my guy's side of it was that he respected Geena Davis's character, who proved she was a ballplayer. I thought that to stick with that was a cool thing."

Doris (Rosie O'Donnell) heads to the plate as Dugan flashes the signs. (Columbia Pictures)

A League of Their Own is a wonderful film. Whoever thought one would find a movie in which Madonna *avoids* upstaging those around her? (She does, in fact, contribute the hit song "This Used to Be My Playground" under final credits.) If there are scene-stealers, they'd probably be Geena Davis and Lori Petty as the warring sisters. Both actresses are terrific to watch, and their charisma negates the corny and obvious plot contrivance which has them facing off against each other for the final out of the World Series.

The film went on to gross over $100 million, making it an undisputed smash. A year after its release, Hanks said, "*League of Their Own* did an awful lot for me, and this is strictly from the crass business point of view. I had any number of people saying, 'What the hell are you doing?' It's not even your movie, you're just a guy passing through. Do you love Penny Marshall so much that you want to spend the summer and listen to her whine? Look what you could be doing!.... I could have done *Popo Goes to the Big Town* and *Oops. I Tripped on a Lawn Chair*. Things like that. I was looking for something to do different, and I think the message got out that he'll do anything. Which is a good thing. He'll get fat. He doesn't have to be the cute guy. He will cut his hair in an unattractive manner. He will be disgusting and sit there. He doesn't have to be the king of every scene that he is in. Well, that's a marvelous message to put out there."

Practical reasoning aside, Hanks did confess to the main reason he starred in *A League of Their Own*: "The whole reason I did this movie was because it was going to be a blast. Come on, play baseball all summer with a bunch of girls? Please! Help me. And get paid for it? Fine. I'm there. When do we start?"

Reviews

"A quick glance at the lineup suggests what one might expect from this comedy of baseball bonding bosom buddies. The agenda here is clearly along the lines of good-natured vignettes, smart one-liners and a healthy does of heartstring tugging.... Hanks, in another gem of a comic performance, is the drunken has-been with disgusting personal habits, reluctantly coaching the Rockford Peaches from a horizontal position

Dugan finally has something to cheer about when his team begins to contend for the championship.

until their abilities, natch, startle him into animation. . . . It's a mostly winning combination of sassy humor and sentiment, enlivened by some fun 'newsreel' recreations that catch the period flavor of a sport adopting show-biz tactics. . . ."

—Angie Errigo, *Empire* magazine (U.K.)

"Awash in sentimentality and manic energy but only occasionally bubbling over with high humor, [the movie] hits about .250 with a few RBI's but more than its share of strikeouts . . . Downside includes contrived plotting, obvious comedy and heart-tugging, some hammy thesping and a general hokiness. Pic is amicable enough to please mainstream summertime audiences, but the reported $50 million budget doesn't show on screen. . . . Adding a little testosterone to the recipe is Tom Hanks."

—Todd McCarthy, *Variety*

"Though big of budget, [this] is one of the year's most cheerful, most relaxed, most easily enjoyable comedies. It's a serious film that's lighter than air, a very funny movie that manages to score a few points for feminism in passing [Hanks's] Jimmy Dugan is a priceless, very graceful eccentric. With his work here, there can be no doubt that Mr. Hanks is now one of Hollywood's most accomplished and self-assured actors. Having put on weight for the role, he even looks jowly and over the hill."

—Vincent Canby, *New York Times*

"As a traditional male placed in a distinctly untraditional role, [Hanks] is given a lot of bluster and vulgarity to play. Too much of it. It forces him away from the reality he's also trying gamely to find. The same could be said of the whole picture. Energetic, full of goodwill and good feelings, it never quite attains the graceful nonchalance and self-confidence with which finely tuned athletes—and comedies—move to enchant us."

—Richard Schickel, *Time*

"A joyous mix of comedy, sports and drama. . . . Marshall works the large cast beautifully. . . . Tom Hanks gives his best performance in years. The movie's funniest scene shows Hanks trying to suppress his anger when Schram again misses the cutoff man during a game. And his exasperated line 'There's no crying in baseball!!!' has made it an instant classic. Hanks and Davis are convincing in their movie relationship, too—it's a rare platonic one, based on mutual respect. They're delightful, talking quietly on the team bus or squabbling by flashing dueling signs to a player up at bat."

—Cinebooks

145

19

Sleepless in Seattle

Tri-Star, 1993

> *"It's truly great not to be playing a guy who has some kooky thing happen to him. This isn't a guy who finds a suitcase full of money that the bad guys really want back. Absolutely no magic potions are injected. This is a guy who has lost his wife and has to deal with it. That's about as pure and clear and easily communicated a setup for a character as you're ever going to come across."*

Cast

Tom Hanks (*Sam Baldwin*); Meg Ryan (*Annie Reed*); Bill Pullman (*Walter*); Ross Malinger (*Jonah Baldwin*); Rosie O'Donnell (*Becky*); Gaby Hoffman (*Jessica*); Rita Wilson (*Suzy*); Rob Reiner (*Jay*) Victor Garber (*Greg*); David Hyde-Pierce (*Dennis Reed*).

Credits

Director: Nora Ephron; producer: Gary Foster; executive producers: Lynda Obst and Patrick Crowley; screenplay: Nora Ephron, David S. Ward, and Jeff Arch, from a story by Jeff Arch; director of photography: Sven Nykvist; production designer: Jeffrey Townsend; editor: Robert Reitano; music: Marc Shaiman.
Running time: 104 minutes.

Sam and Jonah Baldwin are reunited after Jonah takes drastic measures to unite his dad and Annie Reed. (Tri-Star Pictures)

After *A League of Their Own* hit a home run at the box-office, Tom Hanks entered "my modern era of filmmaking . . . because such self-discovery has gone on. My work has become less presentationally fake." Hanks's second entry in his "modern era" was *Sleepless in Seattle*, a modest but heartfelt love story with enough sentiment to make *Miracle on 34th Street* look like *The Wild Bunch*. With this film, Tom Hanks would graduate from being a popular screen presence to being one of the top box-office stars of recent years. The successful streak, reignited by *A League of Their Own*, was reinforced by *Sleepless in Seattle*, the first of an astonishingly successful series of movies which were both enormous critical and financial successes.

Like so many of his previous successes, *Sleepless in Seattle* was originally passed over by Hanks, who was not impressed by the original script. Nor did he consider himself appropriate for the leading role of Sam Baldwin, a Seattle-based, recently widowed husband left with the task of raising his young son, Joshua. Sam mourns day and night over his late wife, until Joshua arranges for him to open up during a nationally aired radio talk show. His expressions of pain are so heartfelt that they result in a deluge of eligible women bombarding the radio station with offers to marry him. Sam—a conventional kind of guy—is inspired to try dating again, but his son insists he meet with Annie Reed, who has written him from Baltimore expressing a desire to meet him. Sam dismisses the idea as ridiculous due to the geographic logistics. Annie also has mixed emotions. She feels in her heart that she belongs with the man she heard on the radio, but she is already engaged to be married.

and how so many of our notions about romance are based on the movies that we've seen. I have a sense that the romantic comedy was probably killed by sex. After all, the words *are* the sex of the romantic comedy. Now it's gotten trickier to show sex in movies. So what is there for people to do but go 'blah, blah, blah' at one another?"

Tom Hanks had also been given the script for consideration while it was in its first draft stage. "The script had actually passed my desk a while ago

As widower Sam Baldwin, who discovers his son, Jonah, is revealing his dad's sadness to millions of radio listeners (Tri-Star Pictures)

The whole affair comes to an astonishing conclusion when—straight out of *An Affair to Remember*—Sam and Joshua finally meet Annie atop the Empire State Building and the inevitable romance blossoms.

The link to *An Affair to Remember* was more than a coincidence. That classic 1957 Cary Grant–Deborah Kerr romantic drama is integral to the plot, and most of the characters are seen watching the movie at some point during the story. Writer-director Nora Ephron initially rejected the first draft of the script but was later impressed by a second one by David S. Ward, who based the screenplay on a story by Jeff Arch. She explained what attracted her to the property the second time around: "It had all these weird, wonderful ideas to play with, including all this stuff about what the movies do to your brain

in another incarnation. Looking at it again after Nora Ephron had rewritten it, all the potential manifested itself." He would later say, "I like that [my character's] motivation was immediately understandable. The guy is enmeshed in grieving, and no one has to work too hard in buying that attractive premise, as opposed to a guy who gets off the airline and picks up the wrong suitcase and it's full of uranium." He also found a certain poignancy and fascination with the script's premise that a chance encounter can change people's lives: "One of the fourteen themes that Nora is trying to examine with her work here is the concept of a second chance. The thing is, you always say, well, there's one person out there for you and eventually you'll cross paths. Well, [Sam Baldwin] did this at one point, and now he's sort of

Annie (Meg Ryan) dreamily listening to Sam's plight (Tri-Star Pictures)

gotta do it again. . . . It's just the human condition." Hanks later expanded on his feeling about fate affecting the most important decisions in our lives, saying, "That whole concept of the second chance is a powerful one to me. There's something wonderful about the notion that if you just hang around long enough, it will all come around. If you just continue to breathe in and breathe out, eat and pay your rent, things *will* eventually get better. You know, I'm thirty-six, and like all of us, I've been through a bunch. It's pretty much pantywaist stuff, nothing terrible. The relative aspect of the human condition being what it is, I've gotten my ass kicked a bunch of times by life. I mean, I've had any number of reasons to have sleepless nights myself, so that helped make *Sleepless in Seattle* a pretty real story to me."

Both Hanks and Ephron realized that the character of Annie Reed was every bit as prominent as that of Sam Baldwin. The role would require an actress talented enough to appear sympathetic even as she plans to dump her frumpy but lovable fiancé for the absurd notion of "snaring" a total stranger whom she has only heard on a radio show. Hanks and Ephron looked beyond the *failure* of *Joe Versus the Volcano* to see his on-screen chemistry with Meg Ryan. It was decided that she would be the ideal Annie Reed—a prospect which immediately appealed to Ryan. She had greatly enjoyed working with Hanks previously and recalled the first time he really impressed her as an actor: "I was a big fan of *Punchline*, and when I first met him, I was amazed how he puts people at ease. It's great for everyone on the set. He's able to find so much in a moment. He can have pathos and make you laugh. His work is very simple, and he always finds the strongest thing to do that says the most. There's something about him where you feel you can just fill in the blanks."

Ironically, the reteaming of Hanks and Ryan occurred in a film in which they share the screen only fleetingly because their characters live on opposite sides of the country. The challenge for the screenwriters and Nora Ephron as director was to fashion a genuine love story in which the two characters do not meet until the final moments of the film. Ephron explained her philosophy of how that obstacle could be overcome: "One of the themes of the movie is the global village. We all live in one place and it's called the United States and it's connected by airplanes, 800-number radio shows, the same jokes and statistics. By the time Tom and Meg are out on their respective piers sitting on their respective benches, you feel like it's a love scene even though they are three-thousand miles apart." Indeed, Ryan was going in one door in Baltimore while Hanks was going through another in Seattle. To seal a bond between the actors, Ephron actually had the same door transported between cities!

As an actor, Hanks was conscious that his character figured into only 50 percent of the screen time: "Since I was only in half the movie, I had to realize that the entire other side of the story was being made without me. It would not be fair for me to come in and say, 'Here's what this is, and here's what I'm doing,' because it may bump with the other work that's been done completely independently of me." Virtually the only time Hanks and Ryan saw each other was during the shots filmed in a studio. Meg Ryan sarcastically recalled how minimal their screen "reunion" time really was: "It left me thinking that it would be nice to work with Tom! We'd pass each other going through the studio door, and it would be a case of 'How's your half going?' 'Oh, great! How's your story coming along?'" She'd later describe *Sleepless in Seattle* by saying, "The whole movie is foreplay."

Nora Ephron said of Hanks to the press, "You don't direct him. You just sit there getting lucky. . . . He has almost no vanity. I think it's very manly." She later added to her feelings about Hanks's masculinity in an interview with *Entertainment Weekly*: "Tom is a man in a very attractive way. He is never going to spill his guts or confess in some intimate way to anybody. He's not like that. [In *Sleepless*] Tom is manly in a part that requires him to be tender—and lot of other things. . . . [He is] one of the few actors who can do tender and irritable and angry all at the same time . . . [he's] completely at home in his skin."

Meg Ryan echoed the compliments, saying, "He's an incredibly dedicated actor, a moral guy. . . . The appeal is about safety . . . What people see up there on the screen, that's him." She marveled at his "ability to deflect attention back onto whoever it is that he's working with."

Ephron couldn't resist the stale notion of comparing Hanks with Jimmy Stewart, but at least she put a novel twist on it: "Tom's got that boy-next-door thing that Jimmy Stewart had, as opposed to Cary Grant, who you knew you didn't live next door

to. But he's also very much his own original version of that. I wasn't old enough to know whether I wanted to have sex with Jimmy Stewart, but I do think that people want to have sex with Tom Hanks." Certainly good news for Mr. Hanks.

As usual, Hanks looked at his personal life to gain inspiration for his character's traits and actions. "My own kids stir up plenty of emotions. But you can only mine these things so many times. I'm running out of references in my own life. I've got to get some more stuff!" One influence from his own life was the presence of his wife, Rita Wilson, in a supporting role, as Sam Baldwin's sister. Because the film concentrates on the influence *An Affair to Remember* has on all the characters, Wilson encouraged Hanks to watch the movie. Like his on-screen alter ego Sam Baldwin, Hanks scoffed at the idea of watching the tearjerker. Wilson recalled, "I asked Tom to watch it with me. He looked at me like *Yeah, I'll be right in— not!* He came in at the end, when I was wiping my eyes. I tried to be pretty objective about the movie, but it's manipulative. I cried, yeah. Anyway, I wasn't sobbing profusely." The battle between the sexes over the merits of *An Affair to Remember* inspired one of the films funniest moments, in which Hanks and his brother-in-law mock the tearjerker by sobbing over "their" sentimental favorite: *The Dirty Dozen.* (Curiously, Meg Ryan takes the traditional male attitude toward the film in real life, calling it "a terrible movie. It's a movie about female masochism.")

Criticisms of *An Affair to Remember* aside, *Sleepless* is equally shameless in its unabashed sentimentalism. It's virtually impossible not be moved by the story, particularly in the scenes between Hanks and his on-screen son, wonderfully played by Ross Malinger. The sensitivity of the sequences in which Hanks tries to explain to the boy about the qualities which attracted him to his mother are beautifully written and enacted, especially when Malinger realizes, almost with a sense of panic, that his memories of his mom are beginning to fade.

To offset the sobriety of the Hanks-Malinger scenes, the script regularly shows us the dilemma faced by Meg Ryan's character. She is trying desperately to convince herself that she is madly in love with her hypochondriac boyfriend. Amazingly, it never seems to strain credibility that this highly stable woman would throw away her relationship on a

Annie and Becky (Rosie O'Donnell) watch *An Affair to Remember* for the umpteenth time, dreaming that true love may someday come their way. (Tri-Star Pictures)

whim to pursue a man she overheard on the radio. Ryan is one of the most watchable actresses on-screen today, and her ability to alternate between sensitivity and physical comedy makes her performances always delightful to watch. Here she is at her peak, and she carries her scenes with no less conviction than Hanks does his.

The supporting cast is particularly good in *Sleepless in Seattle*. Bill Pullman gives a gem of a comedic performance as Ryan's nice but drab fiancé,

Sam learns from his friend Jay (Rob Reiner) that dating has changed dramatically since Sam's been out of circulation. (Tri-Star Pictures)

That fateful moment atop the Empire State Building when Sam and Annie's eyes first meet (Tri-Star Pictures)

and the script refreshingly fails to vilify him to justify Ryan's mad obsession for Hanks. If there is a villain in the piece, it is Ryan's character, who rather bluntly breaks off her engagement to pursue Hanks to the top of the Empire State Building. Rob Reiner steps out from behind the camera for an infrequent acting stint as Hanks's best friend. It's a very amusing performance, particularly when he warns Hanks about the pitfalls of getting back into the singles scene. (Hanks is so out of touch that he confuses the dessert Tiramasu with a sexual act he fears he will not know how to perform.)

The centerpiece of the film is not the Hanks-Ryan relationship but the Hanks-Malinger relationship. The two actors bring the audience on a roller-coaster ride from laughter to tears. As a director, Nora Ephron knows how to manipulate the audience. She fills the screen with classic love songs from the likes of Jimmy Durante and Louis Armstrong, along with Victor Young's memorable "When I Fall in Love," and has cinematographer Sven Nykvist shoot Seattle in such an alluring way that it appears to resemble Shangri-la. The tactics work, as it's tough at times to keep a dry eye.

Only the ending of *Sleepless in Seattle* sacrifices logic for sentiment. We are asked to believe that little Joshua can connive his way onto a plane to New York, where he hopes to force a meeting between his dad and Annie atop the Empire State Building. Hanks follows in hot pursuit on another plane when all he had to do was notify the airline to detain Joshua and return him to Seattle, which would have made for a dull, unromantic ending. Instead, the kid arrives in the Big Apple and finds his way around as though he were Ratso Rizzo. By the time Hanks arrives, however, it becomes clear that biting realism is not what Ephron had in mind. The inevitable meeting between Hanks and Ryan is guaranteed to bring a lump to your throat as you gladly toss away any complaints about the lack of logic.

Sleepless in Seattle was released in the summer of 1993 and quickly became known as the sleeper of the year, ultimately grossing $126 million (despite opening against *Jurassic Park*). Ephron remains puzzled by the film's reputation as a surprise hit, claiming, "We did show it early to a couple of key people, but the main thing, which was done very artfully, was that we had a through-the-roof sneak, news of which somehow leaked instantaneously in the trades. At the same time, [studio personnel] made the movie seem like a sleeper, even though from the time the movie first sneaked, there was nothing particularly sleeperish about the movie. Even the title *Sleepless* was as close as you can get to the word sleeper."

Whether the film was a sleeper or not is irrelevant. What is undisputed is that this became *the* "date movie" of the year, with parallels to the on-screen character's reactions to *An Affair to Remember*. Guys tolerated the sentiment, while girls cried their eyes out. What was unanimous was the praise heaped on Tom Hanks by audiences and critics alike. He had finally escalated to a serious romantic leading man, and he had nary a suitcase of uranium to have to contend with. The movie had such an impact that it resulted in a groundswell of interest in the original *An Affair to Remember*. Indeed, even today videos of the fifties tearjerker sell countless copies due to being immortalized in *Sleepless in Seattle*. And the soundtrack exposed young viewers to the charms of Durante, Armstrong, and others to such a degree that the film spawned *two* soundtrack albums of romantic ballads from days gone by and even returned Durante to the Top Ten pop charts briefly despite the fact that he died in 1980.

Reviews

"*The hippest, frankest and funniest date movie around. . . . In his best work since* Big, *Hanks gives a classic romantic comedy performance, investing the role with sweetness, humor and genuine gravity. Hanks is sensational, but he would have been less so without Ryan , who reacts to Sam's words with a vulnerability that breaks down the cynicism in Annie and the audience; she is wonderfully endearing. In* Sleepless, *[Ephron] breaks your heart without making you feel like a jerk. As date movies go, that's the ultimate compliment.*"

—Peter Travers, *Rolling Stone*

"*[A] sweet but perilously thin love story. . . . The funniest lines and most touching scenes are all near the end. To fill the dead time, director Ephron shamelessly relies on her nostalgia-drenched pop soundtrack to work up feelings that aren't on the screen. For long stretches, this feels like a morose VH-1 video. With its appealing cast (Hanks is in*

top form) and its refreshingly quiet tone, you want [the movie] to sweep you away, but it never quite transcends its synthetic setup."

—David Ansen, *Newsweek*

"*A hugely enjoyable romantic comedy, this attacks both funny bone and tear ducts with equal success. Ryan looks good enough to eat, Hanks women will find hard to resist, and the kid is one of the most appealing on the screen for years. Shamelessly slushy fluff it may well be, but you'd have to be hardhearted indeed to leave the cinema without feeling just that touch gooey inside. A real treat.*"

—Mark Salisbury, *Empire* magazine (U.K.)

"*A gentle meditation on fate, on what must come to pass, but there's no hint of a genial God pulling strings on high; it's up to the characters to plot their own course toward a triumphant union. . . . I like my romantic comedies to wake me up, but this one put me to sleep with its sweet mooching reverie, much of it secondhand. The best reason to see [the movie] is Tom Hanks, but then he's always the best reason to see a movie.*"

—Anthony Lange, *New Yorker*

"*A feather-light romantic comedy. . . . Not since* Love Story *has there been a movie that so shrewdly and predictably manipulated the emotions for such entertaining effect. Be warned, though: [This] is a movie you may hate yourself in the morning for having loved the night before. Mr. Hanks and Ms. Ryan are terrifically attractive, each somehow persuading the audience of the validity of all the things that keep them apart and then miraculously bringing them together.*"

—Vincent Canby, *New York Times*

20

Philadelphia

Tri-Star, 1993

"If what we are dealing with is the dignity of the human spirit and trying to illuminate that and live it, this does it probably better than anything I've ever been involved with."

Cast
Tom Hanks (*Andrew Beckett*); Denzel Washington (*Joe Miller*); Jason Robards (*Charles Wheeler*); Mary Steenburgen (*Belinda Conine*); Antonio Banderas (*Miguel*); Joanne Woodward (*Sarah Beckett*); Anna Deavere Smith (*Anthea Burton*); Lisa Summerour (*Lisa Miller*); Ron Vawter (*Bob Seidman*); Charles Napier (*Judge Garnett*).

Credits
Director: Jonathan Demme; producers: Edward Saxon and Jonathan Demme; executive producers: Gary Goetzman, Kenneth Utt, and Ron Bozman; screenplay: Ron Nyswaner; director of photography: Tak Fujimoto; production designer: Kristi Zea; art director: Tim Gavin; editor: Craig McKay; music: Howard Shore.
Running time: 126 minutes.

Andrew Beckett has just been given a major promotion in the law partnership. (Tri-Star Pictures)

Following his resurgence as a top box-office attraction with *A League of Their Own* and *Sleepless in Seattle*, Tom Hanks was about to embark on the riskiest project of his career—playing a gay, AIDS-infected lawyer in director Jonathan Demme's much-debated and eagerly awaited film *Philadelphia*. Hanks signed to play the part of Andrew Beckett, a prominent, rising young attorney with the city's most prestigious law firm. When his superiors learn he has AIDS, Beckett is summarily fired, presumably because of a sudden deterioration in his work performance. Beckett stuns his former colleagues by filing a lawsuit against the firm, alleging he was the victim of discrimination.

Despite Hollywood's apparent sympathy for the AIDS-afflicted, it is well known that the industry in general limits its support to fund-raisers and wearing red ribbons. In reality, AIDS victims find themselves virtually blacklisted in the entertainment industry, just as they do in other businesses. Hanks spoke about the hypocrisy in the entertainment business: "Hollywood goes back and forth between wearing its altruism on its sleeve and not doing much of anything. The motor for change runs very slow in this town." Hanks remained optimistic that playing a gay man would not result in locking him out of other roles: "I'm not sure I agree it's a stretch. People will still see Tom Hanks because I'm not that kind of chameleon who disappears in a role. . . . I'm probably a good choice for this. I'm non-threatening. There may be people who loathe me but not many who fear me. It's that likability-charming factor I can't shake."

Nonetheless, other actors who played homosexuals found their careers at least temporarily hindered. (Remember Michael Ontkean and Harry Hamlin in *Making Love*?) In fact, the only mainstream gay-themed movie to find much success was *Long Time Companion*, a sensitive look at the gay world in the era of AIDS. Even that film, however, did not play to audiences much beyond the urban art-house crowds.

The idea for *Philadelphia* came from a collaboration between a straight director, Jonathan Demme, and a friend, gay screenwriter Ron Nyswaner. Demme, who had recently won the Academy Award for his direction of *The Silence of the Lambs*, had found that his triumph was somewhat compromised by protests from the gay community, that the film's serial murderer was unnecessarily explained as a transsexual. Demme was quite vocal in his own defense, claiming, "I got all this unfounded abuse on *Silence of the Lambs*. He wasn't a gay character. He was a tormented man who hated himself and wished he was a woman because that would have made him as far away from himself as he could possibly be." Nevertheless, Demme admitted: "I came to realize that, in fact, there is a tremendous absence of positive gay characters in movies."

In the wake of the criticism of that film, many people accused Demme of making *Philadelphia* as a way of placating gay critics. In fact, he had been developing the project since 1988. He recalled the event which inspired him: "I was on a train, in the dining car, around 1987. There was a man sitting two tables away. Then the man looked at this friend and said, 'I have AIDS.' Well! I wanted to dive off the train! But when it's someone you love—a friend, a neighbor—who says, 'I have AIDS,' you finally have to confront your own terror. That's what happened to me. And *Philadelphia* was my way of dealing with the terror."

Demme and Nyswaner first discussed the possibility of bringing an AIDS-based drama to the screen in 1988. Both men had learned that someone close to them was suffering from the disease. Nyswaner recalled that they wanted to make a film which was "not solemn, not dull, not a disease-oriented, issue-oriented, lecturing kind of movie that would preach to the converted. We knew at least what we didn't

want. The positive was harder. Disease movies tend not to work anyway. . . ."

Demme took the idea for *Philadelphia* to Marc Platt, the head of Tri-Star Pictures, after Orion's bankruptcy scuttled plans for that studio to finance the project. Platt insisted that it be geared toward mainstream audiences and told the *New York Times*, "This picture has to be able to play in Wichita, Kansas. It's of no value if it's nothing but politically correct and no one comes to see it but those who already have experience with AIDS." The first decision was that the character of Andy Beckett should have a straight counterpart with whom the general audience could identify. That character turned out to be Joe Miller, a black, conservative ambulance-chasing attorney whom Andy seeks out in desperation to represent his uphill legal battle. Initially, Joe refuses largely due to his homophobic attitude, but he comes to admire his former colleague's determination and courage and decides to go against his instincts and take on the precedent-shattering case.

It was imperative to cast two powerhouse actors to carry the dialogue-heavy script. There are no car chases in *Philadelphia*; nor are there any special effects, karate fights, or alien landings. It is a somewhat claustrophobic story that would depend on the skills of its leading actors to keep audiences riveted. After initially being turned down by Daniel Day Lewis to play the role of Andy, Demme approached Tom Hanks. Hanks was immediately intrigued, and while filming *Sleepless in Seattle*, he received the script for *Philadelphia*. He would later say, "I think you honestly know by page seven what the screenplay is doing and what it's aspiring to. The nature and tone of it all. The quality of it all and what it's going to demand of you as a participant. And I think by page six I was ready to say, 'Please let me be a part of it!'"

Demme was equally enthused about casting Hanks and reflected that he would bring to the role qualities that may have been missing if Daniel Day Lewis had accepted the part: "As a personality, Tom had the trust and confidence of America, which I felt would help us reach across to a mainstream audience. Daniel would have been wonderful in the part. But one of the qualities of people with AIDS is their humor. I don't know if Daniel had played the part if

Andrew poses for a picture with his family at his parents' fortieth-anniversary celebration. Pictured (*left to right*), Mom Sarah (Joanne Woodward), Dad Bud (Robert Castle), and sister Jill (Ann Dowd). (Tri-Star Pictures)

With AIDS ravaging his body, Andrew seeks the help of attorney Joe Miller (Denzel Washington). (Ken Regan, Tri-Star Pictures)

humor would have been captured as completely as it was by Tom."

From the minute Hanks was announced as the lead, controversy ensued. Gay activists protested casting the self-described "poster boy for heterosexuality" in the part of the homosexual lead. Others praised Hanks and Demme for taking a chance. Hanks downplayed the heroic aspects of accepting the role and restated his enthusiasm for the script: "I thought it was a very *real* approach to what is going on. It's not one of those exploitive TV movie things that they always say is ripped right out of today's headlines. I don't think it's an especially brave move. I think of it as a great role that's an honor and responsibility to play. Obviously you can't do what I do for a living and not have a sense of the impact of AIDS. A lot of preparation is just picking up the paper and reading the front page or, in a lot of cases, the obituaries." He later again dismissed the idea that he was taking a risk with the role, saying, "A big bold choice would have been to have Jean-Claude Van Damme play the sensitive homosexual who's fired from his job

because he has AIDS."

For the role of Joe, Demme signed Denzel Washington, largely because of the latter's desire to work with the Oscar-winning director. "I would have been attracted to any project Jonathan was doing because I just wanted to work with him. Then I read the script and saw how wonderful it was and how good Joe's part was and how important the subject matter was." Ironically, Tom Hanks was originally envisioned for Washington's part. Marc Platt said: "We offered Tom the role of Joe. My thinking, and Demme's thinking, was that we wanted someone in the role with a good sense of humor. Tom came back and said, 'I'd rather play the role of Andrew Beckett.' After consideration, it occurred to us that this was a fantastic idea." Hanks previously would have wanted the other role: "In the old days I would have wanted that part because it was flashier, because he's got all the good speeches in the courtroom.... But I never even blinked in reading the script from Andrew's point of view.... I think the characterization is very subtle. They should take the words *less is more* and stamp them on everyone's forehead when they start working in movies. I think that's what I got from portraying Andrew."

"I relished working with Denzel, sparring with him," Hanks said. "He's a very witty guy. Rarely do I get to go head-to-head and toe-to-toe with an actor like this." He later expanded his views in an interview with the gay magazine the *Advocate*, saying "I had never really been able to work with men. Almost all of my work had been done with actresses. Denzel is certainly at the absolute top of his game all the time. So there's no small amount of competition that goes on. I didn't want to be sandbagged by him. And, likewise, I didn't want to sandbag him. So the give-and-take kept things fresh." For his part, Washington found working with Hanks every bit as rewarding as he had hoped: "I already knew what a great actor Tom was, but mostly in comedic terms, and I had a tremendous amount of respect for him. Now I'm even more impressed with what a good dramatic actor he

is. I saw his dedication—how focused and disciplined he was. . . ."

For Demme, having the combined talents of two of the screen's hottest talents proved to be a dream come true. He said "Tom and Denzel: they are both two actors who *know* that they are gifted. So they move right beyond any insecurity and any nonsense. They also move beyond any egotism about it because each one independently, I think, is committed to living up to the gift they acknowledge they've got, and they want to challenge themselves and they go for it one hundred percent."

Jason Robards was signed for the key role of Andrew Beckett's idol, Charles Wheeler, a legendary attorney who acts as his mentor—until he learns Andy has AIDS. Wheeler and his "good old boy" cohorts at the law firm are unrepentant homophobics, although, tragically, they truly believe in their own way that they are on the side of right. Mary Steenburgen elected to play the small but pivotal role of the defense attorney

Attorney Belinda Conine (Mary Steenburgen) defends Charles Wheeler and his prestigious law firm. (Ken Regan, Tri-Star Pictures)

trying to prove that Andy has not been fired because of his affliction. Joanne Woodward was cast as Andy's supportive mother. She recalled: "Jonathan asked if I would come and 'be a presence.' It was wonderful to be part of something that is such a groundbreaker, a very important film."

The key role of Andy's lover, Miguel, was played by Antonio Banderas, who has since emerged as a major heartthrob. Hanks joked at the time, "Because I get to play a man who lives with Antonio Banderas, I am the envy of, I'm not sure of the numbers, but I think it's 95 percent of the women in the world and 22 percent of the men." Nevertheless, there was criticism again from gay activists, that the screenplay diluted the relationship between the characters by failing to include any love scenes. Hanks responded somewhat testily to these charges, saying that the filmmakers were in a no-win situation: "If we had shot a love scene, they'd be saying 'Are we supposed to applaud the fact that Tom Hanks and Antonio Banderas dared to kiss each other?' These guys have been together for nine years. They're once-a-weekers at best. I've been with my wife now for ten years. And the number of times we actually smooch in public is probably declining. It's just the nature of things. I mean, if we have to live up to the kiss-o-meter, how fair is that?" Demme was simplistic in his response to the criticism. "I've heard everything on the relationship, that it skates over too much but also that it's a relaxed portrayal of two men living together nonerotically." Ron Nyswaner said: "Occasionally, one of us would bring up the potential political or social ramifications of these kinds of absences, to which Jonathan had the courage to say, 'We're not going to please everyone.'"

In fact, Demme did shoot scenes showing Andy and Miguel in a more romantic light, but these, like other scenes which dwelled on their life at home together, ended up on the cutting-room floor. "We could have had a lot more of that if it had been gripping enough. But the scenes slowed the movie down. I wish there was more screen time involving the two of them, but I know why it isn't there."

An effective scene which showed the Andy-Miguel relationship was the party held in a gay social club which Joe Miller and his wife attend. Here Miller is amused and enlightened by a lifestyle so far from his own as the participants arrive decked out in elaborate—and sometimes outrageous—costumes. It is also here, as he watches the two men dance and embrace the way he does with his wife, that he begins

to accept the Andy-Miguel relationship as a valid one. The party scene is one of the few truly lighthearted moments in the film. Tom Hanks explains: "You don't expect to see that party scene in this movie. It could have been an incredibly intrusive moment that made no sense at all, but it stayed right on the path of where the movie is supposed to go. And it was a lot of fun to do." Many actors in this sequence were from the Philadelphia gay community. Indeed, fifty-three gay men appear in various scenes in the movie. Tragically, within one year of *Philadelphia's* filming, forty-three of these men died of AIDS.

The role of Andy Beckett required some physical sacrifice on the part of Hanks. He lost over thirty pounds in order to convincingly portray the agonizing decline of his character's appearance. "I had to lose weight," he recalled, "but I had to lose it in a very kind of specific manner which required a pretty rigorous diet and exercise program that never stopped. From the middle of September to February, very specific foods were brought to me every day, and either before or after work, I had an hour in the gymnasium that I had to do." Conversely, Denzel Washington was encouraged to *gain* weight to dramatize the difference between his character's physical appearance and Hanks's. Washington took sadistic pleasure in making sure that the dieting Hanks observed him devouring large quantities of candy: "I know how much he enjoys Snickers, and I knew he couldn't have any, so I wanted to give him the pleasure of at least seeing *me* eat them." "It was an interesting vicarious thrill," Hanks joked.

Hanks's preparation for the role of Andy also motivated him to intensely study AIDS. "I met with Dr. Julian Falutz at the UCLA AIDS Institute," he said, "and had many conversations with men with AIDS. It's not just playing a disease; it's playing a man who is gay, who loves his family, who loves his lover, who loves the world. Thanks to the cachet of being the guy who's going to do this story, I was given the leeway to ask these men incredible questions, like 'What happened when you found out you had the disease? How did the doctor tell you? What got you to the doctor in the first place?' I mean, *Jesus Christ!* Yet that's what the thing requires in order to get there. The whole damn thing was a big psychological process. Any job is, but not to this massive extent." Hanks did draw the line, however, at frequenting actual gay bars. He rationalized, "Having always been around plenty of gay people, I didn't think it was necessary for me to be picked up at

A controversial scene in which an AIDS-stricken Andrew feeds a baby while his lover, Miguel (Antonio Banderas), looks on (Tri-Star Pictures)

Rampage on Santa Monica Boulevard." The research Hanks and the makeup and hair designers did insured that the physical deterioration of Andy's condition was accurately portrayed.

Although the movie could have been set in any American city, Jonathan Demme explained why he chose Philadelphia. "Dealing with the subjects it does, our story could be set in any major city or even, at this stage, in many small towns. But we decided that Philadelphia, known as the City of Brotherly Love, the city where the Declaration of Independence was adopted, brought a special kind of resonance to a story about justice and brotherhood." The filmmakers received the full cooperation of local businesses and city government. They were granted access to Philadelphia City Hall for a full four-week shoot, while trials continued in surrounding courtrooms. Other prominent locations included the Philadelphia library, Mt. Sinai Hospital, the Spectrum Sports Arena, and the law firm of Mesirov, Gelman, Jaffe,

Cramer and Jamieson, which doubled for the law office where Andy is employed. (The actual firm donated its fees to local AIDS charities.) All but one sequence was shot at an actual location.

Artistically, *Philadelphia* is a bold and daring film, one which dares to deal with one of the most emotional issues of our times—how society treats people who are often regarded as modern-day lepers. The movie certainly has its sympathies with Andy's case, and the script alludes to his being framed by his bosses in order to justify his termination. Yet this is never quite proven, and there is a refreshing level of ambiguity about whether his superiors genuinely believe he was fired for work-related reasons. The script also does not canonize Andy and dares to present the opposing viewpoint—does a person with a deadly disease that we do not fully understand have a moral obligation to inform those around him in the workplace? The riveting courtroom scenes in the film tackle these issues head-on, and one begins to understand both sides of the argument, although we clearly are meant to sympathize with Andy. And we ultimately do.

Philadelphia is an "actor's movie" in every sense. While Nyswaner's intelligent screenplay certainly deserves enormous praise, the performances by a stellar cast are what command the most attention. Hanks is superb in the role of Andy Beckett, and he dares to not play the character in a "typically" gay way. In fact, it comes as a shock to his coworkers to learn of his sexual orientation precisely because he has been so mainstream over the years. Hanks imbues Andy with such courage, determination, and wit that the audience is never depressed to see him on-screen. Rather, they are inspired. The scenes in which Andy tries to maintain normalcy around his family and friends despite his rapid physical decline are extremely moving, as are the film's final moments in which Andy's loved ones return from his wake and watch silently as home movies of this once vibrant young man play on a TV to the music of Bruce Springsteen's moving song "Philadelphia." Nothing else in the film conveys the waste of a valued life so poignantly.

Hanks won almost unanimous praise from the mainstream press for his stunning performance. Less kind were members of the gay media, few of which seem to be placated by the olive branches extended to them by Hanks and Demme. Perhaps Hanks's critics failed to realize that by having one of the most popular actors around bring such a story to the screen, the case for treating AIDS victims with sympathy rather than disdain was placed in the spotlight.

Somewhat lost in the Hanks controversy was the outstanding performance of Denzel Washington, whose work in the film rivals Hanks's. Because Washington does not have the more sympathetic role, it could be argued that his challenge was even more difficult than Hanks's. Fortunately, although the character of Joe Miller certainly becomes more sympathetic with AIDS issues and more aware of his homophobia, he does not become an overnight advocate of the gay lifestyle. He is merely a lawyer trying to win a David-and-Goliath battle on behalf of his client. Washington's work should have earned him an Oscar nomination.

The supporting cast is equally good, with Jason

The Wyant, Wheeler, Hellerman, Tetlow, and Brown team: Bob Seidman (Ron Vawter), Charles Wheeler (Jason Robards), Andrew Beckett (Tom Hanks), and Kenneth Killcoyne (Charles Glenn). (Ken Regan, Tri-Star Pictures)

Robards excellent as Andy's mentor—the man who ultimately betrays him. Robards is no cartoon villain, however, and his scenes display his character's genuine belief that he is on the side of right. Mary Steenburgen is also very good as the Marcia Clark–like attorney who can viciously destroy a witness, all the while maintaining a smile. As Miguel, Antonio Banderas is a vibrant screen presence, but the film is not really about him, and he suffers from lack of screen time.

The marketing of *Philadelphia* presented a challenge to the studio. Emphasizing that the story was about AIDS might alienate mainstream audiences or be deemed exploitive. The company developed an ad campaign that was daring for being so understated. The film's one sheet poster featured the faces of Hanks and Washington without divulging a single clue as to what the plot was about. Tri-Star rationalized that all the publicity would certainly have made the public informed. Three trailers were tested—one which dealt with AIDS discrimination directly, one which did not mention the disease at all, and one which emphasized the courtroom drama. In a portent of things to come, audiences responded best to the AIDS-themed trailer.

Philadelphia opened in December 1993 amid the usual wave of high-profile year-end releases. Jonathan Demme, who so masterfully handled the directing of this controversial film, feared the movie would be lost among the "feel-good" competition of the season. His worries were unfounded. Although receiving mixed but respectable reviews, the film shocked the industry by attracting mainstream as well as gay audiences. Ultimately, it would gross over $80 million—not a blockbuster by today's action film standards but an astonishing amount for such a serious film released during the Christmas season.

Although the movie divided critics, Hanks enjoyed widespread acclaim that led to a personal invitation to stay at the Clinton White House. Of "the best damn bed-and-breakfast in the United

Hanks's poignant portrayal of a man fighting for his life and his reputation earned him his first Oscar. (Ken Regan, Tri-Star Pictures)

States," he joked with David Letterman, "I came home with every conceivable shower-bath gel, conditioner, net, bathrobe, towel, stationery—we brought empty suitcases just so we could lug this stuff back on the plane."

On a more personal level, talk of an Oscar for Hanks took a giant leap forward in 1994 when he won for Best Actor at the Golden Globe Awards. The momentum continued to build until the night of the Oscar ceremonies. When Hanks was announced the winner, the audience roared its approval. Hanks would turn the moment into a controversial one, however, with a speech that was denounced by some as rambling while praised by others as refreshingly spontaneous and heartfelt. In the course of the speech, Hanks praised his high school drama teacher, Rawley Farnsworth, for inspiring him earlier in life— then announced the man was gay. Cynics accused him of "outing" Farnsworth without his permission. The protest turned into a tempest in a teapot when Farnsworth praised Hanks for his sincere speech. (The film received other Oscar recognition as well. In addition to being nominated for Best Picture, Bruce

Hanks discusses a scene with director Jonathan Demme and Banderas. (Tri-Star Pictures)

would toss it into the swimming pool and have his kids dive to retrieve it, and he also was planning to have it welded onto the hood of the family Dodge.

Reviews

Philadelphia, *mostly succeeds in being forceful, impassioned and moving, sometimes even riding to the full range of emotion that its subject warrants. But too often, even at its most assertive, it works in safely predictable ways. The courtroom scenes, which lack suspense and too often have a soapbox tenor, will not tell the audience anything they don't already know. . . . In the end, thanks to . . . the simple grace of Mr. Hanks's performance, this film does accomplish what it meant to. Philadelphia rises above its flaws to convey the full urgency of its difficult subject, and to bring that subject home."*

—Janet Maslin, *New York Times*

"An ideal film for people who have never known anyone with AIDS. . . . Intelligent, but too neatly worked out in its political and melodramatic details, [the film] is fronted by a dynamic lead performance from Tom Hanks, but will need top reviews and a superior marketing campaign to make it a must see for members of the general public whose idea of a night out might not be to see a movie about a man dying with AIDS. . . . Hanks makes it all hang together in a performance that triumphantly mixes determination, humor, perseverance, grit, energy and remarkable clearheadedness. Whatever else

Trivia Note

Tom Hanks discussed his role in *Philadelphia* in the acclaimed documentary *The Celluloid Closet*, a historical look at the treatment of gays in motion pictures.

Springsteen's *Streets of Philadelphia*—a top hit on the charts—earned the Oscar for Best Original Song.)

In the wake of his Oscar win, Hanks began to finally be perceived as not only one of the top comedic talents in the American film business but also one of the most talented contemporary dramatic actors as well. Hanks used the publicity from his Oscar to lecture to AIDS awareness groups and try to foster compassion from the public for AIDS victims. Still, despite the seriousness of the issue, he maintained his characteristic sense of humor. He told Jay Leno on *The Tonight Show* that the Oscar was coming in handy in unlikely ways. He joked that he *might nag about the film's treatment of a difficult subject, Hanks constantly connects on the most human level."*

—Todd McCarthy, *Variety*

"Turns out to be a scattershot liberal message movie, one that ties itself in knots trying to render its subject matter acceptable to a mass audience. . . . Hanks has some fine moments, especially when he's testifying in court during the throes of illness; the actor makes you feel the battle between his will and his dying body. But Andrew, as written, is less a character than a file-card hodge-podge of gay characteristics. Certainly, it's hard to feel any closer to him after seeing him discourse weepily on the beauties of Maria Callas singing "La Mamma Morta" from the opera Andrea Chenier, *a showpiece so obviously designed to win Hanks the Oscar that it's an embarrassment to behold. Ultimately, the audiences has only one way to define Andrew Beckett: as a person with AIDS."*

—Owen Gleiberman, *Entertainment Weekly*

"Far from perfect, but it would be hard to imagine the person who could walk away from it unmoved. . . . You can feel the pressure of the filmmakers to design a film that will speak to the widest possible audience, to reach people who may not know anyone who's died of AIDS. But the film pays a price for it. Heartfelt and stylishly made as Philadelphia *is, it has, almost by definition, the feel of a movie made from the outside in. . . . There will be no argument, however, about the film's stars. The superb Hanks doesn't make a false move as the proud,*

The city of Philadelphia embraced the makers of the film and its two stars. (*Philadelphia* magazine)

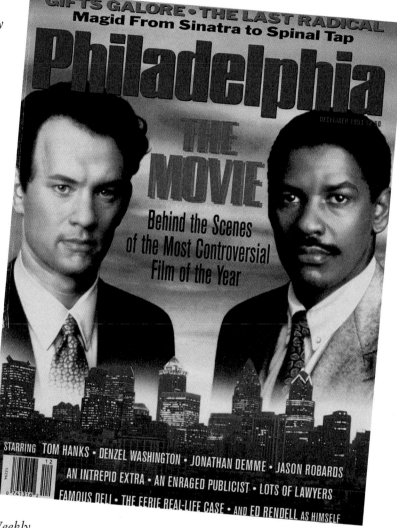

ironic Beckett. . . . Hanks moves us deeply by never begging for sympathy. . . . [This] might not be the film Demme's fans expect—its emotionalism is unfiltered by cool. But it has the power to open more than a few blinkered hearts."

—David Ansen, *Newsweek*

"Above all, credit for the movie's success belongs to Hanks, who makes sure he plays a character, not a saint. He is flat out terrific, giving a deeply-felt, carefully nuanced performance that deserves an Oscar."

Leah Rozen, *People*

21

Forrest Gump

Paramount, 1994

"He lives an amazing life and sees amazing things, but the purity of how he sees the world was what I thought was amazing about the screenplay, and what he goes through to get to the point that we're all at. All the great stories are about our battle against loneliness: Hamlet *is about that; so is* The Importance of Being Earnest. *That's what I always ended up being drawn to."*

Cast
Tom Hanks (*Forrest Gump*); Robin Wright (*Jenny Curran*); Gary Sinise (*Lieutenant Dan*); Mykelti Williamson (*Bubba*); Sally Field (*Mama Gump*); Michael Humphreys (*Young Forrest*); Hanna Hall (*Young Jenny*).

Credits
Director: Robert Zemeckis; producers: Wendy Finerman, Steve Tisch, and Steve Starkey; screenplay: Eric Roth, based on the novel by Winston Groom; director of photography: Don Burgess; production designer: Rick Carter; special visual effects supervisor: Ken Ralston; editor: Arthur Schmidt; music: Alan Silvestri.
Running time: 142 minutes.

Portraying one of the most beloved characters in movie history (Paramount Pictures)

While still basking in the glow of his Oscar triumph in *Philadelphia*, Hanks would follow that film with the most remarkable project of his career and help establish a new American hero in the process. Yet, at the outset, *Forrest Gump* was viewed within the industry as anything but a surefire success. Like so many classic movies, it seemed to provide a very modest basis for a major motion picture. Through one of those all-too-rare occurrences, however, it ultimately fell into the right hands and became a cultural phenomenon.

Author Winston Groom's novel about a simple-minded, completely naive man who chronicles a remarkable journey through the great events of recent decades was only modestly successful when published in the mid-1980s. However, the book attracted the attention of producer Wendy Finerman. "I saw an incredibly cinematic story of a man who is inseparable from the events we've all grown up with. In the same way that children can say the most brilliant things, Forrest Gump is able to bring a rare clarity to what we went through in the fifties, sixties, and seventies. He's a remarkable character who is just as good at making you cry as he is at making you laugh." Finerman became obsessed with bringing

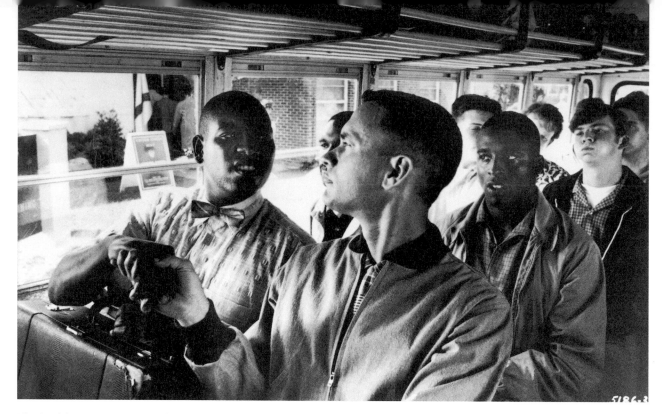

The fateful moment when Forrest meets Bubba (Mykelti Williamson) on the bus to boot camp (Paramount Pictures)

Gump's epic story to the screen but found that "actors, directors, agents, studio people, were just not interested in the project. People would ask me what I was working on, and I'd say Forrest Gump. And they'd get that glazed look. I knew they were thinking, When is she going to give up?" But she re-mained persistent. "There was something magical about the book, and even though I knew it would be an expensive and difficult movie to make, for nine years I always believed it was going to happen."

Finerman eventually made converts of fellow producers Steve Tisch and Steve Starkey, and the trio finally interested a major studio—Warner Bros.—to consider financing the project. Groom was commissioned to write a screenplay, which was later passed over as two other writers tried their hands at the difficult task of condensing the epic scope of the book into a feature film. Eventually, Warners passed on the project despite having spent considerable sums on development. Undeterred, Finerman approached Paramount and convinced the studio to resurrect the film. Writer Eric Roth was hired to write the final screenplay, a task he completed in December 1992. Roth said, "The script broke all the traditional rules of moviemaking. Yes, it was episodic. But it was also told from the point of view of Forrest. . . . He anchored the movie on the love story. That's the spine of the film."

Earlier in her quest to bring Gump to the screen,

Finerman had given the novel to Tom Hanks, who said he would be interested in starring in the film version if a screenplay could successfully convey the offbeat charm of the book. He recalled his first impressions of Roth's script: "I read Forrest Gump when we were on our Christmas break from Philadelphia. . . . I was completely broken. I was absolutely bent. And I thought that if we didn't really screw it up that we could make a movie as good as what was on paper."

When the film was placed on the fast track by Paramount, Hanks signed for the role immediately. He told of why the project appealed to him: "It breaks every rule of moviemaking I know of. There's no quest that anyone's on. There's no bad guy. It's just the spirit of Forrest Gump. That's the backbone of the movie." Steve Tisch recalled his enthusiasm about Hanks signing for the role: "I've been involved in Gump for nine years, and I can't now think of any other actor who should've played Forrest Gump other than Tom. . . . The man is as nice, as honest, as professional, as personal, as he seems to be. His life is not an act. He's an extremely talented actor, and as a human being he is what we should all aspire to be."

Hanks and the producers agreed that the ideal director would be Robert Zemeckis, the creative force behind such high-tech hits as Back to the Future and Who Framed Roger Rabbit. Because the script required Forrest to interact with some of the most notable people of the recent past, it was clear that the film would need a director who could somehow convincingly achieve the feat without the audience being preoccupied by apparent camera trickery. While it is true that Woody Allen's *Zelig* had achieved some remarkable success in blending Allen in with famous historical figures, that film was in black and white, which made the ruse a bit easier to disguise. In *Forrest Gump,* Tom Hanks would have to interact with historical figures on the big screen in color.

Zemeckis recalled being instantly excited by the challenge of bringing *Gump* to the screen: "I read the screenplay and couldn't put it down. It was compelling in a strange way because it didn't have any typical plot devices, and all I wanted to do was find out what was going to happen to this guy." He, Hanks, and the producers decided from the beginning that *Gump* would not be a heavy-handed "message" movie despite having its hero live through some of century's major events. Zemeckis said: "What we were able to do was present this generation without commenting on it or taking a position explaining it." That the filmmakers respected the viewers enough to allow them to formulate their own interpretations of events placed the movie at odds with almost every other recent motion picture. The problem still remained: How do you entice audiences with a film featuring a dim-witted hero, no villain, a rambling, episodic plot, and only hints of sexuality? The buzz was that Tom Hanks was about to make a career blunder starring as Gump. Cynics felt the film was simply too uncommercial to market successfully. Zemeckis, Hanks, and the producers acknowledged that they had an uphill battle but felt that Roth's groundbreaking screenplay could indeed be turned into a popular film.

Long before the cameras rolled, Hanks began his exhaustive research to find the right method to bring Forrest Gump to life. "It was like creating an alien," he said of Gump's unique personality and mannerisms. "What are the rules of his world? It was like creating a whole new take on the universe." He later told the *Hollywood Reporter,* "There's a lot of preparation. I need at least six months now before we go off and shoot. I need at least six months to mull over the particulars in the script, the intangibles. With Forrest we knew right off that this wasn't going to be a line-by-line etching of somebody with an IQ of 75. For Forrest, I went to a place out in La Canada that is doing what I think is the work of God, working with adults who are mentally handicapped, challenged—or whatever the officially accepted terminology. Without question, those people's lives are limited. Hopefully, these folks can have a card from the transit district to ride the bus. They might be able to have a job, but not much more than that. We knew going in we wouldn't be depicting that sort of [person]. In the course of the movie we never really sought to define what Forrest is and what he is not. The guy in school

Forrest's D.I. tells him that he is a "Goddamned genius!" (Paramount Pictures)

says he has an IQ of 75, but no one really knows what that means. He doesn't have cerebral palsy. He's not mentally retarded. He's kind of slow. What was remarkable about the time I spent out there was becoming aware of the individuality of these people. When you sit down with them and the people who work with them every day, they might be shy and nervous, but they have individual characteristics like everybody else does. . . . They were humans who are worthy of dignity and respect."

While Hanks researched the most challenging role of his career, Zemeckis was casting the other pivotal roles in the film. He suggested an unusual choice to play Forrest's protective mother, the individual

Forrest doing one of the things he does best (Phil Caruso, Paramount Pictures)

even during the years in which Jenny goes astray, choosing self-destructive paths in her life. Robin Wright was cast in this demanding role and complements Hanks perfectly with a performance that is both moving and heartbreaking.

For the scenes of Forrest as a grammar school student, eight-year-old Michael Humphreys made his film debut, having won the part through an open casting call in Memphis. It was felt that Humphreys best matched the type that Zemeckis was searching for: "a young Tom Hanks with light eyes and a quirky disposition." Humphreys acquits himself very admirably, as does nine-year-old Hanna Hall, who plays young Jenny. While on location, both families lived together to strengthen the chemistry between the two children.

The key male roles in the film are vitally important to the development of Forrest's character and the road he chooses to take in life. Actor-director Gary Sinise was cast at Lieutenant Dan, Forrest's gung-ho superior officer in Vietnam. Forrest saves Dan's life in a fierce firefight, but instead of receiving thanks, Forrest is cursed by the embittered man because he has had his leg amputated from his wounds. Left a cripple, Dan is furious that he has not been allowed to carry out his destiny of dying in battle, as did all his ancestors. Gradually, however, he develops a bond with Forrest, and when the latter takes him on as a partner in a shrimp-boating venture, the two men become close friends, not to mention millionaires. Sinise proved to be the perfect choice for the role, and his transformation from a foe of Forrest's to a friend is all the more believable because of Sinise's fascinating performance.

Forrest's other friend is Bubba, a similarly slow thinking but affable army buddy who knows only of the shrimping business. He was to be Forrest's original partner in the fishing industry after the war, but when he is mortally wounded and dies in his friend's arms, Forrest vows to carry on without him. Bubba is beautifully played by Mykelti Williamson, and his scenes with Hanks are among the most enjoyable—and moving—in the film.

Budgeted at $40 million, *Forrest Gump* began principal photography in August 1993 in Beaufort, South Carolina. Other major locations included Savannah (site of the classic scenes of Forrest sitting on a park bench telling complete strangers his life

who influences him the most during his life. Hanks recalls, "They called up and said, 'What do you think of Sally Field as Mama Gump?' I said, 'Look, I played Sally's love interest in a movie. I can't call her up and say, 'Would you want to play my mom in this thing?' But it worked out great because, you know, Sally's appearance is so perfect.... She's a brilliant craftsperson at what she does."

A major influence in Field's decision to play Mama Gump was the opportunity to work with Hanks again. She sang Hanks praises to one and all. "He's absolutely the most lovable human being on the planet. ... Top-notch. First-class in every category. So you know the familiarity and the love and all that was just there. Because we'd already worked together; because we were friends. It was just easy to be his mom."

The other key female role in the film is that of Jenny, Forrest Gump's "girl" since grade school. Forrest maintains a crush on her throughout his life, story), Washington, D.C., and Los Angeles. Second-unit photography was done at scenic locations across the country, including North Carolina, Vermont, Maine, Montana, Arizona, and Utah's Monument Valley (the site of so many of the great John Ford westerns). These locations would be primarily needed for the scenes in which Forrest makes his inexplicable but inspiring run across the United States. The Vietnam scenes were actually shot on Fripp Island, South Carolina. Here the extensive battle sequence was filmed amid foliage that convincingly passed for the jungle of Southeast Asia. Computer palm trees filled in any gaps. (Several acres were burned in order to stage the napalm drop on the jungle.) Filming wrapped in early December—a remarkably short period of time for a movie this sweeping in scope.

Forrest and his one true love, Jenny (Robin Wright)
(Phil Caruso, Paramount Pictures)

The special effects presented in *Forrest Gump* are simply astounding. One is initially confounded as to how a film on a relatively modest budget (at least by today's standards) could possibly have employed the thousands of extras seen in the crowd sequences that witness Forrest's triumphs at the football stadium, the peace rally in Washington, D.C., and the Ping-Pong championship in a gigantic hall in Red China. The fact is that those scenes employed only a fraction of the people seen on-screen. For instance, the Washington peace rally consisted of a crowd of fifteen-hundred extras. Special effects supervisor Ken Ralston of Industrial Light and Magic explained; "We take groups of seven-hundred and film them at different positions around the Reflecting Pool so they match each previous position. They're blended together through a process of digital composing done in postproduction." The result was a crowd of hundreds of thousands convincingly replicated on-screen. State-of-the-art technology was also employed by cinematographer Don Burgess, who went so far as to use a Global Positioning System (GPS) to pinpoint the sun's exact position, enabling him to capture some breathtaking sunsets. Burgess said, "Since the

film is practically 85 percent daytime exteriors, the GPS was invaluable in helping us choose the most beautiful lighting for important moments in the film, like the first time we see the Gump house or first meet a character."

The most impressive use of special effects concerned those scenes in which Tom Hanks had to be on camera with famous historical figures. Ralston and his team managed the seemingly impossible—to seamlessly blend the actor into great moments in recent history with such precision that younger viewers would have to be told that he is not really meeting with famous people. Ralston explained, "Our goal was to carefully match or blend Forrest's image to every shadow, every scratch, every moment of the corresponding cuts in the archival sequence. How we choreograph the shot and how we light our work, because the lighting has to match perfectly with the rest of the scene, are very important. It all has to look like one big dramatic moment in the film. That can be very difficult considering that much of the 16 mm archival footage during the early sixties was shot by

Forrest takes on the Chinese Ping-Pong champ, under the watchful eye of Chairman Mao. (Paramount Pictures)

amateurs with very unsteady, handheld cameras. Our footage had to match the movement in the original footage. We shot ours handheld and on the same type of film, such as 16 mm black and white or 16 mm color so that it would look as realistic and documentary-like as possible."

The achievement is nothing less than stunning as we witness Hanks greeted by JFK, LBJ, and Richard Nixon, not to mention intermingling with other prominent celebrities of the day, including George Wallace and John Lennon. Three archival film sources were used for the JFK sequence: footage of Kennedy greeting the Penn State football team in the Rose Garden; shots of Kennedy shaking hands with the first Peace Corps volunteers in the Oval Office, and a scene of the president looking over his shoulder during a ceremony in which he was inducted as an honorary Boy Scout. Using composite digitizing, Ralston and his team isolated and removed JFK's image from the Rose Garden footage and inserted it into the Oval Office scene they had created. Here the other Kennedy footage was also inserted. Tom Hanks was filmed against a blue screen, and his image was later blended in with the Kennedy footage. (A voice double was used to dub Kennedy's words, and the president's mouth movements were manipulated by computer.) Similar techniques were used to create Forrest's meetings with Johnson and Nixon.

Tom Hanks was fascinated by these unorthodox methods of filmmaking. "It's very fascinating. . . . You go in front of a blue screen, and you're pretty much

Mama Gump (Sally Field) shows Forrest the opportunities for product endorsements. (Paramount Pictures)

done in twenty minutes. It's quite funny, actually, because there is this whole crew there from I.L.M. and it's like 'Stop bossing me around, I don't even know who you are.' But for the rest we built the sets and cast them with look-alikes. With Johnson and Kennedy, we were on a White House set. With John Lennon, we recreated the *Dick Cavett Show*, and Dick Cavett came in. We had the set, the whole thing, and the harsh kind of lights, and we had a guy who played Lennon right off, and later on we'd take it and incorporate it into the thing" (A sequence in which Forrest meets Dr. Martin Luther King Jr. was shot but did not make the final cut because it slowed the pace of the film.)

Robert Zemeckis was sensitive about the possibility of being criticized for using so many special effects in such a low-key, personal story. He defended his decisions, saying, "The whole idea of motion pictures is a mechanical gimmick. I don't understand these actors who work in motion pictures and then claim that they must find the 'reality' to do the scene, because the whole thing is ridiculously unreal. I mean, how can you play the reality when you have all this stupid equipment around and thirty or forty guys in T-shirts are watching? We already know that the photographic evidence means nothing today because pictures can be retouched. Now, you can't believe anything you see on TV, either. . . . I think if David Lean were making movies today, he'd say, 'Where has this been all my life?' He used to sit in the desert for months with a thousand horsemen waiting for the perfect sunset. Now we have these very, very sophisticated ways to do shots by certain means that I think are going to be invisible—if we do our job right, no one will know they're looking at a special effect. We have new toys to play with, but every shot, in fact, has always been a special effect because it's all fake. It's all movies."

Not all of the remarkable special effects were limited to historical events and people. The opening shot of a feather floating on the breeze lasted two

Lieutenant Dan (Gary Sinise) apparently finds his sea legs and joins Forrest on his shrimp boat. (Paramount Pictures)

minutes and cost $100,000 to film. It was the longest continuous shot ever done with computer graphics. The feather was tied to a fishing line and shot in front of a blue screen. A second feather was attached to Tom Hank's shoe the whole time, and the floating feather would later blend into the one on the shoe. Other prominent scenes featuring special effects were the sequence in which the doves fly out of a cornfield where Jenny and Forrest hide from her abusive father; the torrential rainstorm which batters the shrimp boat on which Forrest and Lieutenant Dan fight for their lives (although actually shot in a real boat on the water, the vessel was tied to the dock and the water was calm); and the adding of animated Ping-Pong balls to the extensive scenes in which Forrest clobbers his opponents. Most impressive was the method used to simulate Lieutenant Dan's amputated legs. Gary Sinise did not even have to tape his legs behind him— a common method of replicating this particular handicap. Instead, Sinise acted as though he had no legs, even though they were plainly visible the whole time. Through digital blue-screen effects, his legs were "removed" after the fact. The result is nothing less than astonishing.

Forrest and Jenny resume their childhood love affair. (Paramount Pictures)

Hanks would not allow himself to be distracted by the special effects. He was too worried about capturing the essence of this extraordinary character. "I was afraid of the dialect. This was new turf for me. I'm no great linguist. And I wasn't sure the audience would accept it, coming from me. Because Gump talks through the whole damn movie," Ultimately, Hanks echoed the voice mannerisms of his younger, on-screen alter ego Michael Humphreys. "He just had this voice that seemed to come right out of his backbone."

Hanks confessed to being "scared every minute" while filming *Forrest Gump.* "With Bob Zemeckis and I, we more often than not just approached the beginning of every day saying; 'What are we going to do?' And at the end of the day, we say, 'Was that it? I don't know. We'll find out later on.' Bob always said, 'We're walking in a minefield here.' You never have any idea. We didn't know if people would care about this man's life. We didn't know if they'd be willing to sit with him on the bench long enough to hear him ramble on and on about everything that happened to him." Hanks also admitted that he initially tried to eliminate one of the film's most effective scenes: Forrest's cross-country jog. He confessed, "I always said, 'Bob, no one is going to sit still for this run

across the country. You're making a huge mistake, Bob. It's the dumbest thing in the world. No one's going to care. The movie's over. Let's just say he did it and then get on with it.' And it ended up being one of the heartbeats of the movie."

For his part, Zemeckis had his own doubts about the reception the film would receive despite all the pain and suffering in bringing it to the screen: "The hardest thing about this movie was the overall scope and the epic size of it, the logistics we had to handle. We built 150 sets, shot in eleven states, costumed twelve-thousand people. But part of me subscribes to the George Lucas binary theory: Movies are either ones or zeroes—they either work or they don't. When you say, 'I'm going to make this movie,' that's it. That's the decision, and everything that you do after that isn't going to matter if you've signed on to a concept that's faulty. So that's the big fear. You go through all the complication and the suffering, and you wonder, 'What if nobody wants to see a movie about this guy?'"

A *lot* of people wanted to see a movie about a guy named Forrest Gump. The film, however, represented a difficult challenge for Paramount's marketing team. The decision was made to settle on a simple ad campaign showing Hanks sitting on that now-famous

Forrest keeps a bedside vigil for his dying Mama (Sally Field). It felt a little strange having his onetime (*Punchline*) cinema love play his Mama Gump! (Phil Caruso, Paramount Pictures)

of the movie's phenomenal success, however, Paramount granted eager licensees the right to everything from Forrest Gump cookbooks to boxed chocolates. (Even Hanks confessed to being sick of hearing the "Life is like a box of chocolates. You never know what you'll get" line.) Winston Groom's original novel (which sold about 10,000 copies in its initial print run) was reissued with Hanks on the cover. It would sell over 800,000 copies this time around. Eventually Forrest Gump restaurants opened to enthusiastic crowds.

The Gump juggernaut continued through the awards season in 1995. Hanks's remarkable performance won him the Golden Globe Award for Best Actor, and *Entertainment Weekly* voted him "Entertainer of the Year." By the time Hanks was nominated for Best Actor by the Academy, however, he was anything but a "shoo-in." The fabulous success of the film had resulted in a slight backlash, and the film community seemed divided between loyalists for *Gump* and Quentin Tarantino's pop-culture black-comedy hit *Pulp Fiction*, which was being widely hailed as John Travolta's comeback film. On Oscar night, nominees for Best Actor also included Paul Newman, Morgan Freeman, and Nigel Hawthorne. But the *real* contest was between Hanks and Travolta. Hanks seemed to have somewhat of a

bench. No attempt was made to explain what the film was about, but the airwaves were saturated with intriguing and inspiring television spots which whetted the appetite of the audience. When the film opened on the Fourth of July weekend in 1994, it grossed over $24 million in its first few days—a remarkable achievement for a film that had very little advance talk. Within days, the success of *Forrest Gump* became the stuff of Hollywood legend. The film proved to have durable "legs" at the box office. Its grosses continued strong for many months, and Paramount succeeded in making it an "event" picture. Clearly, one would feel like a social misfit if they hadn't seen it. Bu the end of its theatrical run, the movie had earned over $300 million and had become the highest-grossing film ever released by Paramount Pictures. (As of September 1995 it had also become the fourth-highest-grossing film of all time.)

The success of the film caught Paramount's licensing division by surprise. There had been no major product tie-ins planned for *Forrest Gump*. Within weeks

Sharing that famous bench with director Robert Zemeckis. By all accounts, theirs was a rewarding partnership. (Paramount Pictures)

Forrest's memorable words to JFK: "I gotta pee!" (Paramount Pictures)

anywhere from $35 million to more than $65 million.

The praise seemed completely deserved. *Forrest Gump* is a masterful movie in every respect, and it haunts the viewer long after the final credits roll. It is also something unique in film today—a totally original and daring concept, tastefully executed and brilliantly made by a team of actors and technicians with boundless talent. It is to American filmmaking what Norman Rockwell was to American art, and it is one of the few movies that deserves to be called a masterpiece.

Just as Forrest Gump makes his incredible journey through life, so, too, does the film allow Tom Hanks to make a similar journey in terms of his career. Few other actors have displayed such wide-ranging talent over the course of so few years. With *Forrest Gump*, Hanks hits a high-water mark in terms of his acting skills. He could have played the role as a one-note simpleton, but he invests Forrest with such honesty, integrity, and total innocence that—while the character is certainly amusing—he is never cheapened or made to look foolish. Much of this can be credited to Hanks's multi-layered performance.

In 1995, Winston Groom authored a sequel to his book: *Gump and Company*. It met with savage reviews and illustrates the danger of going to the creative well once too often. Perhaps for this reason, Hanks has all but ruled out considering a sequel to the film. "I'll be saying 'box of chocolates' again about the same time Sean Connery says, 'I'm Bond. James Bond.' I have to confess I don't see this as a franchise. A sequel would ruin what we had done. It would be like *Jaws 2*." As for explaining the success of the film, Hanks would say, "It is a moment when lightning struck. I think the confluence of all the energies that went into it—not just me but certainly everybody else who was involved in the movie—that somehow we landed on some sort of magic formula that I don't think will ever be repeated. Other movies will come along, but I think we did land in a certain place with a certain movie."

handicap because he had won the previous year. Only one other actor had won back-to-back Oscars, and that was Spencer Tracy, in 1937 and 1938. Still, *Gump* had earned thirteen nominations—the most for any film since *Who's Afraid of Virginia Woolf?* in 1966. (Although Gary Sinise would be nominated for Best Supporting Actor, some were surprised that neither Sally Field's or Robin Wright's fine performances were recognized by the Academy.) On the "big night," it became clear that *Gump* would prevail. The film won Best Picture, Best Director, Best Adapted Screenplay, Best Film Editing, Best Visual Effects. . . and Best Actor. Hanks received a thunderous ovation as he movingly accepted his second consecutive Oscar. This time he paid special tribute to his wife, Rita Wilson: "I am standing here because the woman I share my life with has taught me every day just what love is. . . . I feel as though I'm standing on magic legs in a special-effects shot that is too unbelievable to imagine and far too costly to make a reality." In addition to Hank's artistic triumph, by forgoing a hefty up-front salary, he owned a percentage of the *Gump* gross. His earnings to date have been estimated to be

Reviews

"This film begins as yet another case of a Hollywood star doing an Oscar-turn playing a mentally disturbed character, but surprisingly turns it into a marvelous, whimsical epic of contemporary America. Forrest Gump is more of a vehicle than a person in the film, a vehicle that drives us through the past forty years of American history like a Candide *mixed with Woody Allen's* Zelig *and Peter Sellers's Chance from* Being There.

—Gene Siskel, *Chicago Sun-Times*

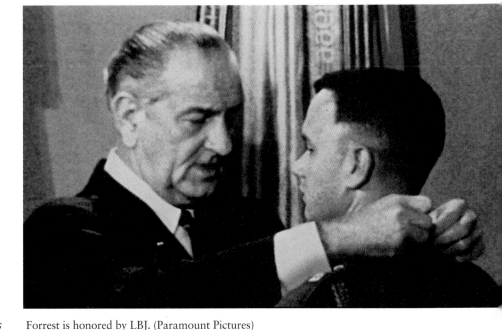

Forrest is honored by LBJ. (Paramount Pictures)

"Zemeckis is exactly the right man to have filmed Forrest Gump. . . . *Hanks, to his credit, never grovels for sympathy. This is a complex human comedy that is heartwarming to the max, both curiously offbeat and oddly disarming."*

—Bruce Williamson, *Playboy*

"A movie heartbreaker of oddball wit and startling grace. There's talk of another Oscar for Tom Hanks, who is unforgettable as the sweet-natured, shabbily treated simpleton of the title. . . . Credit Hanks for not overplaying his hand. He brings a touching gravity to the role. . . . It's Hanks who brings humor and unforced humanity to the literary conceit of Forrest, though the slim actor scarcely resembles the 6 foot 6 inch, 240 pound bruiser of the book."

—Peter Travers, *Rolling Stone*

"As Hollywood summer movies go, this picaresque fable is definitely not the same old same old. . . . [It] is inventive, sometimes hilarious, and it pushes so many nostalgia buttons, you can't help but stay engrossed even when the tale starts to ramble. Yet the whole seems less than the sum of its parts. . . . Hanks, who can do no wrong as an actor, turns this fantastical conceit into funny, touching, flesh and blood; even his elbows are eloquent. . . . It's a tribute to Hanks and Zemeckis that this all-purpose symbol is as fetching as he is. The world according to Gump is certainly an enjoyable place to visit. But its core is disappointingly soft and elusive."

—David Ansen, *Newsweek*

"A picaresque story of a simpleton's charmed odyssey through 30 years of tumultuous American history, Forrest Gump *is whimsy with a strong cultural spine. Elegantly made and winningly acted by Tom Hanks. . . . Zemeckis's technically dazzling new film is also shrewdly packaged to hit baby boomers where they live. Pic offers up a non-stop barrage of emotional and iconographic identification points that will make the post-war generation feel they're seeing their lives passing by onscreen. Paramount's target audience is obvious, and boffo box-office should ensue."*

—Todd McCarthy, *Variety*

22

Apollo 13
Universal, 1995

"I've always wanted to play an astronaut. I've always wanted to shoot a vast stretch of movie completely encapsulated by nothing but metal, glass, and switches, and I finally have a chance to do that, too. So this is really dream-come-true stuff here."

Cast
Tom Hanks (*Jim Lovell*); Kevin Bacon (*Jack Swigert*); Bill Paxton (*Fred Haise*); Gary Sinise (*Ken Mattingly*); Ed Harris (*Gene Kranz*); Kathleen Quinlan (*Marilyn Lovell*); Mary Kate Schellhardt (*Barbara Lovell*); Emily Ann Lloyd (*Susan Lovell*); Jean Speegle Howard (*Blanch Lovell*); Clint Howard (*Eecom White*); Joe Spano (*NASA director*); David Andrews (*Pete Conrad*); Chris Ellis (*Deke Slayton*).

Credits
Director: Ron Howard; producer: Brian Grazer; executive producer: Todd Hallowell; screenplay: William Broyles Jr. and Al Reiner, based on the book *Lost Moon* by Jim Lovell and Jeffrey Kluger; director of photography: Dean Cundey; production designer: Michael Corenblith; visual effects supervisor: Rob Legato; editors: Mike Hill and Dan Hanley; music: James Horner.
Running time: 136 minutes.

As astronaut Jim Lovell (Imagine Entertainment/Universal City Studios)

Prior to the release of *Forrest Gump*, Tom Hanks had already committed to his next film. It is doubtful, even if he had anticipated the phenomenal success of *Gump*, that it would have changed his mind about participating in this particular project despite the fact that it was very much an ensemble piece and not a "star turn" in the way that his last two films had been. The movie was *Apollo 13*, and the appeal of starring in it went beyond the sizable salary Hanks was able to command. Hanks has had a lifelong interest in the space program and as a young boy studied every aspect of the NASA flights. To this day, he can still name most of the *Apollo* and *Gemini* crews. The story of the *Apollo 13* mission, however, was the most dramatic of all, with the exception of the actual first moon landing.

The story was based on the book *Lost Moon* in which the *Apollo 13* mission commander, Jim Lovell, reflected on the nearly disastrous mission which began on April 11, 1970. As an omen of things to come, the *Apollo* flight number 13 was launched thirteen minutes past the thirteenth hour of the day. Lovell and fellow astronauts Fred Haise and Jack Swigert were about to realize their dream of being the next human beings to walk on the moon. For Lovell, it was an obsession he carried since his early days in the space program. However, two days, seven hours,

APOLLO 13

world held its breath until the gut-wrenching moment when the capsule landed safely in the sea.

The *Apollo 13* mission reinvigorated—at least for the short run—the U.S. space program, which had suffered in terms of public and government enthusiasm once the Americans won the much-vaunted "race to the moon." For days on end, people around the world related to the courage of the men who where stranded literally in the middle of nowhere. Ironically, the mission that was the most disastrous from an operational standpoint for NASA also became the agency's finest hour, thanks to the ingenious and dedicated people who worked day and night to overcome a seemingly endless number of obstacles and crises.

After Hanks was approached to play Jim Lovell, he said, "I have this insane job that lets me put on other people's clothes and pretend to be somebody else for a period of time, and they pay me ludicrous amounts of money to do it. This was a chance to play not just somebody that you admire greatly but somebody that I also think went through an almost superhuman experience and at the same time is made up of the flesh and blood you and I are." He would later tell *Time* magazine of his belief in the

and fifty-four minutes into what was expected to be a routine flight, an oxygen tank exploded. The astronauts seemed destined for certain death as the air supply began to run out and the power began to weaken. In one of the most harrowing episodes of space-flight history, NASA technicians worked feverishly to improvise solutions. The astronauts remained calm and cool, figuratively and literally. (To conserve precious energy, the heat in the capsule was turned off, threatening the crew with freezing to death.) A long-shot chance was gambled upon whereby the astronauts used the moon's gravitational pull to bring them around the far side of the planet and put them on course for home. The danger was not over, for it was still unclear as to whether the capsule's heat shields were functional enough to prevent the ship from disintegrating upon hitting the earth's atmosphere. The

The real *Apollo 13* crew: Jim Lovell, Jack Swigert, and Fred Haise...(NASA)

value of the space program and how the film would pay homage to the people behind it: "It gives credit where a great amount of credit has been forgotten. Launching men into space is a fantastic undertaking, which very few people today seem to appreciate. It's ironic that we made a movie about a mission that was a 'failure' because it's probably the best celebration of what NASA did."

Astronaut films were hardly considered surefire at the box office, and there was speculation that even with Hanks on board, *Apollo 13* might be destined for failure. The last NASA-based motion picture—the 1983 epic story of the space program *The Right Stuff*—was critically lauded but a disappointment in terms of its grosses. The origins of the *Apollo 13* film began with director Ron Howard and producing partner Brian Grazer. Both had shown the instinct for turning out box-office hits, beginning with *Splash* a decade before. Hanks and Howard had always been eager to reunite on another project, but nothing suitable had materialized until Howard and Grazer's production company, Imagine Films, purchased the rights to Lovell's book (at a bargain price of only $650,000). The filmmakers had bought the screen rights even though Lovell had only produced a ten-page outline and a sample chapter. Screenwriters William Broyles Jr. And Al Reinert (who had directed *For All Mankind,* the acclaimed documentary about the space program) came up with a draft of a script which was then given to Kevin Costner for consideration. Costner passed on the project, and it was agreed that Tom Hanks would be approached to play Jim Lovell.

Ironically, Hanks was always hoping someone would bring the *Apollo 13* story to the screen. "I talked to my crack staff of show-business experts long ago, and I said, 'Man, we've got to find somebody to write *Apollo 13.* It's an incredible saga.'" Ron Howard would later tell how Hanks became a part of his "dream" project: "Tom's agent (Richard Lovett) was talking to Brian Grazer and mentioned that Tom always wanted to play an astronaut and especially would have liked to have seen a movie made about the *Apollo 13* mission. About a week later, we met in New York while he was promoting *Philadelphia.* He and I have this terrific camaraderie. And I appreciated his point of view on the story and his overall knowledge of the space program. After that, the writers went to work. The more we got deeper into the story,

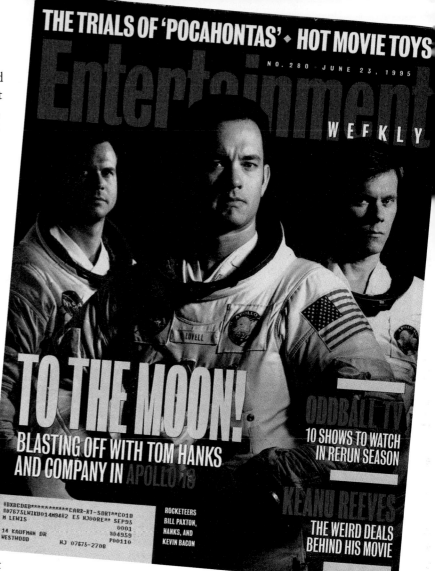

THE TRIALS OF 'POCAHONTAS' ◆ HOT MOVIE TOYS

Entertainment

WEEKLY

NO. 280 · JUNE 23, 1995

TO THE MOON!
BLASTING OFF WITH TOM HANKS AND COMPANY IN *APOLLO 13*

ODDBALL TV
10 SHOWS TO WATCH IN RERUN SEASON

KEANU REEVES
THE WEIRD DEALS BEHIND HIS MOVIE

ROCKETEERS
BILL PAXTON,
HANKS, AND
KEVIN BACON

... and Hollywood astronauts Bill Paxton, Tom Hanks, and Kevin Bacon (*Entertainment Weekly*)

the more we realized that we didn't have to Hollywoodize this movie. The more we stuck to the facts, the more powerful and suspenseful the story became." (Indeed, the screenwriters had to *eliminate* some actual crises situations in the film because there was concern that audiences would not believe these men could actually have survived all that they had to cope with in real life.) Hanks had a slightly more dramatic spin on how he came to terms with Howard about starring in the film: "I was in a restaurant in New York holding a busted beer bottle to Ron Howard's neck, saying, 'You give me that part! You give it to *me*! I was *born* to play Jim Lovell.'" The Lovell role would be the first Hanks would portray a real-life person on-screen.

Many actors vied for the roles of the other astronauts on the ill-fated *Apollo* mission. Among those considered: Val Kilmer, John Cusack, and Hanks's good friend John Travolta. Ultimately, the roles of

181

astronauts Fred Haise and Jack Swigert were given to Bill Paxton and Kevin Bacon. Ed Harris landed the meaty part of Gene Kranz, the tough-as-nails NASA engineer who spearheads efforts to get the crew back to earth. Gary Sinise, Hanks's costar in *Forrest Gump*, would play the role of astronaut Ken Mattingly, an original member of the mission whom Swigert replaced when it was believed Mattingly had come down with measles at the last minute.

Lovell explains the mission to his young son. (Imagine Entertainment/Universal Citiy Studios)

Devastated by being cheated by fate from his chance to walk on the moon, Mattingly would ironically become a heroic figure in the rescue mission.

From the beginning, Hanks was determined to ensure that the script remained completely authentic. Brian Grazer recalls, "Tom was at least 50 percent of the driving force of this movie. Because of his understanding of what actually happened on that mission, he was the truth meter of the movie. He paid attention to how astronauts are, how they should say things, and he made sure we adhered to what really went on and portrayed things with honesty. Astronauts go into space and rely on both their physical and mental capabilities to survive. Tom made it very clear how the tone should be and helped police it. This is completely unusual for a star actor of his caliber." Grazer was also impressed with Hanks's willingness to sacrifice screen time to the integrity of the film: "His biggest problem with the early versions of the script was they had too many movie moments. He was always giving his great moments away. He'd say, 'No, Swigert would do that,' or, 'Hayes would do that.' He didn't want the movie to be all about him."

Jim Lovell himself was brought on as a technical adviser and gave Hanks an aerial tour of Texas in his jet, much to the dismay of Universal executives, who didn't fancy their star and his real-life counterpart dashing precariously through the clouds. Lovell's intention was to give Hanks a feel for experiencing zero gravity prior to filming. Hanks later confessed to not handling the "sneak preview" flight very well: "My mouth started watering, and I was immediately bathed in hot sweat. Even worse, I began to feel extremely nauseous. And I thought, This is going to be sad. I *cannot* let on to Jim Lovell that I'm sick when he's just picked me up from the airport." Hanks survived, however, and Lovell later brought him up for a night flight to get him adjusted to the vast blackness of outer space. To re-create the limited view seen from the space capsule, Lovell installed a triangular cardboard cutout on Hanks's side of the cockpit.

Hanks admitted to being intimidated by having Lovell on the set but soon developed an excellent rapport: "Jim visited the set on occasion. I felt like an idiot. . . . We would be on our teeter-totters, pretending to be flipping switches, doing stuff, and Jim, God bless him, he just said, 'It looks just like the real thing,' and move along. He never said, 'This is it? This is how you're showing my experience? Take it seriously!'" Lovell sympathized with the actor: "It's intimidating for a great actor like Tom Hanks to portray a character who happens to still be alive and is still standing on the back end of the camera."

The four astronaut actors were also trained

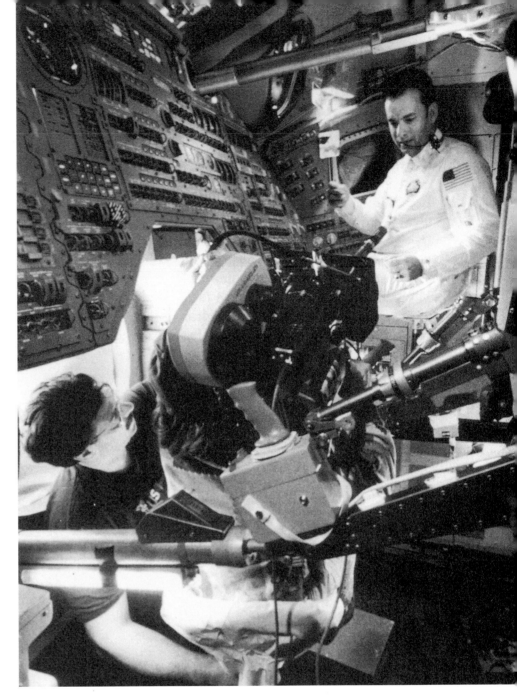

under the guidance of Dave Scott, the commander of the *Apollo 15* mission. At the Houston Space Center, the actors were sealed in a cylindrical altitude chamber, where they prepared for their zero-gravity runs. Two months later, they arrived at the U.S. Space Camp in Huntsville, Indiana, where they flew shuttle missions in simulators.

Ron Howard, determined to make the film as realistic as possible, decided the only way to show the actors in weightlessness would be to actually have them be weightless. All previous astronaut films had the actors float about on wires. For *Apollo 13*, Howard had initially tried to simulate weightlessness by turning the capsule upside down, with the actors strapped into special harnesses. The resulting footage was passable, but all suffered from blood rushing to their heads. Howard went back to the drawing board, and then a "brainstorm" hit him: He would utilize the actual aircraft used to train astronauts for weightless situations. The plane—a stripped-down 707 known as the *KC-135*—climbs at a forty-five degree angle to thirty-thousand feet, then begins a rapid arc back to earth at five-hundred miles per hour. Not surprisingly, the aircraft earned the nickname the "Vomit Comet."

By the time *Apollo 13* would be finished filming, Ron Howard and his cast would have spent more time in the zero-gravity aircraft than any real astronaut. The capsule set had to be built in the interior of the plane, which gave everyone a very limited amount of space in which to maneuver. Complicating matters was that one could only achieve weightlessness for a total of twenty-three seconds per dive. Once this period had elapsed, the crew had to quickly find a place in which to sit before the gravity returned and unceremoniously "dumped" them. Hanks said: "There were times when we's finish shooting a scene and I had no idea which way I was going to fall. It's not a sensation you can liken to anything else. It's not like floating like Superman but kind of floating like an angel."

The cast and Howard were initially nervous about being asked to act naturally in such an unnatural environment. At a cost of $6,500 per hour for use of the plane, there was tremendous pressure on everyone not to waste a single moment. Ron Howard confessed, "As the director, I kept thinking, If I'm the first one to hurl, are they going to lose respect for me or what? Something along those lines was kind of running through everyone's head." The cast discovered that it was preferable to eat prior to embarking on a flight. Hanks recalled the time he opted to be macho and not take an antinausea drug or eat prior to filming: "I was so nauseous, I had an out-of-body experience. My body wanted to throw up so badly, but I didn't have anything in my stomach, so rather than throw up, I just went *ka-kack!* Because it was like a near-death experience, I started hallucinating. I thought I would go back to like swimmin' in the

Ed Harris in a remarkable performance as the heroic Gene Kranz (Imagine Entertainment/Universal City Studios)

swimmin' hole or marrying my wife or the birth of my children. Instead, I imagined myself, and I truly was on-stage playing violin in a scene from *The Man With One Red Shoe.* That was my life flashing before my eyes!" Nevertheless, once Hanks and his comrades became accustomed to zero gravity, they learned to have fun. According to Howard, "Saying something is better than sex rarely lives up to that claim. Weightlessness doesn't quite, either. But it came awfully close."

One other obstacle to avoid in the weightlessness scenes were the props, which became dangerous weapons when floating through the air. The props were built by Max Ary's KCSC Space Works space

museum of Hutchinson, Kansas. This facility built the modules used on the capsule, along with over eight-thousand other items, ranging from pens and flashlights to checklists and fully functioning space suits. A few of the items were actually from the *Apollo 13* flight. Again, every effort was made to ensure that even the smallest details were accurate. This included Mission Control, a set so convincing that when actual technicians from the *Apollo 13* crisis visited the location, they could immediately find their original places at the control boards. NASA was fully cooperative to guarantee that the filmmakers received the best advice and technical support.

After ten days' filming in the Vomit Comet, the cast and crew flew to Universal Studios in Los Angeles to do interior shots of the space capsule. Here Hanks, Bacon, and Paxton had to endure long hours in a very confined space. "It was like shooting a movie in a Volkswagen Beetle," said Paxton. The actors spent fourteen hours a day for eight weeks in the capsule, which measured only seven feet by six feet. Ron Howard's tendency to film multiple takes also prolonged the shoot, but as the director explains, once the shooting is over, you can't get everyone back to the studio if a take is unsatisfactory. Therefore, he tends to shoot a great deal of footage so that he has adequate coverage of scenes. The men tried to fight boredom by pretending they were anywhere but in a capsule. Howard recalls, "I'd be up on the camera crane, and I'd look down, and there were Tom, Bill, and Kevin, looking like any photo from the *Apollo* era. Yet they were discussing their agents, talking about how they used to wait tables—it was strange." The guys also indulged in some raunchy humor. Howard said, "The stories got pretty rank in there. Real locker room stuff going on." Hanks agreed: "The only things that were missing were the girlie magazines and the cigars."

Howard had another challenge for his cast: To

Liftoff! Incredibly, director Ron Howard used miniatures for the remarkable footage of the *Apollo 13* launch. (Imagine Entertainment/Universal City Studios)

stimulate the frigid conditions in the stricken capsule, he ordered the temperatures on the set to be lowered to thirty-four degrees. Hanks joked about this drastic attempt at realism: "I can't wait to hear what people say when this movie comes out. You just know they're going to look at the condensation coming out of our mouths and say, 'I guess they found a big, walk-in refrigerator and the astronauts and the director work in there for a few days. I mean, they wouldn't do something ridiculous like, oh, refrigerate a *whole* set!'" Howard found that the actors' inconvenience paid artistic dividends: "Being jammed in the capsule filming for hours on end, with it chilled down to thirty-four degrees, was pretty debilitating in its own way for these guys. We shot it in sequence so that as we began to physically wear down, which I knew was inevitable, their characters would also." To ease the discomfort, the actors would relax between takes in Hank's trailer and watch mini-film festivals organized by Paxton.

Ron Howard's goal of stark realism extended to exterior scenes of the launch of *Apollo 13*. He watched films of the real space launches but was not happy with the quality. Instead, he ordered that models of the rocket be built and enhanced with special effects. The resulting footage is impossible to distinguish from the real thing. All of this was accomplished by director James Cameron's Digital Domain

unit for special effects. (Cameron himself served as an unbilled adviser on the project.) Although filming aboard the *KC-135* had reduced the need for certain special-effects shots, the movie still required over 150 others (twenty-five for the launch alone). For Howard, the painstaking work was worth it: "It seemed to me that a couple of scenes in *Backdraft* made people feel like they were in an actual fire. I felt we had a similar opportunity to really make you understand what it feels like to be inside a capsule."

Throughout the filming, Hanks endeared himself to his costars and the crew. Brian Grazer said of him, "Every choice he's been making has been both incredibly pure and incredibly smart. I don't think anyone can second-guess Tom Hanks now. He's done three or four hundred-million-dollar-plus movies, and they're all really good. The thing about Tom that's the most amazing is that all his successes have come out of great work. Whereas many other people's successes can and do come in different ways, his has been the product of remarkable performances in good films."

Ron Howard was especially pleased to be working with Hanks once more. He called his old friend "the no-fuss, no-muss superstar" and said, "His belief in the power of the story was his driving point. He was an advocate for the story's real-life drama. He wasn't viewing it as a vehicle. He wanted to portray

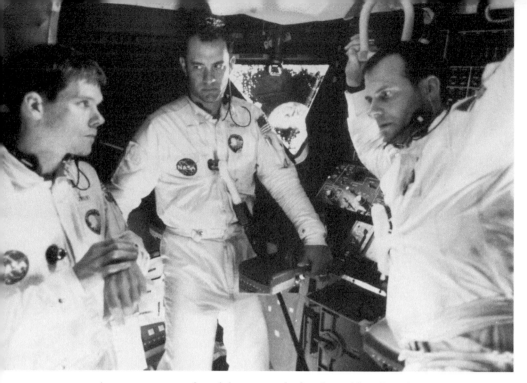

A tense moment on board the spacecraft after the accident (Imagine Entertainment/ Universal City Studios)

Mission Control leader obsessed with bringing his men back to earth safely. Harris commands the screen in his every scene and rallies the audience with the same skill with which Kranz rallied his harried crew in the film. Every other element of the movie works perfectly, and even the smallest roles are expertly cast. James Horner's music, combined with intelligent use of period rock-and-roll classics, fits perfectly the mood of the film, particularly in the moving climactic moments. All other technical work is top-notch, especially Dean Cundey's cinematography and Mike Hill and Dan Hanley's editing. (The latter two had the unenviable task of cutting the 3:30 rough cut to the final running time of 2:15.)

this story as truthfully as possible. He came to this movie an ally and a friend and a true collaborator. Tom is a working guy. He goes to work. There's not a lazy bone in his body. He's there to do the work. He's learned more and more about movies and has smart decisiveness that you can reap huge dividends from. You have to admire Tom in that he's quietly put in a tremendous eleven years in the movies and has arrived as one of the really premier film actors."

Hanks is not being modest when he calls *Apollo 13* an ensemble piece in which no one particular actor dominates the others. The other characters are explored in depth, although Jim Lovell still remains the central figure around whom the story revolves. Artistically and technically, the film is superb on every level. Hanks's best moments are not necessarily in the capsule itself but in the quiet scenes with his wife, beautifully played by Kathleen Quinlan. Hanks *becomes* Jim Lovell, and by the end of the film, despite his heroics during the mission, we can truly sympathize with a man who will be haunted forever by being denied his one dream—to walk on the moon. It's a wonderful, enriching performance.

The other "astronauts" are also impressive, and Bill Paxton, Kevin Bacon, and Gary Sinise all get plenty of moments to shine in the terrific script by William Broyles Jr. and Al Reinert. (Writer-director John Sayles also contributed to the script, although he does not receive screen credit.) The scene-stealer, however, proves to be Ed Harris as Gene Kranz, the

As for Ron Howard's direction, suffice it to say that his cinematic journey has been every bit as remarkable as Tom Hanks's. Howard, a popular actor since age five, decided to switch from acting to directing—an obsession he had since a young boy. Graduating from calling the shots on profitable drive-in fare like *Grand Theft Auto* (1977), he has established himself as one of the most interesting and diversified filmmakers working today.

Apollo 13 had the buzz of a winner long before it opened, although skeptics still maintained that the "dating crowd" would be loath to see a history lesson about a space mission they had never even heard of. The film was premiered before President Clinton at the White House, with Ron Howard and the cast in attendance. A special screening was also held for NASA personnel at the National Space Center in Houston. The movie was originally scheduled for release in November 1995, but Universal was so high on the film that it advanced the premiere date to June 30, making it the studio's most prestigious release of the summer. Despite such high-powered competition as *Batman Forever* and *Pocahontas*, it opened to a huge first weekend gross over the $25 million. The film received virtually unanimous praise from the critics, some of whom claimed it was a masterful piece of movie-making

With Hanks on a popular roll, speculation heated up that he might be nominated for a third consecutive Oscar. Hanks dismissed the notion: "That won't happen. The world is safe. I'm not in a third of the movie because it's Mission Control and we're up in space." He would later add that a nomination wasn't probable because the film is "very much an ensemble piece. Everybody has great moments in it, and everybody's really important to the core of the entire movie. This is not one of those types of very flashy or attention-getting roles." (Indeed, not only was Hanks not nominated, neither was Ron Howard—one of the more controversial omissions in Oscar history. The film was nominated in many categories—including Best Picture—but won only two technical awards.)

Perhaps Ron Howard summed up Hanks's abilities when he discussed how the actor matured in the years since they worked togeth-

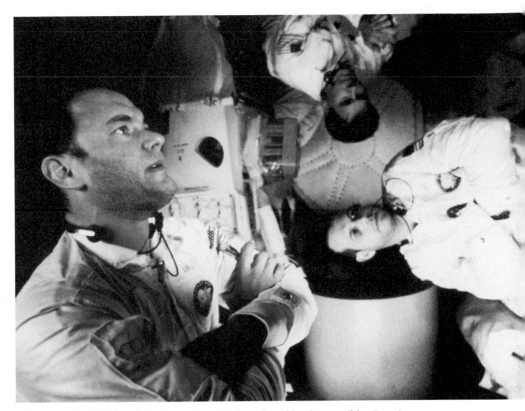

Filming on the NASA training jet made weightless shots like this possible. (Imagine Entertainment/Universal City Studios)

The crew sadly gets one last look at the moon, on which they will never walk. (Imagine Entertainment/Universal City Studios)

er on *Splash*: "He's more confident. He's wiser, not only about his own choices, but he now has the ability to ask very pertinent and valuable questions about story and character, which make him a huge asset on a film set. He's every bit as much fun to work with as he was eleven years ago. He has not lost his passion for the work, and at the same time, he was incredibly relaxed in his very first movie, and he's incredibly relaxed today. He gives 110 percent, and he just hopes that's enough—and he has proven over the years that it's more than enough."

Three men with a date with destiny (Imagine Entertainment/Universal City Studios)

Reviews

"It's easily [Ron] Howard's best film. . . . Hanks gives another great performance—instinctive and assured. He humanizes the hardware and the space speak, shows feeling in Lovell's scenes with his children and wife (a touching Kathleen Quinlan), and subtly draws us into the heartache of a dedicated man who won't fulfill his dream to set foot on the moon. There is nothing showy in the Philadelphia or Forrest Gump mode in what Hanks does here, yet his acting as the unassuming Lovell ranks with his most impressive work."

—Peter Travers, Rolling Stone

"With its rah-rah, gung-ho, can-do attitude, and cast of good-looking white men in buzz cuts, this engrossing account of the nation's most perilous moon shot embodies what many people consider to be old-fashioned American virtues in a virtually pristine state. Sufficiently suspenseful despite its historically preordained happy ending, slightly overlong real life thriller will appeal to mainstream audiences across the board and land a commercial bullseye for Universal. . . . Casting Hanks as Lovell gives the film a human center, someone with whom the audience can feel at home, but his dramatic opportunities are more limited here than has been customary for him of late. His most powerful scene has him calming down his partners when their dilemma threatens to get the better of them."

—Todd McCarthy, Variety

"A throwback to classic Hollywood pictures about men in groups, the new film is also a splendid display of old-fashioned realistic special effects. . . . Hanks provides the anchor. His Lovell—as strong, faithful and emotionally straightforward as Forrest Gump—carries the story like a precious oxygen backpack. His resourcefulness gives Lovell strength; his gift for conveying worry give the film its humanity and a purchase on ordinary Joe heroism."

—Richard Corliss, *Time*

"Directed with single-mindedness and attention to detail that makes it riveting. [Howard] doesn't make a mistake of adding cornball little subplots to popularize the material; he knows he has a great story and he tells it in a documdrama that feels like something filmed on location in outer-space. This is a powerful story, one of the year's best films, told with great clarity and remarkable technical detail, and acted without pumped-up histrionics."

—Roger Ebert, *Siskel and Ebert*

Poster advertisement (Imagine Entertainment/Universal City Studios)

Trivia Notes

Jim Lovell appears briefly in *Apollo 13* as the captain of the naval ship which rescues the astronauts.

As with all of Ron Howard's films, *Apollo 13* is very much a family affair. His father, brother, and mother appear in the movie. Ron's brother Clint has a significant role as one of the NASA Mission Control technicians, and his father appears briefly in the finale in a wordless role as a priest. (Ron cut out his dad's "big scene"!) Ron's mother, Jean, makes the most of her screen time as Jim Lovell's mom and gets the film's biggest laugh when she fails to recognize Neil Armstrong. To prove that nepotism isn't rampant in the Howard clan, Ron made his mother audition for the part!

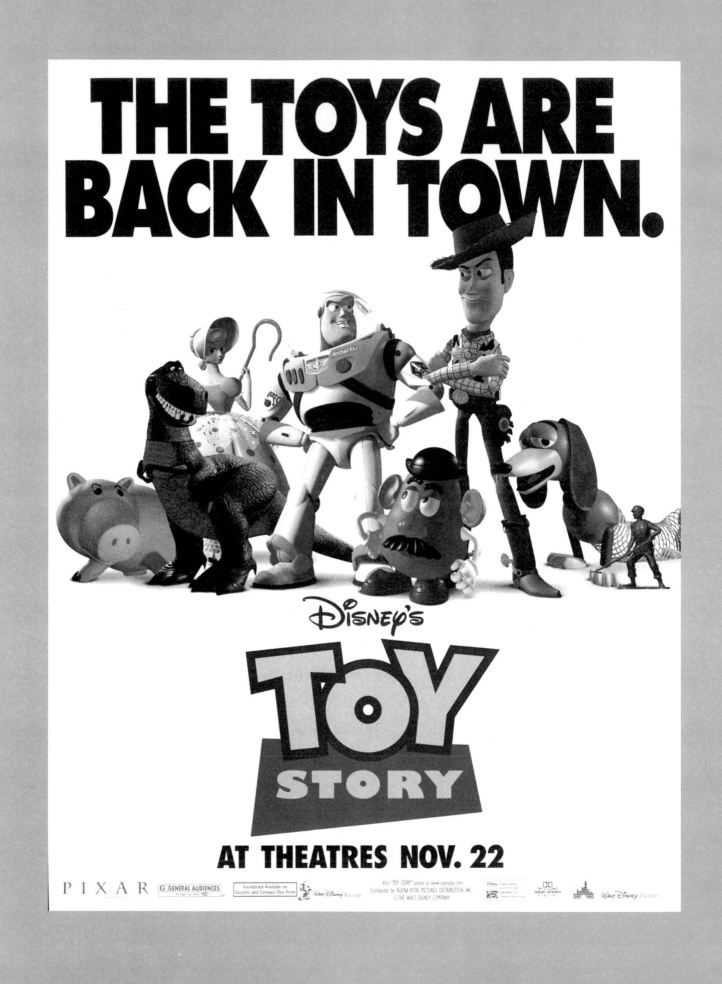

23

Toy Story

Disney, 1995

"I felt like Patrick McGoohan in The Prisoner. *I'm standing there yelling, saying the same things over and over. I was not prepared for how tough it was. I had to get into this almost quasi-hypnotic state of delirium imagining I'm in this other place."*

Voices:
Tom Hanks (*Woody*); Tim Allen (*Buzz Lightyear*); Annie Potts (*Bo Peep*); Don Rickles (*Mr. Potato Head*); Jim Varney (*Slinky Dog*); John Ratzenberger (*Hamm*); Wallace Shawn (*Rex*); John Morris (*Andy*); Erik Von Detten (*Sid*); Laurie Metcalf (*Mrs. Davis*); R. Lee Ermey (*Sergeant*).

Credits
Director: John Lasseter; producers: Ralph Guggenheim and Bonnie Arnold; executive producers: Edwin Catmull and Steven Jobs; screenplay: Joss Whedon, Andrew Stanton, Joel Cohen, and Alec Sokolow, based on an original story by John Lasseter, Peter Docter, John Ranft, and Andrew Stanton; supervising animator: Pete Docter; editors: Robert Gordon and Lee Unkrich; music and songs: Randy Newman. Running time: 80 minutes.

Advance teaser ad for *Toy Story*

By November 1995, it seemed as though Tom Hanks had become comfortably entrenched as *the* motion picture icon of his time. Hanks confessed to being increasingly uncomfortable with the never-ending successes, saying that he feared he was becoming overexposed in the media. He had somewhat successfully managed to make *Apollo 13* the ensemble achievement it actually was and not just the latest Hanks blockbuster. He announced that his next film would be a modestly budgeted comedy called *That Thing That You Do*, centering on a rock band circa 1964. While it would be significant in marking Hanks's big-screen directorial debut, the actor was careful to note that he would only be playing a supporting role in the film. Clearly, Hanks wanted to fade a bit from the media before he suffered the inevitable backlash that overexposure will bring. (Call it the Burt Reynolds syndrome.)

It was therefore most unexpected to find that before 1995 had ended, Tom Hanks would be the star of yet *another* box-office phenomenon, albeit one in which his face never appeared on-screen. The film was *Toy Story*, which arrived with very little advance hype or word of mouth. The brainchild of director John Lasseter, *Toy Story* began as a troubled production which many thought would never be completed.

Lasseter, a onetime animator for Disney, had become disenchanted with the old-line animation policies of the studio during the pre–Michael Eisner era. Simultaneously, Dr. Ed. Catmull and his staff of research-and-development people were feverishly trying to enhance their system of computer-animation techniques for Pixar, a division of George Lucas's production company, LucasFilm. Like Lasseter, Catmull became impatient with the policies of his studio, feeling his techniques were not being used properly. Eventually, Catmull saw Lasseter's work on short films and lured him away from Disney to Pixar. It was always the goal of both men to upgrade the computer-animation process to the point where they could create the first full-length feature film using this technique. However, LucasFilm was more interested in having the Pixar staff work on research and development as opposed to honing their skills as filmmakers. Eventually, Catmull informed Lucas that he was making Pixar an independent production company.

With Pixar now on its own, it attracted interest from Steven Jobs, the Apple Computer founder and magnate. Jobs eventually bought Pixar, and Catmull would serve as president. Jobs had full faith in his team and left them free to use their creative impulses. Together Catmull and Lasseter began to produce some mind-boggling special effects. The Disney Studios, now in the animation-rennaisance period which Michael Eisner had brought to the studio, tried unsuccessfully to woo Lasseter away. However, Disney did sign a three-picture contract with Pixar to create three fully computer-animated feature films, the first of which would be *Toy Story*.

Toy Story tells the tale of the secret life of a group of playthings owned by a young boy named Andy. While no specific time frame is mentioned, all of the toys are endearingly old-fashioned, and one presumes the film is set in the 1950s. Whenever Andy is not around, the toys chat and play with each other, having established their own comfortable community, which includes Mr. Potato Head, a terribly tame *Tyrannosaurus Rex*, Little Bo Peep, and Woody, a pull-string cowboy who prides himself on being not only the unofficial leader of the group but also Andy's very favorite toy.

Into this sacred hierarchy comes Buzz Lightyear, a snazzy new battery-operated spaceman who immediately captivates Andy and threatens Woody's status. The film follows the antagonistic relationship between the streetwise Woody, who recognizes he is indeed a toy, and the heroic but naive Buzz, who real-ly thinks he is a spaceman. However, when the chips are down, the two come to each other's aid to escape the grasp of Sid, a young punk with a penchant for destroying toys.

Originally, the concept for *Toy Story* was not quite as warmhearted. The characters were not clearly defined despite Disney's insistence that they all behave like adults for fear of alienating mature audiences. Catmull and Lasseter were succeeding on the technical level but admitted that the story was not working on an emotional level. The filmmakers' rough-cut screening of an early version of the film left the Disney brass disappointed. Undaunted, the Pixar team of animators and writers continued to work painstakingly. Eventually, the various elements began to jell, and everyone could sense that the movie was coming together beautifully.

Lasseter, who was serving as director, was determined to get "name" actors to provide the voices for these marvelous toys. His first choice for Woody was Tom Hanks, because he "has the ability to take emotions and make them appealing, even if the character, like the one in *A League of Their Own*, is down-and-out and despicable." A goateed Hanks met with Lasseter shortly after having completed filming of *Philadelphia*. Lasseter showed him thirty seconds of a computer-animated Woody accompanied by Hanks's voice from *Turner & Hooch*. The actor howled with laughter and asked simply, "When can we start?" Hanks described Woody as "a classic piece of Americana. He's an old-fashioned, loose-limbed marionette without the strings. His vocabulary is stored in his chest." He was further encouraged by a fellow actor: "I met Matthew Broderick about the time he was doing *The Lion King*. He told me what a wonderful experience it was. I had never done a voice before, but I'd always been interested in trying it."

Hanks certainly did not accept the "gig" for the cash. He and fellow star Tim Allen (who was providing the voice of Buzz Lightyear) were paid slightly more than union scale. While neither actor complained about the pay, it became obvious very quickly that this would prove to be an arduous assignment. In fact, the voice-over work would extend over two years. Hanks and Allen were kept separated from each other, partly because of their ability to crack each other up. The actors had to endure countless sessions of rerecording dialogue, for the script constantly changed to enhance the character's personalities. Hanks would later recall it being one of the most unexpectedly challenging assignments of this career.

On the technical side, dozens of the best animators in the film industry labored nonstop to ensure that the characters moved smoothly and flawlessly. Their efforts required over two-hundred years of collective efforts! The results, however, were beyond anyone's expectations. *Toy Story* is a superb achievement on every level and a personal triumph for Lasseter, Catmull, and the entire Pixar team. By backing the commercially uncertain project, Disney also showed the type of daring and insight which Walt Disney originally brought to the studio. The film works flawlessly, and there are too many individual contributors to acknowledge here. Suffice it to say that this is the most original film in decades and one which will revolutionize animation forever.

Tom Hanks, Tim Allen, and the other talents who provided the brilliant voice-overs (including Don Rickles as Mr. Potato Head!) deserve kudos as well for so perfectly capturing the essence of their characters while never actually interacting with each other in the studio. Equally wonderful is Randy Newman's catchy score and songs. (Disney reluctantly agreed to drop plans to make the movie a full-fledged musical at the filmmakers request.)

Toy Story opened without much advance fanfare during Thanksgiving, 1995. The public and critical response, however, was overwhelming. The film grossed over $38 million in its opening weekend, a phenomenal achievement. *Toy Story*—along with the surprise resurgence of the James Bond films with the smash hit *GoldenEye*—became the talk of the winter film season. Now, as its grosses eclipse over $150 million in North America alone, Tom Hanks can add another blockbuster to his already impressive and diverse resumé.

Toy Story underscores the fact that in the world of animation nobody does it better than Disney. Appropriately, it does for animation in the nineties what *Snow White* did for the art form in the late thirties.

Reviews

"*This year's most inventive comedy. . . . Sheriff Woody is wonderfully voiced by Tom Hanks. . . . Like a Bosch painting or a* Mad *comic book,* Toy Story *creates a world bustling with strange creatures and furtive, furry humor. When a genius like Lasseter sits at his computer, the machine becomes just a more supple paintbrush. Like the creatures in this wonderful zoo of a movie, it's alive!*"
—Richard Corliss, *Time*

"*A richly entertaining comedy adventure that represents the coming of age of a new art form: computer animation. . . . Though [it] is dazzling in its execution, presenting fully-rounded figures moving fluidly through complex spaces, it's also a beautifully told story, full of appealing, complex characters and imaginative situations. . . .* "
—Dave Kerr, *New York Daily News*

"*A landmark in computer-generated imagery,* Jurassic Park *had six minutes of CGI,* Casper *had forty minutes.* Toy Story *is all CGI and astonishing fun. Without paper or pencil, director John Lasseter and his team bring characters to life. . . . Woody and Buzz dis each other royally and the voices of Hanks and Allen spark a brisk hilarity . . . a toy story that makes art of computer science.*"
—Peter Travers, *Rolling Stone*

"*Watching the film, I felt I was in at the dawn of a new era of movie animation, which draws on the best of cartoons and reality, creating a world somewhere in between, where space not only bends but snaps, crackles and pops.*"
—Roger Ebert, *Chicago Sun Times*

"*Hanks, believe it or not, gives a more arresting dramatic performance here than he did in* Apollo 13. *Woody's jealousy sucks us right into the movie, even as his attempt to get Buzz out of the way results in the space ranger's being knocked out the bedroom window. . . . The beauty of* Toy Story *is the way it expresses the essence of child's play— that pretending is the art of dreaming when you're wide awake.*"
—Owen Gleiberman, *Entertainment Weekly*

About the Authors

LEE PFEIFFER has written several highly successful books for Citadel Press, among them *The Official "Andy Griffith Show" Scrapbook* and *The John Wayne Scrapbook*, as well as *The Films of Harrison Ford*, *The Ultimate Clint Eastwood Trivia Book* (the latter two with Michael Lewis), *The Incredible World of 007: An Official Celebration of James Bond*, *The Films of Clint Eastwood*, and *The Films of Sean Connery*. Pfeiffer is one of the founders of T.W.I.N.E. Entertainment, a production company which specializes in documentaries about the making of classic motion pictures. The company's initial productions—*The Making of "Goldfinger"* and *The Making of "Thunderball"*—were released by M-G-M/UA Home Video in 1995. He resides in Piscataway, New Jersey.

MICHAEL LEWIS is a career marketing executive. An avid student of the cinema, he has contributed to the marketing campaigns for many successful books. In 1996 he became a published author with *The Films of Harrison Ford* (Citadel Press). Following *The Films of Tom Hanks*, Lewis coauthored *The Ultimate Clint Eastwood Trivia Book*, *The Ultimate James Bond 007 Trivia Book*, and *The Cheapskate's Guide to Walt Disney World*. He resides in Fair Lawn, New Jersey.